Why Fascism Is on the Rise in France

From Macron to Le Pen

Ugo Palheta

Translated by David Broder

VERSO
London • New York

English-language edition first published by Verso 2025
First published as *La possibilité du fascisme: France, la trajectoire du désastre*
© La Découverte 2018
© Ugo Palheta 2018, 2025
Translation © David Broder 2025

All rights reserved

This work received support for excellence in publication and translation from Albertine Translation, a program created by Villa Albertine and funded by FACE Foundation

The manufacturer's authorized representative in the EU for product safety (GPSR) is LOGOS EUROPE, 9 rue Nicolas Poussin, 17000, La Rochelle, France Contact@logoseurope.e

The moral rights of the author have been asserted

1 3 5 7 9 10 8 6 4 2

Verso
UK: 6 Meard Street, London W1F 0EG
US: 207 East 32nd Street, New York, NY 10016
versobooks.com

Verso is the imprint of New Left Books

ISBN-13: 978-1-80429-095-8
ISBN-13: 978-1-80429-097-2 (US EBK)
ISBN-13: 978-1-80429-096-5 (UK EBK)

British Library Cataloguing in Publication Data
A catalogue record for this book is available from the British Library

Library of Congress Cataloging-in-Publication Data
A catalog record for this book is available from the Library of Congress

Typeset in Minion Pro by MJ & N Gavan, Truro, Cornwall
Printed and bound by CPI Group (UK) Ltd, Croydon CR0 4YY

Contents

Preface: 'The Womb Is Still Fertile'   v

1 The Return of (the Concept of) Fascism   1
2 A Hegemonic Crisis   35
3 The Neoliberal-Authoritarian State and Fascisation   71
4 The Nationalist and Racist Offensive   111
5 A Fascist Party on the Road to Power   161

Conclusion: Fend Off Disaster, Revive Anti-fascism   229

Preface

'The Womb Is Still Fertile'

The far-right vote has risen steadily in every French election since 2012, reaching 41.5 percent in the runoff of the 2022 presidential contest. This is no isolated phenomenon. The traditional right has become extremist; civil liberties have been curtailed in the name of the fight against terrorism; more and more demonstrations have been banned in the last ten years and all dissent increasingly criminalised; Islamophobic laws and decrees have been accompanied by media campaigns targeting Muslims; and a mass reactionary movement has developed against equal rights and educational programmes promoting gender equality. In today's France, migrants are systematically hunted down and bludgeoned by the police (on the orders of successive governments), when they are not kidnapped, beaten up and left for dead by violent mobs.[1] Observers count an increasing number of physical attacks by far-right groups against members of ethnic minorities and activists involved in social movements. An ever-wider array of publications across all platforms – from online articles to videos, podcasts, books and so on – promote a conspiratorial racism (the 'great replacement' theory) and calls for the establishment of an

---

1 This book benefited from the critical reviews and advice of Gilbert Achcar, Isabelle Bruno, Cédric Durand, Isabelle Garo, Stathis Kouvelakis, Henri Maler and Rachel Renault. I would like to thank them all. However, the author alone must be held responsible for the arguments in this book and for any errors.

See Stéphanie Maurice, '"Ratonnades" en série chez les migrants de Calais', *Libération*, 1 October 2015.

authoritarian government able to strike back against minorities and the left ('the party of foreigners'). There is constant public harassment of Muslims and anti-racist, feminist and LGBTQI+ activists.[2] All this is rounded off by the intensification of repressive policing of working-class neighbourhoods and the structural impunity of police violence.

Fascism is announcing its arrival – not as an abstract hypothesis but as a concrete possibility. Here we have mentioned some of its disparate, still embryonic forms – and even just to list them speaks to the sclerosis of French politics in the neoliberal age. This possible return of fascism is generally dismissed out of hand by the commentariat: how could the French Republic, the self-proclaimed homeland of human rights, give rise to fascist barbarism? Was not France 'allergic' to fascism throughout the twentieth century, as many mainstream French historians have long argued?[3] Does not the Front National (FN), which became the Rassemblement National (RN) in 2018, claim to have abandoned the political project that it upheld since its foundation in 1972? Has not this party hit an electoral glass ceiling, as has been so routinely claimed across the past three decades? Are we not actually seeing a revival of French capitalism, helmed by a young president who is finally carrying out the 'reforms' France supposedly needs?

This book sets out to dismantle these false truisms, and a few others. It does so in an attempt to describe a *possible* disastrous course, rooted, in particular, in the decomposition of the French political field (of which Emmanuel Macron is both the symptom and the leading agent), but which is also *resistible*, provided that the danger is recognised in time and fought with determination, unity and strategic sense. To avoid any misunderstandings, I should make clear at the outset that this is not just, or even primarily, a book about the French far right. While we must take it seriously as a threat, it is equally important that we place its resurrection and its growing strength within a wider historical process: the neoliberal, authoritarian and racist radicalisation of the French ruling class as a whole.[4] Both product and producer of a seemingly interminable political crisis, this radicalisation has encouraged the rise of a new kind

---

2 For an analysis of this harassment, see for example: Miguel Shema, 'Médine, Maryam, Rokhaya, Mennel: montrez patte blanche ou taisez-vous!', *Bondy Blog*, 13 June 2018, bondyblog.fr; Claude Askolovitch, 'Zemmour, Mennel et l'anti-France', *Slate*, 10 February 2018, slate.fr.

3 For a critique of this 'immunity' thesis, see Michel Dobry (ed.), *Le Mythe de l'allergie française au fascisme*, Paris: Albin Michel, 2003.

4 As will be emphasised later, this process is at work in other societies, each in its own specific way.

of fascism, incomplete at this stage – particularly in its ability to mobilise the masses – but already in a position to largely dictate the political and media agenda and capable of winning coming elections, including the presidential contest set for 2027. It has given confidence to violent individuals and groups who share the worldview of the institutional far right but want to accelerate what they see as the ongoing 'race war'.

Fascism in France is currently embodied in organisations such as the FN/RN[5] (a party that is now more than fifty years old), Reconquête (founded in 2021 by the Islamophobic pundit Éric Zemmour), and a number of other movements and sects (Action française, the Identitaires, 'revolutionary-nationalists' and so on). It doesn't mean that any of these organisations is a fully fledged fascist mass movement. Yet each is a vehicle – or more precisely a collective producer, organiser and amplifier – of fascist desires, ideas, strategies and practices. The idea is hard to accept, because we've probably given too much credence to the idea of 'never again'. Or rather, because many people misunderstood it: this should have been seen as a call to action, aimed at opposing all resurgences of a fascism lurking at the heart of capitalism. Instead, it has been mistaken as a promise or a guarantee that the 'democracies' that had defeated Nazi fascism in 1945 could not, by their very nature, give rise to fascism. We have not taken seriously enough playwright Bertolt Brecht's warning: 'The womb is still fertile, hence arose the foul beast.'

After 1945 and decades in which the heirs of Hitler and Mussolini were marginal, fascism has survived and been reborn. It has done so while getting rid of the outward markers of the particular fascism that developed in the interwar context: the *style* with which fascism is so stubbornly associated in our minds, because it was so evocative, could be abandoned or considerably overhauled. From this point of view, we have to agree that neither Marine Le Pen, Éric Zemmour or their respective lieutenants, nor the far-right YouTubers and influencers who have emerged in recent years, are fans of brown shirts and swastikas. But they appear as the diverse avatars of a neofascism for the present moment, and more exactly, in the case of the FN/RN, as a more institutional branch of fascism, such as has *always* existed within this political current. It is, indeed, already present at the heart of French society (and more broadly of neoliberal capitalism), but biding its time and preparing the ground to become a *practice of power*.

---

5 To emphasise the continuity between the Front National and the Rassemblement National, in this book we will refer to the FN/RN.

But fascism is not limited to these organisations. It also manifests itself through a series of molecular shifts and transformations, at both the ideological and institutional levels, which pave the way both for an electoral victory of the far right and for a qualitative transformation of the state in an authoritarian and racist direction. These shifts and transformations can be encapsulated in the concept of *fascisation*.[6] In conclusion, this book argues for an anti-fascism that fights both the far-right organisations that give the neofascist project its political crystallisation, and the threefold neoliberal, authoritarian and racist offensive that is fostering its rise.

Since 2007–8, with the great financial meltdown and its aftermath, capitalism has plunged into a crisis from which only the blindest of business-press pundits thinks they see the way out. Indeed, this crisis regime seems to have become the normal way of managing the economy and society. Surely one expression of this crisis is the weakening of what we call democratic institutions. In France, the civil liberties and social rights won by the working class and its organisations over the last two centuries have been worn down by a series of governments. The traditional mechanisms of parliamentary democracy are systematically undermined, marginalised or hollowed out by the ruling class itself, in favour of unelected bodies or procedures to circumvent its processes (for instance, constitutional Article 49.3, used to pass laws without a vote, or else rule by decree). In other words, the current political forms of capitalist domination, which guaranteed certain rights to social protest or parliamentary opposition, and whose main function was to build broad social compromises that could have a stabilising effect, are breaking down. Moreover, racism is increasingly visible in the public arena, notably in the form of anti-migrant xenophobia and Islamophobia.[7] Currently ubiquitous reactionary ideologues make excuses for systemic discrimination against non-European immigrants and their descendants, while introducing the idea of the possible deportation of millions

---

6   See Ugo Palheta, 'Fascism, Fascisation, Antifascism', *Contretemps*, 28 September 2020. In English translation: 'Fascism, Fascisation, Antifascism', *Historical Materialism*, 7 January 2021. For further arguments on this count, see also: Ludivine Bantigny and Ugo Palheta, *Face à la menace fasciste. Sortir de l'autoritarisme*, Paris: Textuel, 2021, Chapter 3.

7   See Abdellali Hajjat and Marwan Mohammed, *Islamophobie. Comment les élites françaises fabriquent le 'problème musulman'*, Paris: La Découverte, 2013.

of Muslims (now rebadged 'remigration').[8] Finally, far-right forces have made significant electoral gains in France and beyond.

However, over the last ten years or so the possibility of a fascist threat has often been too readily dismissed, simply because of the way this spectre has been used for several decades. It has, indeed, been cynically wielded by a Socialist Party (Parti Socialiste, or PS) that became social-liberal in the 1980s and then liberal-authoritarian under François Hollande in the 2010s, but also by the right, particularly in the days of Jacques Chirac. 'Refuse to vote for us, in the first or second round, and you will have the return of fascism on your conscience,' their leaders have constantly told us. Such blackmail, combined with the policies pursued by these parties (borrowing in many respects from the far right's own agenda), has had the effect of trivialising the specific danger represented by the FN/RN: what good is sounding the alarm, if those who talk about a threat and claim to avert it are also clearly working to make it a reality? We only have to compare the massive popular reaction when Jean-Marie Le Pen reached the second round of the presidential election in 2002, and the lesser response when his daughter did the same in 2017 and 2022, even though the latter's score ended up much higher (41.5 percent in 2022 compared with 18 percent in 2002), to see that this election-night pseudo-anti-fascism is increasingly losing its hold.[9]

In recent decades, we have seen a constant worsening of the working and living conditions of millions of employees; a state of emergency wielded to prevent social mobilisation and then to manage the pandemic; the use of authoritarian procedures to undermine labour rights and pensions; migration and security policies that are increasingly indistinguishable from the ones advocated by the far right; and an Islamophobia that is today endemic in French society. These shifts were pushed by the Gaullist party under Jacques Chirac and then Nicolas Sarkozy, by the Socialist Party under François Hollande and Manuel Valls (among others),

---

8   To the question posed by a journalist from Italy's *Corriere della Sera* (in an interview published on 30 October 2014) – 'But then what do you suggest we do? Deport 5 million French Muslims?' – Éric Zemmour had this to say:

   I know, it's unrealistic but history is surprising. Who would have thought in 1940 that a million *pieds-noirs* would have left Algeria twenty years later to return to France? Or that after the war, five or six million Germans would have abandoned Central and Eastern Europe, where they had lived for centuries?

9   It should be pointed out, however, that the huge mobilisation against Le Pen and the FN in the run-up to the 2002 elections was hardly reducible to Chirac's instrumental purposes: this was a genuine, popular anti-fascist movement, undoubtedly the most powerful of the last fifty years.

and since 2017 also by Macronism. All this has weakened public sensitivity to the real threat posed by the FN/RN, including among those who surely have the most to fear from today's neofascist dynamic in France. Why should anyone fear a party that is known to be violently hostile to liberation movements, foreigners and Muslims, and more broadly to minorities, when successive governments have already laid the foundations for emergency legislation targeting so-called 'enemies within'? These policies have struck at Muslims, Roma people, migrants, residents of working-class and immigrant neighbourhoods, but also those whom the Macronist right has described in recent years as 'eco-terrorists' or 'Islamo-leftists'. Pandering to the FN/RN electorate all year round, only to denounce the far-right threat in the days ahead of some decisive electoral runoff, has been a losing strategy. This is quite unambiguously demonstrated by the electoral progress of Marine Le Pen and her party.

Did not François Hollande himself legitimise the FN/RN by inviting it to the Élysée Palace after the terrorist attacks in November 2015? Did not Emmanuel Macron endorse the far right by granting a lengthy interview to *Valeurs actuelles*, a reactionary weekly magazine recently convicted of racially insulting La France insoumise MP Danièle Obono? Has not the French ruling class, led by Macron and his ministers, already borrowed heavily from neofascist language, when it speaks of 'growing savagery', 'de-civilisation', the 'great replacement', or of a France 'drowning in migration'? Is it any wonder that there are too few people left who think it's worth confronting the far right head-on, and that the proportion of voters willing to vote against it in runoff elections is slowly but surely being whittled down? Moreover, a vote for Macron's party Renaissance, and even more so for traditional right-wing party Les Républicains (LR), which has sunk ever deeper into a fusion of neoliberalism and nationalist identity politics, can only temporarily ward off the danger.[10] It is an illusion to expect anything from them. In the long term, the logic of the 'lesser evil' is disarming because it systematically postpones any attempt to develop and implement an emancipatory policy. Such an alternative must have its centre of gravity among the working classes, already subjected to steadily worsening living conditions, but also among those who face all forms of oppression.

Inevitably, as illusions fade, the call for a 'pragmatic vote' or a 'vote to block the far right' has ever less sway over the populations whom it

---

10 Vincent Geisser, 'Le "bon filon" des primaires: la question identitaire au cœur de la future campagne présidentielle?', *Migrations société*, 2016, vol. 4, no. 66.

is supposed to mobilise. The Socialist Party long supposed that this was the way to push back the far right and to hold together its own electoral base, notwithstanding its own past record of using the FN to divide the right-wing camp. The Socialist Party has clearly failed on two counts. First, because its electorate and its activist base (more or less reduced to its local elected officials and their retinue) have dried up to an extent that would have been hard to imagine just a few years ago. Second, because the FN/RN has continued to grow, even if it is still far from a mass movement. The electoral weaponisation of the fight against the far right has backfired on its promoters (from both the Socialist Party and the right): the working classes and the parts of the middle classes who are becoming increasingly precarious can now easily see through their ruse. For it is too obviously functional to making people forget about a politics that does all it can to serve the dictates of capital and the interests of the propertied classes.

The anti-fascist struggle is thus urgently in need of renewal. However, this first means abandoning certain comfortable but impotent ideas about how to fight the far right. To oppose the FN/RN, we need something more than 'republican values' – which most people's everyday experience shows to be far from a reality – or a 'republican front' made up of organisations directly responsible for the destruction of social and democratic rights, for trivialising racism and, consequently, for the rise of the far right. Anti-fascism only has a chance of success if it abandons a strictly defensive stance. Its action must be part of the patient but determined, united but radical, building of a broad movement capable of putting an end to neoliberal, authoritarian and racist policies, halting the immiseration of the working classes and, more profoundly, breaking with the capitalist organisation of our lives.[11]

---

11   On the alternative to capitalism, see (among many other works): Stathis Kouvelakis (ed.), *Y a-t-il une vie après le capitalisme?*, Paris: Le temps des cerises, 2008.

1

The Return of (the Concept of) Fascism

At the end of World War II, it looked like there was a consensus on the idea of 'fascism'. There seemed to be a common view of what it was, not only on the left (across its various reformist or revolutionary, Stalinist or anti-Stalinist, anarchist or Trotskyist wings) but also across both left and right (or at least, that part of the right which had not collaborated with the fascist regimes). But this apparent consensus relied on many things being left out of the picture. Anti-fascist unity, especially in such countries as France and Italy, could only hold together so long as there was an ongoing struggle against Nazism and its accomplices. As the Axis camp disintegrated, so too did a certain understanding of the fascist phenomenon which had been tied to the palpable existence of enemy movements and regimes. These were the conditions in which it had been possible to agree, at least, on what fascism was and was not – and on the need to unite against it.[1]

The Cold War shattered this apparent consensus. Right-wingers and social democrats increasingly tended to put communism and fascism on an equal footing, casting these as different faces of the same 'totalitarian' menace. The communist movement, for its part, was quick to see a

---

1   This was not always the case: we know that, before the Communist International's turn in the mid-1930s, centred on the so-called 'popular front' policy (that is, seeking alliances with social democracy but also with certain bourgeois parties considered to be 'progressive', such as the Radical and Radical-Socialist parties in France), the official international communist movement considered social democracy to be 'social fascism'. On the variety of communist theories of fascism, see John M. Cammett, 'Communist Theories of Fascism, 1920–1935', *Science & Society*, 1967, vol. 31, no. 2. For a critique of the theory of 'social fascism', see Leon Trotsky, *Fascism: What It Is and How to Fight It*, New York: Pathfinder, 1969.

resurgence of fascism in the re-emerging conservative right, even as both Christian Democrats in Italy and Gaullists in France shied away from the label 'right wing'. The concept of 'fascism' thus became both less analytically powerful and more of a polemical tool, in national contexts where the far right – now reduced to a maelstrom of tiny groups – seemed firmly condemned to the political margins. The endurance into the 1970s of the Franco and Salazar dictatorships, clearly each within the 'magnetic field of fascism',[2] as well as the military coups in Greece and Chile,[3] nevertheless kept alive anti-fascist memory and the fight against fascism, at least as far as the left was concerned. Still, debates on fascism – whose terms had been set out in the interwar period, mainly within the workers' movement and among Marxist intellectuals[4] – offered few genuinely new developments, at least up until the early 1970s.

When the heirs of historical fascism raised their heads again – in the Italian Social Movement (MSI), the Freedom Party of Austria (FPÖ), the National Front in Britain or in France's FN – a pervasive anti-fascist culture inherited from the Resistance fed a certain shared vision of these forces, at least for some decades. It was easy for anti-fascist activism to claim political and theoretical continuity with the anti-fascism of the interwar period. However, when these parties began to evolve ideologically in the 1980s and 1990s, left-wing and anti-fascist movements proved unable to update their understanding of fascism. More than that, they generally struggled to get a serious grip on racism as something more than an individual prejudice or moral flaw. They failed to see that neo-colonial and institutional racism was, in fact, one of the main vehicles for the far right to push an alternative hegemonic politics based on processes of systemic discrimination and racialisation. They also failed to take seriously the far right's tendency to move on from the theme of racial superiority and instead focus on cultural incompatibility, clash of civilisations or conflicting identities. The result was that the rise of Islamophobia – across the political field, and not just on the far right – was not properly grasped as one of the fundamental focuses of the anti-fascist struggle, and, more broadly, of the left's battle for hegemony. Moreover, as far-right ideas and organisations began to make electoral headway,

---

2   Philippe Burrin, *La Dérive fasciste*, Paris: Seuil, 1986, pp. 61–94.

3   Augusto Pinochet's coup d'état created a military dictatorship which – while not, strictly speaking, fascist – served as a laboratory for forcing through neoliberal 'therapies', in collaboration with the economist Milton Friedman and the 'Chicago Boys'. See Naomi Klein, *The Shock Doctrine*, London: Picador, 2008.

4   David Beetham (ed.), *Marxists in the Face of Fascism*, Chicago: Haymarket Books, 2019 [1983].

French specialists on this political camp, from historians to political scientists, soon resorted to other concepts like '(national)-populism'. This not only limited a proper understanding of the far right but also played down the danger which it represents.[5]

The reading of these phenomena in the specific terms of fascism seems to have been permanently undermined by this mix of both disorientation faced with a changing far right and radicalisation among more traditional political forces. But it has also been hit hard by the academic and media consensus around the category 'populism'. For many, the very word 'fascism' is today off-limits – and even when it is used, it appears more as a slogan than a real tool of analysis.

Abandoning the Concept of 'Populism'

The concept of 'populism' is so vague and generic that it lumps together forces which are opposed in almost every other regard, for instance the RN and La France insoumise in today's France. If, during the Cold War, the 'totalitarianism' paradigm was used to equate the far right and the radical left, today the category 'populism' fulfils this same function.[6] This label thus tends to be applied without distinction to all movements said to be enemies of 'democracy'. When Syriza reached power in January 2015, Europe's various neoliberal ideologues joined in branding Alexis Tsipras a 'populist' or even a 'national populist',[7] because his party called for a break with the unprecedentedly harsh austerity measures imposed on

---

5   The concept of 'national-populism' was first outlined by Pierre-André Taguieff in the 1980s but was quickly taken up by others. For many examples, see Michel Winock (ed.), *Histoire de l'extrême droite en France*, Paris: Seuil, 1994; Jean-Yves Camus and Nicolas Lebourg (eds), *Les droites extrêmes en Europe*, Paris: Seuil, 2015. For Taguieff's first formulation of this idea, which is interesting in many respects, see 'La rhétorique du national-populisme. Les règles élémentaires de la propagande xénophobe', *Mots*, 1984, no. 9.

6   For an in-depth discussion of the concept of totalitarianism see in particular Enzo Traverso, 'Le totalitarisme. Histoire et apories d'un concept', *L'Homme et la Société*, 1998, no. 129. See also the collection of texts, coordinated by Traverso, *Le Totalitarisme. Le XXe siècle en débat*, Paris: Seuil, 2001.

7   Symptomatic of the many such statements by establishment pundits between January and July 2015 was former *Le Monde* editor Jean-Marie Colombani's 'L'imposture Tsipras', *Slate*, 29 June 2015, slate.fr. He wrote, among other things, that

> Alexis Tsipras and his Syriza party have shown their true colours: that of a radical, anti-system, anti-capitalist and ultimately anti-European group, whose model, if it exists, is surely found in the late Hugo Chavez's Venezuela. Instead of denouncing the American devil, this is a national-populist movement driven by intense anti-German propaganda, blaming Angela Merkel alone for all Greece's ills.

Greece from 2009 onward. Yet these accusations of 'populism' stopped as soon as Tsipras betrayed the programme on which he had been elected.[8] This served to demonstrate this label's basic function (at least in public debate), which is to put in the same basket all and any forces who criticise globalisation and/or the European Union, even if they have opposite motivations and political objectives.

Even the moderate left may be denigrated in such terms, if it dares challenge the hard limits of neoliberalism. When Jeremy Corbyn became Labour leader, he was accused of having succumbed to 'populism', because he broke from the project that Blairism had imposed on the party (and then on Britain in general) in the 1990s. Never mind the reality that Corbyn pursued a traditional centre-left Keynesian programme. It could be said that these are polemical uses of the term 'populism', used as weapons of political combat – and that they are, above all, used by politicians and ideologues trying to fend off any kind of criticism. But that would be to overlook the success that this notion has had also in the academic world.[9] And we can hardly fail to note the extraordinarily diverse phenomena which this concept is supposed to capture: ranging from nineteenth-century Russian and US populisms to twenty-first-century Islamism (from the Islamic State to Hezbollah), not to mention Mussolinian fascism, Stalinism, authoritarian movements in Brazil in the latter half of the twentieth century, the French and Italian left (all varieties included), Sukarno's regime in Indonesia and so on. But, while it is often acknowledged that this categorisation is rather vague, few draw the conclusion (however logical) that 'populism' is useless as a generic concept.

In France at least, Pierre-André Taguieff is doubtless one of the figures who has most constantly pushed the term 'populism' – an endeavour of his since the 1980s. This is not only aimed at replacing the concept of 'fascism' but also finding a name for all 'demagogic' trends, more broadly, in contemporary politics. Thus, Taguieff has bracketed the radical left together with the far right, distinguishing them only in terms of the different types of populism that each of them supposedly practise: a 'protest populism' in the former case, an 'identitarian populism' in the latter.

---

8   Providing a perfect illustration of the about-turn in political and media elites' view of Alexis Tsipras, *Le Monde* recently published an editorial singing his praises, while passing over in silence the fact that living conditions for most Greeks have continued to worsen: 'Grâce au courage des Grecs et de Tsipras, la Grèce a survécu', *Le Monde*, 22 June 2018.

9   See for instance *Vingtième siècle*, 1997, no. 56, special issue edited by Jean-Pierre Rioux entitled 'Les populismes'.

Taguieff has himself continually bemoaned the vagueness of this concept and its 'demonising' instrumental use;[10] but he has done so in a formal (epistemological) way, not prompting him to draw any further conclusions. So, even having raised well-justified doubts over this concept, he arrives at a definition of it which plunges right into the traps and pitfalls which he has himself noted:

> By the word 'populism', I mean the form taken by demagogy in contemporary societies whose political culture is founded on democratic norms and values treated as absolutes. This is a specific form of demagogy, which presupposes the principle of popular sovereignty and the focus on mobilising the people in a united nation.[11]

Such a definition seems bound to apply to far too many different phenomena to be of any use – and it is hard to see how it allows for any worthwhile distinctions to be made. This is especially true given how often the accusation of 'demagogy' is itself used to denigrate political and ideological opponents. Moreover, even apart from the xenophobic demagogy which we often hear in the mouths of various political leaders (from the far right to the mainstream right and the centre-left), we can quite easily identify a powerful neoliberal demagogy, which is also widely used by establishment pundits and many politicians. In their effort to justify attacks on some of the most militant sectors of the working class (rail workers, teachers and so on), this form of demagogy stirs up a popular feeling that such categories enjoy unfair privileges. Thatcherism was a master of this operation, whose deeper aim is to mask the capital/labour antagonism and instead draw focus towards divisions within the workforce. Macronism simply provides the latest version of this rhetoric. The allegation of 'demagogy' is always part of a strategy for delegitimising an opponent – and whether it works depends on whether the person making the accusation has the required symbolic authority (and media space). But a concept with such a strong polemical intent, and which is also so precarious and unstable, is clearly not a good basis for a definition of a specific political force.

Taguieff adds a few pages further along that populism 'can be defined, in summary, as the act of publicly taking sides with the people against

---

10 See in particular Pierre-André Taguieff, *L'Illusion populiste. Essai sur les démagogies de l'âge démocratique*, Paris: Flammarion, 2007, pp. 93–118.

11 See Pierre-André Taguieff, *Le Nouveau National-Populisme*, Paris: CNRS Éditions, 2012, p. 23.

elites, or even the "cult of the people".[12] Certainly, this is indeed a 'summary' definition. In this reading, what is distinctive about 'populist' movements is their repeated and emphatic appeals to the 'people': but is not that a dimension of *all* politics in the age of democracy? In a society where reaching power depends on the popular vote, anyone bidding for high office will tend to use rhetoric appealing to the people, and cast themselves as the people's natural spokesperson.[13] French conservative François Fillon is rarely suspected of 'populism', and yet when he came under judicial investigation during the 2017 presidential campaign he constantly referred to the verdict 'of the people'; for instance, he insisted that 'I now appeal to the French people and it alone, over and above the judicial process.'[14] Equally, if we imagine that opposition to 'elites' or 'the system' is an inherent characteristic of populism, distinguishing it from other political movements, how are we to explain the fact that Emmanuel Macron – generally presented as an alternative to 'populism' – claimed at his rallies that his rise would 'upset the established order, because it troubles the system'?[15]

In truth, no one really knows what 'populism' is, or could mean. This is also, doubtless, one of the (bad) reasons, as well as its function in demonising certain political currents, that this concept has enjoyed such success in politics, the media and academia. Reputed to be present everywhere from far right to far left, precisely because it is itself neither right nor left wing, and definable on the basis of considerations so generic as to make it undefinable, populism ends up nowhere to be found: as Jacques Rancière aptly puts it, it is left 'untraceable'.[16] The only reasonable way to use 'populism', from a scholarly point of view, would be to sharply circumscribe its usage. This would involve an outright abandonment of this concept's all-inclusive, generalising pretensions.[17] Indeed, whether we define populism in terms of an identitarian obsession with cultural uniformity or racial purity, in terms of a certain style of political

---

12   Ibid., p. 39.
13   See Pierre Bourdieu, 'Delegation and Political Fetishism', *Thesis Eleven*, 1985, vols 10–11, no. 1.
14   See Béatrice Bouniol, "L'appel au peuple' de François Fillon décrypté', *La Croix*, 3 March 2017.
15   Fabien Piliu, 'Macron ou la fausse naïveté', *La Tribune*, 31 August 2016.
16   See his chapter in *Qu'est-ce qu'un peuple?*, Paris: La Fabrique, 2013, pp. 137–43.
17   Even attempts at a typology are problematic insofar as we never really know why these particular objects of study should be compared and thought as a group. For a classic example of this type of approach, see Margaret Canovan, *Populism*, New York and London: Harcourt Brace Jovanovich, 1981.

intervention claiming to appeal to or directly commune with the people or in terms of an ideological orientation that counterposes the virtuous people to corrupt elites, it is hard to see what would justify lumping together Le Pen and Tsipras, Trump and Sanders, Meloni and Mélenchon, Berlusconi and Corbyn, Sarkozy and Iglesias or even Thatcher and Chávez.[18]

We could also add that the logic of political delegitimation mentioned above also seeks to keep the 'people' at arm's length, if not demonise it outright. The general use of the concept of 'populism' reflects the elitist prejudice that the people is ignorant and irrational, impulsive and incoherent, easily manipulated and prone to authoritarian excess and frenzies of xenophobia.[19] So, while the people is ostensibly recognised as the source of all political authority, it is meant to remain passive and settle for electing its shepherds, who are alone up to the task of leading it towards happiness, generally despite itself. In this way of seeing things, 'populists' are pied pipers who use demagogy – flattery and trickery – to lead the popular classes on a quest for unreasonable demands and turn them away from rational thinking (on which the ruling class supposedly has a monopoly). Of course, this rhetoric is now commonly heard – in varying forms, depending which establishment pundit or politician is voicing it – whenever any large social movement emerges or whenever the popular vote goes against the more or less unanimous will of the dominant political forces (we need only think of the victorious 'No' vote in France's 2005 referendum on the European Constitutional Treaty). The accusation also allows the extreme centre to shake off any responsibility for its own authoritarian and racist policies, on the pretext either that it is simply responding to the will of the people, or that it is at least avoiding the worst 'populist' excesses.[20]

---

18   Even in its slightly more sophisticated version, speaking of 'national populism' or 'right-wing populism' the concept tends to mix up organisations and leaders anchored in very different political traditions and pursuing distinct projects (Front National and UKIP, Haider and Berlusconi, Le Pen and Sarkozy and so on).

19   See Annie Collovald, *Le 'Populisme' du FN, un dangereux contresens*, Bellecombe-en-Bauges: Le Croquant, 2004; Federico Tarragoni, 'La science du populisme au crible de la critique sociologique: archéologie d'un mépris savant du peuple', *Actuel Marx*, 2013, vol. 2, no. 54. For a thought-provoking in-depth reflection on the many uses and meanings of the word 'people' see Gérard Bras, *Les Voies du peuple. Éléments d'une histoire conceptuelle*, Paris: Éditions Amsterdam, 2018.

20   Tariq Ali (in *The Extreme Centre*, London: Verso, 2015) explains how this idea applies to the British case:

Westminster is in the grip of an extreme centre, a trilateral monolith, made up of the Conservative–Liberal Democrat coalition plus Labour: yes to austerity, yes to imperial

Politically confused and useless for any analytical purposes,[21] the category 'populism' does not only end up heaping all the blame for the far-right resurgence on the working classes. For, as well as that, it also allows the far right to dissociate itself from historical fascism. Being demonised as a 'fascist' is far from the same as being dismissed as a 'populist' force. In the first case, the accused party is attached to a label which is near-universally despised, given the crimes committed by the movements from which they apparently draw a certain ideological and political inheritance. The recent election of Donald Trump should remind us that this specific type of demonisation isn't enough anymore to disqualify and beat the far right. But the stigma of being called 'populist' is much easier to deal with, by turning the accusation on its head and saying that they are indeed the only true representatives of the people. It is sometimes claimed that the demonisation of the Front National has inadvertently helped this party by allowing it to cast itself as the only popular alternative to political elites. But this assistance comes not from demonisation per se, but rather from that demonisation which relies on the label 'populism'. The Front National has drawn two benefits from this: it rids the party of its troublesome air of 'fascism', which it has been unable to shake off ever since it was founded by nostalgists for Nazism, Pétainism and *l'Algérie française*; but it also implicitly casts the party as standing on the side of the people, at a time when, with the decline of the communist movement and the gentrification of the Socialist Party, the left was losing its roots in the working class.

---

wars, yes to a failing EU, yes to increased security measures, and yes to shoring up the broken model of neoliberalism.

For a discussion of this idea see also Grégory Salle, 'À propos de l'extrême centre', *Contretemps*, 13 July 2017, contretemps.eu.

21   This confusion has been fed by the fact that some left-wing forces – especially Podemos but, following in its footsteps, also La France insoumise – have identified with the 'left-populism' theorised by Ernesto Laclau and Chantal Mouffe. In fact, the 'populism' on which they base themselves has little to do with what specialists working on the far right generally take this word to mean, beyond the (quite commonplace) opposition between 'the people' and 'elites', and the central place assigned to the leader. Moreover, it seems that the decision to self-define as 'populist' is often most of all an attempt to overturn the thrust of this accusation, or even a simple renewal of their political language. This choice does not make it any more legitimate, in either political or scholarly terms, to bracket these movements in the same category as the far right, for their programmes are fundamentally at odds with each other.

What Approach to Fascism?

What we instead need is a conceptual framework that does maintain a link with the category 'fascism' (whether this means speaking of neofascism, protofascism or fascisation). The main reason for this is that this concept points to a much more appropriate political characterisation of the contemporary far right, of its genealogical and ideological links with the past far right, of the factors that continue to distinguish it from other political forces, and the type of dangers raised by its rise. That is, a *Weltanschauung* made of: an obsession with demographic decline and moral decay; a mix of ultra-authoritarianism and extreme nationalism; a racial-civilisational paranoia which necessarily secretes xenophobia and racism (whose forms and targets vary according to the national context); a radical hostility towards equality and movements which support egalitarian demands; and an appeal to a national, racial and/or civilisational rebirth or regeneration that may only happen through a form of purification dispensing with the enemy within (minorities, immigrants, unions, left-wing activists and organisations). And it is notable how with the generic concept of 'populism', these ideological characteristics melt away, or are, at least, considerably diluted.

The use of the concept 'fascism' obviously bears the risk of anachronism, especially if we imagine the resurgence of fascism as its repetition in every detail, or as the product of an openly claimed historical continuity. The historian Robert Paxton notes that 'if we understand the revival of an updated fascism as the appearance of some functional equivalent and not as an exact repetition, recurrence is possible.'[22] History never serves up exactly the same dishes again, seasoned in the same way, in the same order and with the same names on the menu. This is especially true in fascism's case. Given the near-universal repulsion that fascism (particularly in its Nazi variant) has earned since 1945, far-right leaders seeking to breathe new life into ideas that flourished in the interwar period have had to become masters of the art of rhetorical dissimulation, euphemism, nods and winks and other more or less subtle repackaging of their ideas. They have also had to develop a language that somehow differs from the classical fascist one, even though there are some inherent continuities: for instance, when reactionary ideologues claim to have unearthed the 'Islamo-leftist' grip on France's universities or the influence of 'cultural Marxism', it readily brings to mind the past myth of

---

22 Robert O. Paxton, 'The Future of Fascism', *Slate*, 6 April 2017, slate.com.

'Judeo-Bolshevism' or what Nazis used to call 'cultural Bolshevism'. But we need to more clearly specify what is the same and what is different in this repeat performance, beyond inevitable variations in its political forms and historical trajectories. This requires that we first reach a definition of what fascism is.

Indeed, among those who do persist in using this concept, its meaning often tends to be overly elastic. Hence in its most caricatural usage, it can be reduced to the state as such – sometimes considered fascist in essence or tendency – or even with any form of power and/or violence. Some currents, like the Maoists of the Gauche prolétarienne (GP) in the 1970s – went as far as to characterise the right, from Pompidou to Giscard d'Estaing, as a 'new fascism'; they thus ignored the difference between a strong (capitalist) state and a fascist regime (which belongs to the category of 'exceptional capitalist states', to use Nicos Poulantzas's term). This distinction is no mere academic quibble, for it has immediate political consequences: one does not fight in the same conditions and with the same strategies under (and against) a fascist state as under (and against) a liberal one, even when this latter is becoming more repressive.[23] Fascism has, moreover, been theorised as the consequence of a particular psychological characteristic (an 'authoritarian personality'[24] or 'microfascism'[25]) or even as the product of aggressive tendencies inherent to human nature itself. Even if it can be useful to question the psycho-affective structures that encourage the penetration of fascism in certain sectors of the population, this may have two consequences: on the one

---

23   'Nouveau fascisme, nouvelle démocratie', *Les Temps modernes*, May 1972, no. 310 *bis*.

24   Here, we could obviously think of Wilhelm Reich, Erich Fromm or certain works by members of the Frankfurt School. In his *Mass Psychology of Fascism*, Reich wrote that 'fascism' is only

> the politically organised expression of the average human character structure, a character structure which has nothing to do with this or that race, nation or party ... the basic emotional attitude of man in authoritarian society, with its machine civilisation and its mechanistic-mystical view of life.

Here we will not attempt to discuss these positions in detail, but we will note that they tend to underestimate the objective social tendencies and historically constituted forces, the combination of social relations (of exploitation and oppression) but also social and political struggles, in particular the intensity and outcomes of the class struggle. Reich, moreover, concludes by stating that 'international fascism will never be vanquished by political manoeuvres. It can only be vanquished by the natural organisation of work, love and knowledge on an international scale'. See Wilhelm Reich, *The Mass Psychology of Fascism*, New York: Orgone Institute Press, 1946, pp. 5–6.

25   See Gilles Deleuze and Félix Guattari, *A Thousand Plateaus*, London: Bloomsbury, 2013.

hand, decontextualising fascism means isolating it from the sociopolitical forces and dynamics that produce it; on the other, it means suggesting that what we first and foremost need to do is get rid of the fascist nestling within us, just as some used to advise us to 'kill the cop in your own head' if we wanted to fight the police state.

Moreover, after 11 September 2001, 'Islamofascism' entered the vocabulary – a neologism which would die hard. It has been used both to legitimise Islamophobic policies at home and to launch military interventions abroad, especially in France's former colonies and in the Middle East. The European far right has itself been compared to terrorist organisations of claimed Islamic inspiration, while many reactionary ideologues (often ones coming from the left) reduce contemporary fascism to these terrorist organisations alone. But, in all of these cases, their reasoning usually starts out from superficial analogies and hasty generalisations. Even beyond the use of extreme violence – something no one would consider minimising, but which is hardly the province of fascism alone (we need only think of the imperialist wars or deadly repression imposed by liberal democracies) – the historian Enzo Traverso is right to emphasize everything that distinguishes Daesh, in its political profile and the conditions under which it emerged, and Hitler's Nazi Party or Mussolini's National Fascist Party. Indeed, these latter regimes had much more in common with the Ba'athist dictatorships in Iraq and Syria (who, by the way, were supported by a large part of the global far right) than with their fundamentalist opponents.[26] The less fascism is used as a rigorous analytical category, the more it is used for narrow, polemical ends. This doubtless owes to the fact that as far as most of the public's thinking is concerned, fascism still represents the very heights of political disgrace. So, everyone has cause to use this accusation against their enemies, often at odds with all logic.

Some even dismiss the hypothesis of a fascist danger, the better to focus on the immediate threat represented by neoliberalism (in the form of Macronism in France). This logic establishes a hierarchy between the 'main enemy' and 'secondary enemies'. In a bid to drive home this point, neoliberalism is sometimes itself taken for a form of fascism.[27] Clearly, such an equivalence is drawn more because of its denunciatory power

---

26 For a more in-depth discussion of this question, see Enzo Traverso, *The New Faces of Fascism*, London: Verso, 2019. See also Anne Alexander and Haytham Cero, 'Fascism and ISIS', *International Socialism*, 5 October 2015, isj.org.uk.

27 See, for instance, the column by Manuela Cadelli, president of the magistrates' association, 'Le néolibéralisme est un fascisme', *Le Soir*, 3 March 2016.

and ability to provoke than because of its analytical accuracy. This means overlooking or minimising some of fascism's fundamental characteristics (not least its suspension of political and civil liberties, its violent destruction of all opposition and counter-powers, or even the purging of the state) – but also the great variety of political-institutional configurations through which capitalism is able to make whole populations bend to its logic. Not just any authoritarian form of capitalism, any strong state, any increase in the power of the executive or in the repression of social movements amounts to fascism; and the concern to highlight, analyse and denounce neoliberal capitalism's authoritarian shifts is not at all conditional on us being able to call it 'fascism'.[28] Lastly, to claim that neoliberalism is the only enemy that it is important to fight against – or even that we are already subject to a more or less insidious form of fascism – obscures the reasons why, if neoliberalism is not fought and defeated, it could indeed lead to fascism. Moreover, this also means overlooking the margins of action we still have open to us to stop such a dynamic playing out.

If we want to avoid such overly elastic uses of the concept 'fascism', we need to rediscover – or better, reconstruct – its meaning. At the most general level, this category has to do with a specific set of political practices, strategies, ideas and even desires which emerge in particular socio-historical circumstances (and, indeed, these circumstances themselves need specifying). Fascism cannot, therefore, be considered the essence of just any form of power, and still less the product of a regressive and repressive psychological tendency. Its programmatic contours, its modes of action, its style and the forms in which it appears can all vary – not only is fascism as a movement rather distinct from fascism as a regime, but it also varies depending on the national context and its degree of development.[29] But we could hardly include under this label all organisations centred on a charismatic leader, all conservative or authoritarian movements, or any state of exception (for instance, military dictatorships). To do so would again risk losing any grip on its particular meaning.

If we did have to agree on a definition of fascism[30] – even the most basic and provisional one – we should consider it a mass movement

---

28 See Chapter 2.
29 On this, see Robert O. Paxton, *The Anatomy of Fascism*, New York: Knopf, 2004.
30 This is a fraught task, given how heavily it depends on which varieties of fascism we choose to include under this name (in other words, on how extensively we wish to apply this concept). Much of the historiographical debate on fascism revolves around this very question. What about Francoism and Salazarism, for example, or the

that claims to work towards the regeneration of an 'imagined community' which is considered organic (the nation, 'race' and/or civilisation)[31] through ethno-racial purification and the elimination of any form of social conflict and dissent (whether at the level of politics, trade unions, religion, journalism or the arts) – in short, by getting rid of anything that appears to endanger this community's fantasised unity (and, in particular, the visible presence of ethno-racial minorities and of left-wing activism). Fascism purports to impose a principle of monolithic unity – the basis of the mythologised community it claims to regenerate. But this unity is not necessarily racial, in the pseudo-biological sense that this assumed in the Nazi case.[32] It may be cultural (pushing discrimination, violence and exclusion in the name of a supposed ethnolinguistic and/or religious community, allegedly rooted in a millennia-old past) or even political: Mussolinian nationalism largely based itself on an incoherent mix of references to the Roman Empire and an absolutist and exclusivist conception of the General Will.[33]

Such a project is realised through a political practice centred on systematic violence and repression. More specifically, this means recourse to both state and extra-state *terror*, which combines the state's repressive apparatuses with the mobilisation of sections of the population enrolled in mass militias. This 'militarisation' of politics, as the historian Emilio Gentile calls it, distinguishes fascist tyranny from military dictatorships; it relies on a highly unstable alliance between the declining petty bourgeoisie (its sociological core), the most conservative fractions of the propertied classes (or those with most interest in fascism) as well as

---

military dictatorships that spread throughout Latin America in the postwar decades? As Poulantzas suggested, we could also consider that all these far-right dictatorships included various components (fascist, military, Bonapartist), with different social roots, and that in each case we need to ask which is the hegemonic faction.

31 Drawing on numerous studies regarding very diverse movements, Roger Griffin persuasively emphasises the idea of (national, racial and/or civilisational) regeneration or renaissance as fascism's ideological cornerstone, and the source of its dynamism. See in particular R. Griffin, *The Nature of Fascism*, London and New York: Routledge, 1991. See also Roger Eatwell, *Fascism: A History*, London: Penguin, 1997; S. G. Payne, *A History of Fascism*, London: Routledge, 1996.

32 It should be noted that, in the case of Nazism, the racial (or biological) aspect is not opposed to the cultural aspect but constitutes its necessary foundation. Admiring Greek antiquity, fantasizing about their civilization and claiming to be its heirs, the Nazis considered the ancient Greeks to have descended from Nordic peoples. See J. Chapoutot, *Le national-socialisme et l'Antiquité*, Paris, PUF, 2012.

33 Hence the complex relationship between Mussolinian Fascism and the French Revolution, unlike the Nazis who presented this revolution as the source of evil. See George L. Mosse, 'Fascism and the French Revolution', *Journal of Contemporary History*, 1989, vol. 24, no. 1.

plebeian elements pauperised by the transformations of capitalism, who are generally without ties to the trade union movement and left-wing parties. But, at a deeper level, it presupposes a social and economic crisis that mutates into a particularly acute, brutal and profound political crisis – what Antonio Gramsci called an 'organic' or 'hegemonic' crisis[34] – combined with the presence of a far-right force politically independent of the traditional bourgeois right, and which is more or less actively supported by a section of the population. Only a crisis of this kind, married with the presence of such a force, can put a fascist dynamic on the agenda.

While such a definition avoids a purely ideological or cultural characterisation of fascism as a phenomenon,[35] and lays emphasis on the practices of both fascist movements and fascist regimes (and in particular, on the use of violence),[36] it nonetheless takes seriously fascism's ideas, symbols and myths – in a word, its ideology (in a broad sense of the term), or we could say its *Weltanschauung*. So, it is important to avoid two potential traps. One is based on indifference to fascist ideology and is thus unable to interrogate the persistence and/or transformations of a fascist 'project' (instead reducing fascism to methods of intimidation, violent practices or even terror). The other has an exclusive focus on ideology, which could lead us to take fascists' word for what they are, what they do and what their objectives are – or, at least, lack sufficient critical distance from their past and present discourse (especially their 'antisystemic' rhetoric). Seeking to conquer souls, hearts and minds, fascists have developed their own vision of modernity, an alternative to both liberal capitalism and materialist socialism, combining hyper-modernist accents (including a fascination with technology, particularly in its military applications) and reactionary tones (nostalgia for ancestral tribes, small-scale production and the good life in the country), revolutionary pretensions and ultra-conservative or restorationist desires. In this sense, it is worth following Mihály Vajda in remembering that fascism's utter programmatic opportunism (Mussolini declared that 'our doctrine is

---

34   The historian Geoff Eley rightly emphasises this type of crisis, which he calls a 'fascism-producing crisis'. See *Nazism as Fascism: Violence, Ideology, and the Ground of Consent in Germany 1930–1945*, New York: Routledge, 2013.

35   A tendency that we especially find, albeit in different forms, in many eminent fascism specialists, from Zeev Sternhell to George L. Mosse and even Roger Griffin. For an analysis of the consequences of such a focus on ideological and/or cultural aspects of fascism, and in particular a tendency to downplay the role of violence, see Enzo Traverso, *L'Histoire comme champ de bataille*, Paris: La Découverte, 2012, pp. 112–25.

36   On this key aspect of Nazism, see Enzo Traverso's fundamentally important work *The Origins of Nazi Violence*, New York: The New Press, 2003.

action') does not mean that it is without ideology or that this ideology played a marginal role in its rise. As he put it, 'fascism never hesitated to modify its declared programme in the most radical way, even to reverse it completely if its power interests demanded such a tactic. But it never renounced its own ideology'.[37]

The definition suggested above also allows us to avoid an instrumentalist conception of fascism. Such a conception, which can be seen in many approaches claiming a Marxist inspiration, prevents us from grasping fascism's complexity and autonomy. Thus, fascism is too often reduced to a mere tool wielded by the capitalist class – or some fraction of it[38] – so that it can confront an imminent revolutionary threat. This presents fascism as a purely reactive phenomenon (in short, a simple response to the rise of the revolutionary workers' movement)[39] which has no political autonomy from the dominant classes. This thesis is today contradicted by all serious historical studies of fascism and Nazism, which, on the contrary, emphasise not only the central role that the declining petty bourgeoisie played in fascism movements,[40] but also its multi-class character. They thus show the variety of bases of support which fascism could count on, at different moments of its rise and its consolidation of power. Originally, it was based on the petty bourgeoisie and veterans of World War I, but then it also won support from declassed elements of the working class and certain sectors of the dominant classes (including big landowners and most of the powerful capitalists, just before and even more after accessing power).[41]

---

37 Mihály Vajda, *Fascism as a Mass Movement*, London: Allison & Busby, 1976, p. 16. His analysis of fascism doubtless represents one of the most convincing Marxist theoretical offerings in this regard.

38 A definition memorably proposed by Dimitrov in his famous report to the now-Stalinised Communist International in 1935, according to which fascism is 'the open terrorist dictatorship of the most reactionary, most chauvinistic and most imperialist elements of finance capital'.

39 Paradoxically, this was also the argument made by the German historian Ernst Nolte, whose notorious anti-communism led him to propose the revisionist-apologetic thesis that Nazism was an understandable reaction to the 'Bolshevik danger' and did nothing but borrow (and radicalise) this latter's methods. Aside from his erasure of Nazism's particular German roots, and in particular the roots of its pan-Germanism and genocidal antisemitism, Nolte never seriously addresses the fact that the violence he imputes to the Bolsheviks was itself a reaction to the invasion of Russia by a dozen foreign armies (representing tens of millions of soldiers) deployed in Russia to support the White reaction and fight the new government that had emerged from the revolution.

40 One of Leon Trotsky's great merits lies in his emphasis on this point. Indeed, his texts on Nazism represent a high point of twentieth-century Marxist political analysis. See his *Fascism*.

41 See in particular Jairus Banaji, 'Fascism as a Mass-Movement: Translator's

It has rightly been emphasised that, despite fascism's 'socialist' pretensions, it did not revolutionise the economic systems of either Italy or Germany. Rather, it made capitalism dramatically harsher, as it suppressed both workers' rights and their defence organisations.[42] It intensified the concentration of capital and destroyed not only the communist movement – which was, at that time, a real threat to the capitalist system – but the workers' movement as a whole (including its most moderate elements), and even bourgeois parties of the liberal or conservative right. We cannot, however, *reduce* fascism to a mere creation of capital in urgent need of counter-revolutionary repression.[43] This would be to overlook the reasons for fascism's own dynamism, to deny the relative autonomy of the political-ideological plane, and thus to underestimate the role played by nationalism and racism – and in particular, antisemitism – in interwar Europe. In what is, in many aspects, a different context, over the last fifteen years nationalism and racism – this time, in the form of Islamophobia – have again represented decisive factors in the far right's resurgence in Western countries.[44]

Twentieth-century fascism triumphed not only because it was financed by German captains of industry or Italian landowners and politically supported by leaders of right-wing parties, even if this support has everywhere been crucial, or simply thanks to the armed gangs that harassed left-wing parties and trade unions. Similarly, it did not keep itself in power through brutal repression alone, although this did allow it to rapidly weaken, demoralise and gag the workers' movement – the only social and political force that could have put a stop to its rise. It did not stop at exploiting an exceptional economic and political crisis, which led many to feel that capitalism was succumbing to its own internal contradictions. Rather, fascism built its strength by transforming the despair of declassed social layers into millenarian hope in a new order – an alternative to the established one.[45] It thus found a dynamism of its own,

---

Introduction', *Historical Materialism*, 2012, vol. 20, no. 1. On the relations between fascism and different class fractions, see Nicos Poulantzas, *Fascism and Dictatorship*, London: Verso, 1979.

42   See Daniel Guérin, *Fascism and Big Business*, New York: Pathfinder Press, 2000.

43   For an old but still compelling critique of the reduction of fascism to a mere variant of capitalist power, see Claude Lefort, 'L'analyse marxiste et le fascisme', *Les Temps modernes*, 1945, no. 2.

44   On the comparison between interwar political antisemitism and today's Islamophobia, see Enzo Traverso, 'La fabrique de la haine. Xénophobie et racisme en Europe', *Contretemps*, 17 April 2011, contretemps.eu.

45   As Trotsky said of the Nazi base in 1933, 'Despair has raised them to their feet, fascism has given them a banner.' See his 'What Is National Socialism' (June 1933), marxists.org.

in competition with that of the socialist and communist movements. Sometimes considered a 'conservative revolution', in our eyes, fascism can be better understood as a *counter-revolution disguised in revolutionary forms*[46] – whether through the symbolism of the 'new order' and the 'new man', its rhetoric about a break with the established order, or even its recourse to mass mobilisation. Its main enemy was never the state or capital or the propertied classes – only financial capital is generally the focus of fascist critique, which always carries an odour of antisemitism, because, in this ideology, finance is almost always implicitly or explicitly associated with Jews. Rather, its main enemy was the workers' movement and all it had won: civil liberties, fundamental political rights, gains in terms of social legislation and so on.

Having formed a mass movement, fascism managed to rise to power – and stay there – by establishing a robust alliance with society's conservative powers that be (the capitalist class, religious institutions or, in the Italian case, the monarchy), finding a modus vivendi with the army, and moulding the consent of the majority of the population. Never monolithic, this consent could take the most varied forms (from enthusiastic support to mere resignation, passing through various degrees of more or less critical or indulgent acceptance of the regime). But even if it was sometimes eroded, this consent was real, and it extended across all social classes.[47] If, for example, Nazism was able to secure the passivity of the industrial working class, this mainly owed to its measures to absorb unemployment, through state intervention in the economy (and especially via war industries). Yet it also satisfied the big capitalists, in particular in heavy industry, by an enormous increase in profitability which allowed vast fortunes to be amassed and powerful firms to be built, most of which survived World War II and the Nazi defeat.[48]

---

46 Angelo Tasca authored an early, crucially important book on Italian fascism. He rightly emphasises the fact that this counter-revolution was not a reaction to a determined offensive by the workers' movement, but rather a 'preventative and posthumous' action. Preventative, because it sought to pre-empt any future workers' revolution; posthumous, because it came after the proto-insurrectionary experience of the *biennio rosso* of 1919–20, during which the workers' organisations proved incapable of breaking bourgeois power and imposing a socialist political solution. See Angelo Tasca, *The Rise of Italian Fascism, 1918–1922*, London: Routledge, 2010.

47 Neither Mussolini nor Hitler managed to satisfy the bourgeoisie, petty bourgeoisie and proletariat all to the same extent. On the relations between Nazism and the working class, see Tim Mason's classic study *Nazism, Fascism, and the Working Class*, Cambridge: Cambridge University Press, 1995. See also Alf Lüdtke, *Everyday Life in Mass Dictatorship: Collusion and Evasion*, London: Palgrave Macmillan, 2015.

48 See David De Jong, *Nazi Billionaires: The Dark History of Germany's Wealthiest Dynasties*, Glasgow: William Collins, 2022.

Fascism moreover established its authority through an ideological offensive which was deployed at all levels. With this, it cobbled together an extremely powerful variety of nationalism, based on cultural, aesthetic and intellectual ingredients drawn from very diverse sources.[49] This nationalism was further radicalised through the particular contribution of antisemitism (especially in the Nazi case, though we should not underplay its place in Italian fascism),[50] which allowed the fascists to galvanise their supporters by mobilising them against an absolute enemy, considered inferior yet threatening.

The specific seductive force of nationalist and racist ideas was often downplayed on the left. This often owed to a reductive economism: it was admitted that nationalism and racism were used to divide the working class, but they were ultimately considered secondary compared to the class interests that did unite workers. Similarly, a sometimes obtuse rationalism made it hard for the left to take seriously nationalism's more nebulous charms, or indeed the dark satisfactions of antisemitic conspiracy theories. It was thus imagined that nationalism and racism could do no more than superficially mislead the workers, and even then only momentarily. If they were seduced by fascism, this was blamed on the leaders of the left and the workers' movement who had betrayed them. Such a reading failed to understand the power of ideologies which, in historical circumstances marked by the collapse of the old balances, could gain hold over the masses and – as Marx might have said – themselves become 'a material force'.

The Actuality of the Fascist Danger

What is distinctive, then, about our approach to fascism is that we want to understand it as both an expression of the crisis of capitalism – and more specifically, a *crisis of hegemony*[51] – and as a mass movement with its own relative autonomy towards dominant classes.[52] With a specific ideology, organised forces and sources of legitimacy (electoral or militant), fascism should be considered fully a political actor in and of

---

49 See George L. Mosse, *The Fascist Revolution: Toward a General Theory of Fascism*, New York: Howard Fertig, 2000.

50 On this aspect, see in particular the final part of Marie-Anne Matard-Bonucci's recent book *Totalitarisme fasciste*, Paris: CNRS Éditions, 2018.

51 For further elaboration of this point, see Chapter 2.

52 Nicos Poulantzas provides an energetic and unremitting (and itself Marxist-inspired) critique of this trend in his *Fascism and Dictatorship*.

itself – one which, once this crisis has reached an advanced stage, may appear as a solution for certain fractions of the propertied classes, but also for wide layers of the population. The German and Italian bourgeoisies, through their organic political representatives (the traditional right), allowed fascists into power both to restabilize the political power and to quell the workers' resistance, with the objective and obsession of maximizing profits. The rise of fascists also relied on the fact that, amid a generalised ideological crisis that they had themselves skilfully fuelled, they had already conquered a mass popular audience, in promising all things to all people, in proving their activist dynamism and ability to counteract the workers' movement, and in popularising their perspective of national-racial rebirth.

This inevitably raises a question: does the (generic) concept of fascism as defined above refer to a situation which is too historically unique for this same concept to be useful for us today? Should we not, then, restrict its use to that era, which now lies in the past? To take such a line of argument to its full conclusion would necessarily mean using the category 'fascism' for the Italian case alone. For Ernst Nolte and Renzo de Felice, two historians of fascism whose works have been widely debated and subjected to critique, the fascist movements and regimes were phenomena inextricably linked to a particular context – the 'European civil war' of 1914 to 1945. Further, De Felice came to consider (as did Zeev Sternhell) that Mussolinism and Hitlerism did not belong to the same category, given how central antisemitism was in the latter case.[53] We would then limit the application of this term to Italy alone, because even in the interwar period, the political movements that were generally labelled as 'fascist' showed a great degree of variation.

Restrictive definitions or interpretations of fascism ask us to tick boxes to confirm that this or that criterion is satisfied – and more criteria can always be added. This often limits us to a mere survey of particularities, while overlooking dynamic processes or deeper continuities.[54] Of course, the genocidal, conspiracy-theorist and pseudo-biological form that antisemitism took on in Germany is a specificity of Nazism; and, if

---

53   On the historiographical and political debates surrounding fascism, see in particular Renzo de Felice's classic *The Interpretations of Fascism*, Cambridge, MA: Harvard University Press, 1977. See also the much more recent survey by Olivier Forlin, *Le Fascisme. Historiographie et enjeux mémoriels*, Paris: La Découverte, 2013.

54   For an energetic and convincing critique of an approach to fascism that consists of ticking off so many criteria, or identifying the stages meant to lead the way to fascism, see Alberto Toscano, *Late Fascism: Race, Capitalism and the Politics of Crisis*, London: Verso, 2023.

we take this dimension in isolation, it would be difficult to consider it as belonging to the same *type* of movement or regime as Italian fascism, in which state antisemitism came rather more belatedly.[55] Equally, it could be claimed that the contemporary far right has, however partially or rhetorically, broken with the visceral antisemitism with which it was indivisibly linked from the end of the nineteenth century onward, and thus there are no grounds for comparing it to Nazism. But that would be to forget that fascism is not politically defined by the particular groups it happens to target (and, indeed, the fact that the far right should never be taken at its word and that today Islamophobia functions rather like the antisemitism of yesteryear).[56]

What allows them at least to be considered in combination is the fact that not only Mussolinism and Hitlerism but also most contemporary far-right movements are essentially variants of a certain type of nationalism, which affirm the obviousness of national-civilisational decay and the necessity of its regeneration through a vast effort in purification. This type of nationalism necessarily tends towards forms of exclusivism which do, in certain historical circumstances, overlap with racism: in such cases, this latter will provide nationalisms with a 'counter-type in order to sharpen their own sense of community'.[57] 'Racism was the catalyst which pushed German nationalism over the edge, from discrimination to mass extermination'[58] – and there is no reason to think that anti-Jewish racism alone could have played this catalytic role, or could do so even now. In today's Western Europe, and particularly in France, Italy and indeed Germany, the demonisation of Muslims has largely replaced Jew-hatred, in particular on the far right but also in right-wing and centre-left parties. And we may indeed fear that Islamophobia has the same potential to radicalise nationalisms as did the antisemitism of yesteryear.

Some historians of fascism, especially George L. Mosse and Emilio Gentile, emphasise the extreme brutalisation process that began with

---

55   Marie-Anne Matard-Bonucci nonetheless emphasises the specifically Italian roots of this state antisemitism, which was not a mere by-product of the alliance with Nazi Germany. See Matard-Bonucci, *Totalitarisme fasciste*. For its part, the Vichy regime was antisemitic from top to bottom; and, contrary to what was long the received wisdom, this was not in fact the direct product of German demands. See Michael R. Marrus and Robert O. Paxton, *Vichy France and the Jews*, Stanford: Stanford University Press, 2019.

56   See Ugo Palheta, 'L'antisémitisme tourne toujours à droite', *Contretemps*, 12 December 2023, contretemps.eu.

57   Mosse, *The Fascist Revolution*, p. 64.

58   Ibid., p. 66.

World War I, and its effect in sharpening and militarizing nationalisms, as key to understanding fascism's genesis.[59] So, without an event of the same type, there is no possibility of a resurgence of fascism. This argument is not to be ignored. But if we do not assume that neofascism means the simple return of an ever-identical fascism, is it not possible that renewed forms of brutalisation – including ones linked to climate turmoil[60] and the 'new Cold War'[61] – could produce effects equivalent to those seen in the interwar period? Violence has not disappeared so much as taken different forms:[62] indeed, while interpersonal physical violence is ever-less tolerated, violence perpetrated by states, increasingly from a distance,[63] seems widely accepted, insofar as it targets populations or groups that have already been identified as enemies (whether domestic or foreign), as a threat to the nation's or world's security, or as a threat to 'our' identity or interests. Here, again, racism undoubtedly plays a crucial role, particularly Islamophobia in the West. By demonising the enemy (who is always named in deliberately vague terms) and casting them as less human, it legitimises the exceptional treatment (the use of violence, the suppression of freedoms) to which they will be subjected. By extension, this also applies to all those who may (in the self-reproducing and often frenzied logic of racism) be lumped in together with them. It ensures that the majority will be indifferent towards their fate or even support their oppression.

Theories designed to explain fascism thus all too often alternate between extremely general philosophical approaches and historical studies excessively concerned with the uniqueness of each variety of fascism.[64] The former tend to dissolve fascism's historical specificity, banalising it and ignoring the conditions in which it could emerge, take root and conquer power. The latter inevitably lead to an assertion of

---

59   George L. Mosse, *Fallen Soldiers: Reshaping the Memory of the World Wars*, Oxford: Oxford University Press, 1990.

60   Andreas Malm and the Zetkin Collective, *White Skin, Black Fuel: On the Danger of Fossil Fascism*, London: Verso, 2020.

61   Gilbert Achcar, *The New Cold War: The United States, Russia and China – From Kosovo to Ukraine*, London: Saqi Books, 2023.

62   François Cusset, *Le Déchaînement du monde. Logique nouvelle de la violence*, Paris: La Découverte, 2018.

63   Grégoire Chamayou, *Théorie du drone*, Paris: La Fabrique, 2013.

64   A whole analytical tradition presents fascism as the product of survivals of preindustrial traditions and social layers, in Italy as well as in Germany (the *Sonderweg*) and, more generally, as the result of the 'belated' arrival of bourgeois democracy and the 'Rechtsstaat' relative to the capitalist modernisation process. On the wider problems of characterising Nazism politically, see I. Kershaw, *The Nazi Dictatorship: Problems and Perspectives of Interpretation*, London: Bloomsbury, 2015, especially Chapters 1 and 2.

the radical non-actuality of fascism – the impossibility of its resurgence in the present-day context. More generally, the concept of fascism and the theories designed to explain it are subject to the same fate as any concept or theory that seeks to subsume necessarily disparate political phenomena and propose an interpretation of them. Incapable of grasping the complexity and specificities of each political movement and each national situation, they are doomed to remain partly unsatisfactory. But we do think it useful and productive to draw parallels between classical fascism and the contemporary far right if it allows us to grasp the fascist danger of our time, in terms of the socio-economic conditions that make it possible, the political dynamics that have set underway, the structural complicities that it can find among dominant social actors, and also the ideas that allow the far right to influence and sometimes mobilise a section of society.[65]

Moreover, the interwar period is the only one in which fascist or parafascist organisations developed to the point of reaching power and forming more or less stable and enduring dictatorships (and in Spain and Portugal they lasted for almost half a century). It is, in our view, rather irresponsible to refuse to draw parallels between classical fascism and the contemporary far right – even if only as a hypothesis, and also in order to emphasise what differentiates them. For this is to refuse to understand the means by which the movements of this type, once created, manage to take root, mobilise heterogeneous social layers, win power and wield it over the longer run.[66] What were the conditions of possibility for the fascist catastrophe? How did fascist movements manage to conquer power and stay there? Why did their opponents on the left, despite having mass organisations, fail to stop this process? What mistakes did they make? What were the fascist movements and regimes' strengths and weaknesses? Why, and how, did they end up themselves being defeated?

It seems to us, then, that, from both a scholarly and a political point of view, the interest in the comparison is hard to deny. Unless, that is, we imagine that this far right has not inherited anything from the past. Such a supposition seems especially hazardous when we are dealing with organisations that were indeed created by historical fascist militants, who in some cases took part in or collaborated with the fascist dictatorships (the FN, the Austrian FPÖ, the Italian Social Movement and

---

65   Frédéric Lordon, *Les Affects de la politique*, Paris: Seuil, 2016.
66   Here the reader will have recognised Robert O. Paxton's three stages of the onset of fascism. See his *Anatomy of Fascism*.

today's Fratelli d'Italia and so on).[67] Furthermore, using the concept of fascism may allow us not only to uncover the continuities in an apparently chaotic and incoherent history, but, moreover, to build a common understanding and shared memory that ties together the struggles of the past and the fight in the present and future. Without such an effort, it seems impossible to find any political moorings and to formulate strategic objectives: for how could we know where we are and where we are headed, if we indulge the illusion that we come from nowhere and are always starting again from scratch? Daniel Bensaïd liked to remind us – citing Deleuze – that we 'always start again in the middle'. He rejected both the mirage of absolute novelty and the no-less illusory idea of political models that history provides us ready-made, including the user's guide.[68]

Enzo Traverso and G. M. Tamas both make such a comparison between historical fascism and the contemporary far right.[69] However, in their explanations of why they use the category 'postfascism' rather than 'neofascism'[70] they are too quick to close down the necessary, two-pronged debate on both far-right movements and our historical situation. They do this by claiming that we are dealing with essentially unprecedented movements and a previously unseen situation, or, at least, that what we face today is radically different from the interwar period. But is there not a strategic and political project within the contemporary right – and not simply in explicitly neofascist currents, which are almost everywhere marginal[71] – that represents a renovated version of the 'fascist synthesis'? And does our present period really make the renaissance of fascism – at least conceived in terms of a 'functional equivalent' – so improbable?

It is not enough to say that far-right movements in general, and the FN/RN particularly, 'no longer claim their fascist heritage', or to insist

---

67 On Fratelli d'Italia and Italian fascism, see David Broder, *Mussolini's Grandchildren: Fascism in Contemporary Italy*, London: Pluto Press, 2023.
68 On this point, see Daniel Bensaïd, Ugo Palheta and Julien Salingue, *Stratégie et parti*, Paris: Les Prairies ordinaires, 2016.
69 Gaspar Miklos Tamas, 'On post-fascism: The degradation of universal citizenship', *Boston Review*, 1 June 2000, bostonreview.net.
70 See Traverso, *The New Faces of Fascism*, pp. 3–8.
71 None of the far-right movements with an audience in today's Europe claim continuity with the fascist past. This includes even Greece's Golden Dawn, which seems the closest 'stylistically' to classical fascism but denies this association. On Golden Dawn, see D. Psarras, *Aube dorée. Le Livre noir du parti nazi grec*, Paris: Syllepse, 2014. We could also mention Hungary's Jobbik, which has, for some years, pursued a 'de-demonisation' strategy which has led it to swear off any kind of continuity with fascism as well as all explicitly antisemitic discourse.

that their ideological transformations amount to a defascisation, because they apparently 'no longer exhibit an ideological continuity with classical fascism'.[72] While there are indeed changes going on in the Le Pen party, they make it a contradictory and unstable political object whose future development is hard to foresee. It is true that the FN/RN has moved away from historical fascism on certain points. It has toned down the antisemitism, homophobia and anti-feminism which characterised the party up until the 2000s, obviously for the purposes of making it more respectable. This has also helped it to stigmatise Muslims, who are now blamed – against all evidence[73] – for the persistence of antisemitic prejudice, homophobic speech and acts and the oppression of women in France. But, if it has moved away from Mussolinian or Hitlerite fascism, this is perhaps most visible in the fact that it does not form militias to violently attack its political opponents (though small groups gravitating not far from the FN/RN do attempt to do so).[74]

Yet other developments show that the FN/RN has drawn closer to fascism on other grounds. It has coupled its xenophobic ultra-nationalism and its authoritarianism with ideological ingredients which belong more to the fascist register than did some of the positions that used to characterise the party. Marine Le Pen's 'neither Right nor Left' attaches her more to Doriot, and thus to historical French fascism, than Jean-Marie Le Pen's 1970s–80s bid to embody the 'national, social and popular right'; its reappraisal and even celebration of the state, breaking with the zealous anti-statism that characterised the FN up to the 1990s, have also brought the party rather closer to Italian fascism, even if this does not reach Mussolini-style 'statolatry', or what he called founding a 'totalitarian state'.[75] Marine Le Pen's (very partial) critique of free market

---

72 Traverso, *The New Faces of Fascism*, p. 6.

73 Even apart from the many studies reminding us that sexism and homophobia are hardly the sole preserve of any one social or ethno-racial group, it is worth noting that the vast majority of participants in France's movement against equal rights (more specifically, against same-sex marriage) were recruited from among the Catholic population.

74 See Nicolas Lebourg, 'Bastion Social, le mouvement néofasciste qui s'implante en France', *Slate*, 28 March 2018, slate.fr.

75 See in particular the text coauthored by Mussolini and the Fascist regime's official ideologue Giovanni Gentile, purporting to expound *The Doctrine of Fascism* (New York: Howard Fertig, 2006). Still, a note of caution is needed, here, given that, when this text was written, Mussolini was seeking an alliance with conservative circles and big industrialists and thus mounted a sharp critique of all state intervention in the economy, even to the point of declaring himself an enemy of statism. Such was fascism's programmatic opportunism. On this point, see Tasca, *The Rise of Italian Fascism*. So, we cannot agree with Michael Mann when he presents overt statism as a decisive criterion

economics and rhetorical defence of labour (or at least, 'French workers') more resemble the claims universally made by movements within fascism's orbit, than the harsh, Reagan-inspired neoliberalism that the FN used to promote. Lastly, the party's tactical break from antisemitism and Holocaust denial is aimed at masking the virulence of its Islamophobia. This latter pays off much more electorally, given that in today's French political field this appears as a 'respectable racism'.[76] It constantly parades this break with the past,[77] generally with the acquiescence of indulgent journalists, because it serves a dual function: to 'de-demonise' the far-right party (as Marine Le Pen sought to do when she became party leader in 2011), and, in turn, to demonise Muslims and the left as the sole source of antisemitism in France.

As for the fact that the FN/RN (and at least some of Europe's main far-right parties) have abandoned mass violence, we can surmise that this is part of their 'war of position' strategy (as Antonio Gramsci would say). Essentially electoral-institutional in nature, this strategy embraces the forms of parliamentary politics in order to gain state power and then attempt to bring about qualitative transformations within the state. Yet this decision also reflects a common constraint they face in today's Western societies. Since World War II, but also since the experience of the 1970s (particularly in Germany and Italy), these societies have seen a powerful de-legitimisation of political violence, which normally condemns to electoral marginality all those political forces that use violence or (even more so) set up paramilitary structures. In addition, the absence of a brutalising experience comparable in any way to the World War I era means that there is simply not the kind of mass subjectivity that would make it possible to form militias on a large scale; yet historical fascism would have been difficult to conceive of in its paramilitary forms without this *sui generis* group constituted by veterans (even if not all veterans were fascists – far from it). We should also mention the weakening of the workers' movement and its capacity to structure and organise the

---

for terming this or that movement as fascist. See Michael Mann, *Fascists*, Cambridge: Cambridge University Press, 2004.

76 See in particular Saïd Bouamama, *L'Affaire du voile, ou la production d'un racisme respectable*, Lille: Éditions du Geai Bleu, 2004; Pierre Tevanian, *Dévoilements. Du hijab à la burqa, les dessous d'une obsession française*, Paris: Libertalia, 2012.

77 For example, every FN/RN leader today makes a point of commemorating the Vélodrome d'Hiver roundup of July 1942, even though the first number two of the FN, when it was founded, was himself one of the organisers of that roundup: namely, Victor Barthélemy. See Joseph Beauregard and Nicolas Lebourg, *Dans l'ombre des Le Pen. Une histoire des numéros 2 du FN*, Paris: Nouveau Monde, 2012.

working classes in their own trade union and political ranks. Today's fascists no longer really face an adversary that they need to break by force in order to gain a foothold or impose their will, or an adversary with the kind of social power that would demand that they develop an apparatus of mass violence.

Finally, it can be argued that states now have instruments of surveillance and mass repression that are far more sophisticated than the states of the interwar period. Neofascists may well feel that state violence is quite sufficient to control and annihilate – physically if necessary – any form of opposition. The crucial point thus becomes the conquest of the state and its fascisation by purging the dominant bourgeois-democratic elements within it, by transforming the way it functions, and by stifling the elements of counter-power in the state and in civil society (trade unions, human rights associations, activist collectives and so on). All this corresponds to processes which depend on the social and political balance of power, and therefore on popular struggles and their outcome.

The formation of mass militias was both necessary and possible for fascist movements in the peculiar context of the interwar period. But neither the formation of armed gangs, nor even the use of political violence, is the hallmark of fascism, either as a movement or as a regime. These are, indeed, centrally important elements, but other movements and other regimes, by no means belonging to the world of fascism, have also resorted to mass violence to conquer or maintain power, sometimes murdering tens of thousands of opponents (and that is not to mention the legitimate and strategic use of violence by liberation movements). The most visible dimension of classical fascism, extra-state militias, were, in reality, a subordinate element of fascist leaders' strategy, tactically using them according to the requirements of organisational development and the legal conquest of political power. In the interwar period, and even more so today, the latter presupposed a degree of respectability, which meant keeping the most visible and brutal forms of violence at arm's length. Mussolini and Hitler constantly insisted (during the conquest of power, but also sometimes afterwards) that the violence committed by their supporters organised into militias was either a lie invented by their political enemies or a simple defensive reaction against 'communist barbarism'. The strength of fascist or neofascist movements can, in fact, be measured by their ability to use either legal or violent tactics, 'war of position' and 'war of movement' (to use Gramsci's categories), as the historical conjuncture demands. The fact that the main parties of the contemporary far right do not have militias can hardly itself be used to demonstrate that they have *ipso facto* broken with fascism, that they are merely more or less 'radical' varieties of the right or mere nationalist and reactionary fringes of an omnipresent 'populism' which would also include parts of the left.

But what about the historical period itself? Fascism made up part of the modernist 'galaxy' of its time. It claimed to represent a rupture and set forth the utopia of a 'new man' inhabiting a world transformed from top to bottom; this is also what distinguished it from other varieties of authoritarian nationalism. Yet Enzo Traverso and Michael Mann[78] rightly emphasise the contemporary obliteration of any 'horizon of expectations', of any 'transcendence' – in other words, the enfeeblement of populations' and political movements' capacity to project themselves into a desirable and possible future. In this view, the dominance of neoliberal ideology, one of whose particular characteristics is that it presents its reign as 'the end of ideologies', has brought about an era in which all political projects aiming for rupture with the established order – now considered unthinkable – and any utopia – which would implacably lead to totalitarianism – are delegitimised in advance.

On this reading, the contemporary far right is thus incapable of recreating a utopian drive towards rupture, and instead has to settle for calling for a return to the stability of times past: a retro-utopia that finds its model in Trump's 'Make America Great Again', or else in going back to the 'Golden Age', to the protective state, to national currencies, borders and so on. But this, again, is surely getting ahead of ourselves a bit. While neoliberal ideology may have appeared totally dominant right after the collapse of the Eastern Bloc, today it has fractured. Capitalism does not currently face any opponent able to confront it on an equal footing, but it *is* increasingly under challenge. It is often challenged in partial ways, regarding this or that aspect or effect of capitalism, but even its basic logic is sometimes put into question. As the illusion of the end of ideologies dissipates, little by little, new utopias are emerging; some of them are emancipatory, while others are regressive. We should thus steer clear of a static reading of the far right and the political situation. Not only is the resurgence of ultra-nationalisms and the rising strength of racism, in particular Islamophobia, doubtless (sadly) only just getting started;[79] but the crisis of capital accumulation, the climate crisis, the hegemonic instability at the global level (in particular as a consequence

---

78   See Mann, *Fascists*, p. 364.
79   See Chapter 4.

of the relative decline of the US hyperpower and the rise of China), as well as the revival of social and political revolt, could drive the propertied classes to intensify their authoritarian and xenophobic turn. More than that, it could also encourage – in reaction to the progress made by emancipatory movements – the rise of new far-right utopias or even fascist eschatologies like those we find in authors such as Julius Evola.

Of course, this is not a 'return to the 1930s' – a counterproductive formulation, for it suggests an idea of fascism coming back in identical form. But fascism is a concrete possibility in our era. This is the sense in which we will here speak of the *actuality* of fascism, even while strongly distinguishing this category from talk of the *imminence* of fascism, which would suggest the immediate advent of fascist-type dictatorships. To speak of the actuality of fascism means that the cogs are already in motion – and thus our time is running short. But this also allows us to emphasise that this dynamic is far from inevitable, and that it can still be stopped, even if for the moment we are very poorly armed – politically, intellectually, organisationally – to confront it. An awareness and an understanding of this threat should allow us to rally forces and bring them together in the interests of a wide-scale social transformation. Without that, there is every chance that capitalism – in its neoliberal, authoritarian and racist configuration – will drag us towards the abyss.

The Conditions of Possibility for Fascism

So, here, we have no interest in making the umpteenth prophecy and thus satisfying the taste for cheap fear – or, indeed, the need for cheap reassurance. Fascism is not an irresistible force any more than the 'coming insurrection'. It is important not so much to interpret the warning signs as to uncover its conditions of possibility – without thereby succumbing to the temptation of a catastrophism that is more likely to disarm us than spur mobilisation. This is not about political sci-fi, but of grasping what is today only a potential future. At the heart of this study is the category of the possible, which enriches our understanding of reality: 'it is through the possible that we discover the real,' wrote Bachelard. It highlights certain hidden virtualities in the transformation of societies and gives pride of place to the uncertain and unpredictable dynamics of social and political power struggles. While this category has been the subject of an eminently positive reappraisal in recent years,[80] we should

---

80 For a discussion of this category, see Laurent Jeanpierre, Florian Nicodème

be careful not to restrict its use to the emergence of emancipatory politics or the construction of progressive alternatives in the here and now. The possible can also be the sudden onset of disaster or the gradual slide towards catastrophe. If the 'chapter of forks in the road remains open to hope', as Blanqui said at the end of the Paris Commune, it is also open to chaos, oppression and despair.[81]

This book is, then, rooted in a conception of history that refuses to contrast contingent events (moments of salvation or disaster) to the inertia of economic, social, institutional and cultural structures. For it is precisely when structures head into crisis that the event becomes possible. Marx wrote that 'history does nothing'; it constitutes a field of possibilities, some of which are clearly a nightmare for millions of individuals and entire peoples. This condemns us to act urgently – but even then, nothing is promised or guaranteed. History offers model(s) only to those who have been orphaned by the great prophecies (be they religious or secular), and who are desperately looking for a path that has already been set and the promise of a radiant future. For others, it offers a glimpse of possible, contingent ways forward, which are always subject to conditions – including disastrous futures like that described in this book. And we already have a lot to deal with! Indeed, one crucial factor, here, is the possibility of collective action by the millions of exploited and oppressed people who – in each nation as well as among humanity as a whole – make up a social majority. It is they who are capable of transforming the world. If we do not think that that is the case, then how can we imagine any way out of the reign of oppression and coercion? If men and women 'make history' in circumstances they have not chosen, there is no doubt that a shared understanding of these circumstances and an acute awareness of the dangers ahead can be a useful, even irreplaceable, tool for action.

Of course, this book does not claim to be either a theoretical treatise on fascism or a survey of the contemporary far right. Rather, it draws on theory and existing research to analyse the political situation in France and ask the following questions: How can we explain the return and the rise of the French far right since the 1980s? How did the changes in class relations and the political arena resulting from the neoliberal transformation of capitalism contribute to this? What relation is there between this political dynamic, the authoritarian turn of the French capitalist

---

and Pierre Saint-Germier, 'Possibilités réelles', *Tracés*, 2013, no. 24. See also: Quentin Deluermoz and Pierre Singaravélou, *Pour une histoire des possibles*, Paris: Seuil, 2016.
 81   Bensaïd often cited this comment on *bifurcations*.

state, and the transformations of nationalism and racism? More generally, what about the present situation is giving renewed impetus to the fascist project of regenerating a nation considered to be in 'decline', of forcibly restoring a unity perceived as under 'threat', and of re-establishing a hierarchical order deemed only 'natural'? The main aim here is to offer an analysis of the political situation, exploring the conditions that give rise to the fascist threat, and asking in particular what about contemporary French society has made (and can make) a neofascist political offer credible.

While the RN will feature prominently in this book, it is not its core focus.[82] The fascist dynamic described here stems from major trends in neoliberal capitalism and French politics, not from an alleged 'essence' of the Rassemblement national, and recalling its fascist origins is not sufficient to determine its true nature to fascism or establish its eventual fate. Depending on how the social and political balance in France develops over the coming years, on what happens within Marine Le Pen's party, but also on the attitude of the propertied and the actions of the subaltern classes, the RN could make further progress or decline; it could become a more or less traditional right-wing party, become more radical or even pave the way for a new, more violent far-right force. The RN is thus important as a vehicle – even if perhaps a temporary one – for a historical dynamic that stretches beyond it. It has established itself over the last forty years as the main political representative and organiser of different forms of social resentment and fears, succeeding in giving them a national/racial rather than an anti-capitalist and class-based direction. It thus seems worth analysing this party's discourse and activity, its strategy and its electoral influence.

Still, we will also seek to give due weight to the underlying forces which are the vectors of the RN's rise, and which relate both to the crisis of neoliberal capitalism, particularly acute in the case of French capitalism, and to the strategic choices made by French politicians over the last forty years. Only an analysis of the transformations of class relations and the political field, of the state and ideology, can properly explain these

---

82 On this party and its sociology, see in particular: Sylvain Crépon, *Enquête au cœur du nouveau Front national*, Paris: Nouveau Monde Editions, 2012; Alexandre Dézé, *Le Front national: à la conquête du pouvoir?*, Paris: Armand Colin, 2012; Sylvain Crépon, Alexandre Dézé and Nonna Mayer, *Les faux-semblants du Front national*, Paris: Presses de la FNSP, 2015; Valérie Igounet, *Le Front national. De 1972 à nos jours, le parti, les hommes, les idées*, Paris: Seuil, 2014. Older studies are equally worthy of mention: Alain Bihr, *Le spectre de l'extrême droite*, Paris: Editions de l'Atelier, 1998; Guy Birenbaum, *Le Front national en politique*, Paris: Balland, 1992.

forces. Only a dynamic in which the people regain political mastery and the economy is placed under social control can overcome this crisis, from which the 'morbid phenomena' evoked by the communist thinker and activist Antonio Gramsci, himself imprisoned by a fascist dictatorship, have resurfaced. As Frankfurt School co-founder Max Horkheimer famously put it: 'If you don't want to talk about capitalism, you should keep quiet about fascism'. But capitalism understood abstractly as a mode of production can only be a starting point. To go beyond this and produce a concrete analysis requires an understanding of the way in which the class relations, conflicts and struggles inherent in capitalism are translated, in a distorted (and sometimes unrecognisable) way, into the form of political relations, conflicts and struggles within a particular social formation, in this case French capitalist society. The central focus of this book is therefore not the RN itself, but the way in which a fascist danger has been generated and strengthened by a certain political configuration of French capitalism.

This configuration is the product of a series of dynamics: the neoliberal turn in public policies; the authoritarian hardening of the state; the increasing presence of nationalism and racism; the rise of the various elements of the far right, which has been able to structure the political agenda largely around its own obsessions (immigration, national identity, insecurity and Islam); and, last but not least, the political weakening of the working class (a sharp fall in its level of organisation, particularly trade union organisation, ideological disorientation, the collapse of the communist movement, the almost total integration of social democracy and its satellite organisations into neoliberal capitalism and its subsequent decline and so on). The fascist threat arises from the interaction between these different dynamics, each of which has its own specific logic, temporality and actors, while at the same time feeding each other in a vicious cycle from which it seems impossible to escape at present. The buildup of neoliberal counter-reforms is leading to the impoverishment of the working classes and the growth of inequality, but it is also indirectly generating anger and protest. Yet, in response, the French ruling class has steadily stepped up its repressive efforts over the past forty years. This first struck at (and still above all targets) working-class and immigrant neighbourhoods, whose residents suffer overexploitation, racial discrimination, spatial relegation and police harassment. But, more recently, it has also taken aim at social movements (the yellow vests, anti-racist, environmentalist, anti-fascist, trade union and so on). It has also resorted to nationalist and racist demagogy that has continued to fuel the electoral successes of the far right. In turn, the audience acquired by the far right has legitimised the stepping up of securitarian policies by successive parties of government, while encouraging and legitimising the use of a warlike and racist rhetoric against Muslims, Roma and migrants. All this is aimed at winning back the slice of the electoral pie nibbled away by the far right over the last few decades.

Finally, we should make clear that this study will focus on France. Political and ideological power relations are still today condensed in national terms, and most social movements continue to develop at the national scale, notwithstanding the process of capitalist globalisation and forms of regional integration (in particular the European Union). It is, therefore, at this level that the neofascist danger must first be understood and described. Nevertheless, the threat is emerging on a much wider scale and is becoming more pronounced in many countries, and this in turn has prompted important debates on the character of the forces at work and the nature of these transformations. Over the last ten years, we have seen the radicalisation of forces historically belonging to the conservative right;[83] but so, too, the rise to power of forces undeniably rooted in fascism like in India, Austria, Italy and France; and the emergence of new far-right forces in Brazil, Argentina, Germany or Spain. This combination of trends suggests that the conditions for the development of neofascist forces or the fascisation of right-wing organisations are present in many different societies.[84]

But, at a deeper level, it indicates that the bourgeoisies, or at least significant sections of them, are prepared to use increasingly authoritarian means to resolve the long-term stagnation of their economic system, the crisis of political legitimacy and the great destruction of the environment at the expense of the working classes and minorities (whether ethno-racial, national, religious, sexual or gender-based).[85] The fact that the Big Tech magnates came to pledge allegiance to the new tenant of the White House during his inauguration ceremony signals a major change in strategy within the dominant factions of the capitalist class: the rule of law and a certain degree (however minimal) of social compromise may

---

83   We are thinking here of the Republican Party in the United States, Vladimir Putin's United Russia, Viktor Orbán's Fidesz in Hungary, Benjamin Netanyahu's Likud in Israel (in alliance with the Orthodox or secular far right) or Recep Tayyip Erdoğan's AKP in Turkey (allied with the historical fascists of the MHP).

84   For references on most of the countries and movements mentioned here, see Ugo Palheta, *La Nouvelle Internationale fasciste*, Paris: Textuel, 2022.

85   Gilbert Achcar, *Clash of Barbarisms: September 11 and the Making of the New World Disorder*, New York: Monthly Review Press, 2002.

have appeared functional to them in the postwar decades. The neoliberal turn, with its obvious authoritarian impulse, paved the way for a qualitative break with the liberal-democratic state and new dictatorial forms of exercising power.

On the far right itself, over the last fifteen years or so, we have seen the rise of a kind of neofascist common sense: a set of tactics, words, ideas, memes, jokes and 'theories', shared and elevated to the status of self-evident facts, but also affects and desires for change or even redemption, in some cases. This is being done not only by political parties properly speaking but also well outside their ranks, by neo-reactionary intellectuals, militant movements (identitarian, neofascist, supremacist and so on) and ultraconservative think-tanks, via a wide range of online outlets, also using the new possibilities offered by social media.[86] From this point of view, the presence of Steve Bannon – a former strategic adviser to Donald Trump, and follower of the fascist philosopher Julius Evola – at the 16th Congress of the FN in 2018 did more than just reveal an ideological dynamic which jars with this party's more respectable trappings. For it also spoke to exchanges which, while they had always been going on within the far right,[87] have intensified over the last decade and now more than ever include the extremist fringes of the established political right. While these forces are both partners and rivals, their objective is sufficiently shared, clear and dangerous enough to be taken seriously. Faced with the crisis of the ideology that has dominated the political scene for several decades as the handmaiden to the capitalist offensive – that is, neoliberalism – they are seeking to form a new hegemony.

---

86   Pablo Stefanoni, *La rébellion est-elle passée à droite?*, Paris: La Découverte, 2022.
87   From its foundation, the FN enjoyed considerable strategic assistance, but also funding, from the main Italian neofascist party, the MSI: see Igounet, *Le Front national*.

2
A Hegemonic Crisis

Liberal ideologues have tended to think of fascism as a radical departure from capitalist modernity, as if irrationally veering away from the inexorable march of progress. The foremost Italian liberal intellectual of the first half of the twentieth century, Benedetto Croce – who, as a senator, voted confidence in Benito Mussolini's government in 1924[1] – cast fascism as a 'parenthesis' in his country's history. If the liberal tradition thus seems to have repressed its bad memories,[2] in responding to its claims the communist movement and certain Marxist intellectuals have sometimes tended to bend the stick too far in the other direction, describing the relationship between capitalism and fascism according to a mechanical and simplistic logic. This approach centres on the understanding that, faced with the rising mass revolutionary threat, the propertied classes

---

1   Zeev Sternhell recalls not only this episode but also the justification given by Croce himself in an article published at the time. In particular, in the context of the assassination by the fascists of the reformist-Socialist MP Giacomo Matteotti, he stated: 'it can hardly be said . . . that the avalanche of punches is not, in certain cases, usefully and opportunely administered'. The historian also recalls how 'Croce never ceased to wage a bitter daily polemic against democracy, the philosophy of the Enlightenment, natural law and humanist ideologies'. See Zeev Sternhell, *Ni droite ni gauche. L'idéologie fasciste en France*, Paris: Gallimard, 2012 [1983], pp. 25–9 (*Neither Right nor Left: Fascist Ideology in France*, Berkeley, CA: University of California Press, 1986).

2   The invention of the concept of 'totalitarianism' – which from a liberal standpoint, particularly in the context of the Cold War, had the great merit of binding fascism and 'communism' together in a great Other counterposed to 'Democracy' and so-called 'Western' values – was a further instrument of this repression. After all, it drew an unsinkable line between 'Western' or 'liberal' democracies, or the 'free world', on the one hand, and (fascist or 'communist') 'totalitarianism' on the other. For an overview of the disputes over the concept of 'totalitarianism', see Enzo Traverso, *Le Totalitarisme. Le XXe siècle en débat*, Paris: Seuil, 2001.

chose to call on fascism's services in order to defend their position. These classes are said to have handed the fascists the 'job' of annihilating these movements once and for all – authorising the utmost brutality to execute this mission, such as the imperialist bourgeoisies had previously used only in the colonial context.[3]

Hence, the critical understanding of fascism is too often reduced among the left to a kind of stereotypical image, in which the bosses financed and armed fascist gangs in order to crush a popular uprising or pre-empt it happening to begin with: fascism as the bourgeoisie's last defence. In this vision, fascism is little more than an instrument of capital, a tool whose particular nature and strength can be reduced to the single task with which it was entrusted: namely, to crush the left, the workers' movement and all forms of social protest. On this reading, fascism had no real ability to build its own forces, and thus both its early successes and final victory must necessarily be considered the results of a bourgeois conspiracy. Yet such an understanding not only ignores fascism's dynamism and its relative ideological and political autonomy from the propertied classes but also denies the possibility of a fascist threat in our own present. For, if the only thing that can push the ruling class towards fascism is the fear of imminent revolution, then, seeing the weakness of revolutionary forces today, we would necessarily conclude that there is no fascist danger. Indeed, once the problem is framed in these terms, it is also hard to understand why the bourgeoisie would 'need' fascism, when it can in any case draw on sizeable, well-drilled forces (the police and the army) prepared to crush any popular uprising. In fact, it has never failed to use these forces when this was a necessary and possible option. In the French case, we could cite such instances as the bloody repression of the workers' uprisings of June 1848 and May 1871 (the Paris Commune), or later of anti-colonial mobilisations (17 October 1961).

By tying everything to the supposed needs of the bourgeoisie and what is imagined to be its chosen course of action (giving no consideration for

---

[3] We should remember Aimé Césaire's words to the
very distinguished, very humanistic, very Christian bourgeois of the twentieth century that without his being aware of it, he has a Hitler inside him, that Hitler *inhabits* him, that Hitler is his *demon*, that if he rails against him, he is being inconsistent and that, at bottom, what he cannot forgive Hitler for is not *the crime* in itself, *the crime against man*, it is not the humiliation of man as such, it is the crime against the white man, the humiliation of the white man, and the fact that he applied to Europe colonialist procedures which until then had been reserved exclusively for the Arabs of Algeria, the 'coolies' of India, and the 'niggers' of Africa.

See Aimé Césaire, *Discourse on Colonialism*, New York: Monthly Review Press, 2001, p. 37.

its internal cleavages), an economistic and instrumentalist approach fails to understand either the 'classic' fascisms or the far-right forces that are developing in capitalist societies today. If fascism does indeed maintain close relations with capitalism – something which clearly contradicts the liberal postulate of a natural affinity between capitalism and democracy (even understood in a restrictive, that is, liberal, sense) – fascism is not the simple product of the despicable choices of the capitalist class. It is no mere tool over which this class has complete, top-to-bottom control, or a purely functional necessity when the capitalist system is threatened with overthrow. Fascism must, first of all, be understood as one of the expressions – one of the 'morbid symptoms', as Gramsci would have said – of an epoch of capitalist decomposition (declining economic dynamism, intensified competition between imperialist powers, the weakening of democratic institutions, the discrediting of traditional political representatives and so on).

If this decomposition, to which we will return later, is a real factor, this does not imply that capitalism is doomed to collapse under the weight of its internal contradictions, or that fascism is the inevitable end point ahead of us. But it does create the conditions for an acute and multifaceted crisis – a not only economic but also social, political, environmental, ideological and even more broadly 'spiritual' (to use Gramsci's term) crisis. In certain (both national and regional) political contexts, this is opening up space for developments that even just a few years ago would have seemed like products of dystopian fantasy. This chapter seeks to more specifically examine the form that this political crisis takes in the context of contemporary French capitalism. This latter's declining position within the capitalist world economy,[4] combined with a level of social conflict that has remained at much higher levels than the other main European powers (Germany, the United Kingdom, Italy) have surely fed into the country's instability, political elites' deep loss of legitimacy and the reordering of the political field in recent years. Today, French sociopolitical life is organised around three blocs: a neoliberal-authoritarian bloc (still under the hegemony of Emmanuel Macron's Renaissance), a

---

4   Here, it is not our intention to advance any hypothesis concerning France's (or any other country's) position in the international balance of power (particularly in economic terms) and its connection with the probability of fascism. One lesson from the interwar period is that there is no automatic link between a country's level of economic development and the political strength of far-right forces. This does not mean that economic development is a merely irrelevant consideration. But this factor only bears effect through a series of mediations, particularly at the political and ideological level, and under the influence of the relations of power between the different classes.

nationalist-identitarian bloc (totally dominated by Marine Le Pen's RN) and a left-wing bloc (whose unity is constantly threatened by the opposition between a pole supporting neoliberal capitalism, centred around the Socialist Party, and an anti-neoliberal left embodied by La France insoumise).

Here, we will advance a quite simple argument: it was the triumph of capitalism in the 1980s and 1990s, repeatedly hacking away at previously won social gains, that allowed the far right to revive and take root.[5] It is the crisis of capitalism – particularly as manifested and intensified by the financial crisis of 2007–8 and its aftermath – that is putting fascism back on the agenda, albeit evidently in new forms. More precisely, if there is a possibility of neofascism in contemporary France, this is primarily because of the ruling-class response to the crisis of capitalism, which began in the late 1960s but erupted in the mid-1970s. Time and again, it has opted for neoliberal solutions that have been wilfully socially destructive (mass unemployment and precariousness, privatising public services, rolling back social protections and so on), at least for large parts of the working class and growing segments of the middle classes. Yet these solutions have also had the deeper effect of eroding the foundations of bourgeois hegemony, by breaking down the political and ideological balances inherited from the post-1945 period. We can, then, properly grasp the fascist danger only if we take seriously the effects that the neoliberal offensive has had on French society – a process that has been ongoing for over four decades and has only accelerated under the reign of Emmanuel Macron.

To better understand this, we need to analyse the reproduction of capitalism as a system, and more specifically of the role played by mainstream parties – in other words, the main organisational expressions of the ruling class in the strategic field of the state. These parties must not only ensure the conditions for maintaining or increasing the profitability of capital, through the policies enacted by the state and its economic role. They also need to establish a form of political domination in a stable and lasting way. This itself presupposes several other things. It demands a series of (state or para-state, coercive and ideological) apparatuses able to lead and discipline the population, using violence if necessary. But it also requires a set of representatives considered to have a certain legitimacy in running the nation's affairs. It likewise demands a political system

---

5 In the most varied forms, depending on the political and ideological specifics of each country and their place within the international division of labour.

sufficiently flexible to channel popular demands or expectations, but also able to express the interests and needs of the different fractions of the ruling class and ensure the possibility of compromise among them. Finally, it is crucial to obtain the effective subordination of workers – the employers' imagination is particularly fertile, not to say inexhaustible, in this regard – and even their active consent to a system which, in objective terms, exploits them and generates monstrous inequalities. But workers' integration into the production and reproduction processes, and the submission of citizens to the socio-political order, cannot be achieved or maintained by physical coercion alone, nor simply by pure ideological indoctrination in the service of capital, however refined its propaganda operation may be.

Capitalism therefore needs a series of cultural, ideological, political and institutional mediations to ensure not only coordination among the – sometimes contradictory – interests of the different fractions of the ruling class, but also a partial consideration of the needs and aspirations of workers (or at least a large proportion of them). These mediations were built mainly through mass organisations (parties, unions, churches and so on) but also through what Pierre Bourdieu called the 'left hand of the state', that is, the likes of public education, public healthcare and social services.[6] Over the course of the twentieth century, the bourgeoisie achieved a considerable work of symbolic and material integration, without which it would have been impossible to build a 'historical bloc' (as Antonio Gramsci calls it). This bloc integrates certain segments of the working classes – obviously in a subordinate position – into the organisation and functioning of the machinery of capitalism, and thus allows the bourgeoisie to exercise its domination as peacefully as possible. When these mediations are seriously undermined by economic, social and politico-institutional transformations, this produces *a hegemonic crisis*.[7] French capitalism is indeed facing such a 'prolonged hegemonic

---

6   These mediations are hardly just ruses used by the bourgeoisie to gull workers into ignoring the exploitation of their labour power and the class nature of state power. They are always also contradictory: both the product of the struggles waged by the working classes over more than two centuries, and a set of conquests which validate their participation in the political and social life of the country on an institutional level – however partially, since this 'validation' does not call into question capitalist domination. The contradictory nature of these gains can be seen in the periods when, for various reasons, the ruling classes strive to get rid of these mediations.

7   This can be a long-enduring crisis. It may in certain specific circumstances – marked by a division of the ruling classes, a defection of entire segments of the intermediate strata and by mass political intervention by the subaltern classes – turn into a crisis of the regime, or even into a revolutionary crisis. On the notion of revolutionary

crisis',[8] as a result of the very transformations sought and undertaken by the French ruling class across the last several decades.

In striving to impose a new, *neoliberal,* socio-institutional configuration of capitalism, the French ruling class has not *only* done much to undermine the social compromise on which postwar capitalist accumulation was based. It has also seriously shaken France's established political field, and the major ideological balances on which it is built. However, the decisive factor that really distinguishes France, as compared to Britain or Germany, is the combativeness of the subaltern classes, not just since the strike of winter 1995, but in the whole period since the mid-1980s.[9] These mass struggles were strong enough to delay the full imposition of the neoliberal agenda on French society and to revive a radical left after the decline of the French Communist Party (PCF). But they remained too weak to open a way beyond neoliberalism, and still less – so far – to mount a real challenge to neoliberalism (or still less capitalism). They thus served to heighten the hegemonic instability in France, virtually wiping out the political forces which had governed French capitalism for decades, but without allowing a left alternative able to conquer power, at least at this stage.

Neoliberalism Triumphs, Capitalism Rots

The starting point for any analysis of the political situation must be the state of capitalism itself. More than fifteen years after the explosion of the subprime crisis, which rapidly turned into a fully fledged financial crisis and then into a sovereign debt crisis (insofar as states had become almost

---

crisis, which must be clearly distinguished from that of a hegemonic crisis, see Daniel Bensaïd, 'La notion de crise révolutionnaire chez Lénine', 1968, danielbensaid.org.

8   See Stathis Kouvélakis, 'Une crise d'hégémonie prolongée', *Contretemps*, 2009, no. 1. As early as the 1990s, Alain Bihr analysed the rise of the FN as an expression of the hegemonic crisis: *Le spectre de l'extrême droite. Les Français dans le miroir du Front national*, Paris: Éditions de l'Atelier, 1998.

9   Stathis Kouvélakis shows that the student and public service struggles of the 1986–8 period played a crucial structuring role, bridging the gap between the period opened by May 1968 and the one that began on a wider scale with the major strikes of winter 1995. See Stathis Kouvélakis, *La France en révolte*, Paris: Textuel, 2007. On these issues of worker combativity, see also: Sophie Béroud, Jean-Michel Denis, Guillaume Desage, Baptiste Giraud and Jérôme Pélisse, *La lutte continue? Les conflits du travail dans la France contemporaine*, Bellecombe-en-Bauge: Le Croquant, 2008. On immigration and anti-racist struggles in France from the 1970s to the 2000s, see Sadri Khiari's account in *La contre-révolution coloniale. De Gaulle à Sarkozy*, Paris: La Fabrique, 2009.

entirely subservient to capitalist finance),[10] neoliberalism seems to have triumphed in every respect, taking advantage of the crisis to deepen its reign.[11] Pierre Dardot and Christian Laval report that 'the 2008 crisis, which in the minds of many should have ushered in a *post-neoliberal moderation*, has instead allowed a *neoliberal radicalisation*'.[12]

No structural reform has seriously challenged the omnipotence of capitalist finance, and still less has any overall political alternative to neoliberalism emerged in this period. In particular, governments – especially in France – have systematically rejected any serious regulation of the activities of financial players – investment banks, pension funds, sovereign wealth funds and so on. In the United States, during his first term Donald Trump rolled back even the (modest) financial sector regulations introduced by Barack Obama (the Dodd-Frank Act). In France, the law that was supposed to separate retail and investment banking – a very moderate reform that featured in François Hollande's 2012 programme as a proposal to break with Nicolas Sarkozy's legacy – turned into a mere trifling measure, what Frédéric Lordon calls 'barely better than nothing'. As Lordon reminds us, 'Frédéric Oudéa, the head of Société Générale [bank], . . . finally let the cat out of the bag by admitting that the "separation" law would only separate him from 1.5% of his total activities'.[13]

The moment for pearl-clutching, crocodile tears and promises to 'make capitalism moral', made especially by Nicolas Sarkozy (president at that time), is thus long behind us. On the contrary, for the last ten years or so governments have been pumping in heavier doses of the neoliberal cure. From pension reforms (2010 and 2023) to measures to 'modernise'

---

10   On finance and financial crises, see in particular, among an extremely rich bibliography: Suzanne de Brunhoff, François Chesnais, Gérard Dumesnil, Michel Husson and Dominique Lévy, *La finance capitaliste*, Paris: PUF, 2006; Frédéric Lordon, *Jusqu'à quand? Pour en finir avec les crises financières*, Paris: Raisons d'agir, 2008; Cédric Durand, *Fictitious Capital*, London: Verso, 2017; François Chesnais, *Finance Capital Today*, Leiden: Brill, 2017.

11   Among the many works on neoliberalism, choosing different lines of approach variously focused on economics or ideology, see David Harvey, *A Brief History of Neoliberalism*, Oxford: Oxford University Press, 2014; Pierre Dardot and Christian Laval, *La nouvelle raison du* monde, Paris: La Découverte, 2009; François Denord, *Le néolibéralisme à la française. Histoire d'une idéologie politique*, Marseille: Agone, 2016.

12   Pierre Dardot and Christian Laval, *Ce cauchemar qui n'en finit pas*, Paris: La Découverte, 2016, p. 25 (for the English translation, see *Never Ending Nightmare: The Neoliberal Assault on Democracy*, Verso: London, 2019.)

13   See Frédéric Lordon, 'La régulation bancaire au pistolet à bouchon', Les blogs du 'Monde diplomatique', La pompe à phynance, 18 February 2013, blog.mondediplo.net.

public services,[14] from the Macron law (2015) to the El-Khomri law (2016), from Macron's decrees (2017) to the unemployment insurance reform (2023), France's governments have eroded all the past social gains won by the working class. These range from public services (which have been privatised, sold off, liberalised and subjected to the 'new public management', that is, recipes taken from private enterprise) to employment law (thus gradually destroying its ability to protect employees from the whims of their bosses and to even slightly rein in exploitation) and social security (deliberately undermined in favour of private insurance).

The programme to destroy the postwar social compromise was vigorously pursued by Nicolas Sarkozy during his presidency from 2007 to 2012, and before that by Jacques Chirac's governments. The Socialist Party's François Hollande criticised this policy record during the 2012 presidential campaign, albeit with the sole aim of using the anger at these right-wing governments to build up his own electoral base. Hollande's famous 'Le Bourget speech' of 22 January 2012, which damned the subservience of public policy to finance – and which was later often cited as a reminder of how he had betrayed his promises – had the precise intention of kindling hopes in 'another politics'.[15] Yet, the real surprise is not so much the scale of Hollande's election-campaign gambit, but that this worked once more even after the Socialist Party's unbroken record of disappointing the expectations placed in it, ever since the 1980s. It has betrayed the essence of its programme, even when this was particularly moderate (in the case of Hollande, or even Lionel Jospin before him in the 1990s). Hollande pursued and even accelerated the course of neoliberal transformation, as he worked both to protect corporate profits (in the name of the necessary 'restoration of profit margins') and to satisfy employer demands, in particular, the liberalisation of the job market. Seemingly uninterested in cloaking this U-turn in false modesty, Michel Sapin – the 'Socialist' finance minister – proclaimed just two years after Hollande's election that 'our friend is finance'.[16]

---

14   See Laurent Bonelli and Willy Pelletier, *L'Etat démantelé. Enquête sur une révolution silencieuse*, Paris: La Découverte, 2010.

15   Here is what François Hollande had to say:

> I'm going to tell you who my real opponent is in this battle that's about to begin. He has no name, no face, no party, he will never present his candidacy, so he won't be elected, and yet he governs. This opponent is the world of finance. These last twenty years, right before our eyes, finance has taken control of the economy, society and even our lives.

16   See 'Sapin: "Notre amie c'est la finance: la bonne finance"', *AFP*, 6 July 2014.

At first sight, Emmanuel Macron's 2017 victory sounded like an unexpected triumph for the neoliberal camp. Over the previous five years, he had been Hollande's adviser, deputy secretary-general at the president's office, and then minister of the economy and finance. But he proved at least partly successful in dodging the broad mood of antipathy towards the Socialist Party – a public hostility so powerful that in 2017, for the first time in the history of the Fifth Republic, the sitting president did not even dare stand for re-election, fearing humiliation. It is at least a little surprising that Macron managed to save his own skin, insofar as he was himself one of the main figures who inspired the Hollande administration's much-loathed policies. However, his triumph in the 2017 presidential election proved, from the outset, to be a rather fragile achievement. This owes not only to the political exhaustion of the neoliberal camp (of which Macron's election was, paradoxically, itself a symptom) but, more fundamentally, to the long-term collapse of capitalism's capacity for expansion. From this point of view, the crisis of 2007–8 was a *crisis of neoliberal solutions to the crisis* that capitalism entered into over forty years ago.[17] The structural counter-reforms that neoliberals have promoted and implemented since the late 1970s have not re-invigorated the engine of capitalist growth in any sustainable way. Rather, they delayed the explosion of its contradictions and prepared the way for a crisis on an altogether different scale: that is, the crisis of 2007–8, from which the world economy has still not really recovered and which the ruling classes are still scrambling to find solutions for.

Growth in the global capitalist economy has slowed considerably over the last fifty years. World Bank data[18] tells us that it averaged around 6 percent in the 1960s, around 4 percent in the 1970s, before falling to 3 percent in the 1980s and stagnating below 3 percent since the 1990s.[19] Declining growth is especially clear in the core of the world capitalist economy, in North America and Europe, especially since the 1990s.[20] In other words, neither wage compression (leading to a significant fall

---

17 Here, I am drawing on an expression from Michel Husson. See 'La crise en perspective', *Inprecor*, nos 556–7, January 2010.
18 See Group de la Banque Mondiale, 'Croissance du PIB (% annuel)', donnees. banquemondiale.org.
19 See Cédric Durand and Philippe Légé, 'Vers un retour de la question de l'état stationnaire? Les analyses marxistes, post-keynésiennes et régulationnistes face à la crise', in Arnaud Diemer and Sylvie Dozolme (eds), *Les enseignements de la crise des subprimes*, Paris: Clément Juglar, 2011.
20 See Tristan Gaudiaut, 'Comment le PIB a évolué dans les régions du monde', Statista, 11 October 2022, statista.com.

in the wage share of global GDP), nor the financialisation of economies, nor the globalisation of trade (in capital and goods), nor new technologies or rising household debt, have been able to stimulate a new *long wave of expansion*.[21] Worse still, for the first time since 1945, global GDP fell in 2009 (following the financial crisis) and again in 2020 (during the COVID-19 pandemic). Yet capitalism's economic and political health greatly depends on its ability to constantly increase production and to find markets for the goods actually produced, in order to generate profits. This presupposes not only sufficient solvent demand – which is hard to achieve when wage compression becomes its highest law – but also the constant revolutionisation of production techniques and the constant opening up of new fields for capitalist accumulation.[22]

In addition to these long-term factors, we might add that, since the 2007–8 financial crisis, capitalism has been short of breath – and even seems to be gasping for air. Central banks were on life support throughout the period from 2008 to 2022, with quantitative easing[23] and zero or even negative interest rates designed to stimulate investment. This had no convincing result other than to fuel financial speculation. Faced with this sluggishness and the absence of a significant and lasting rebound (not to mention the continuing threat of further stock market crashes), many economists are discussing the danger of secular stagnation. This possibility was raised by former US Treasury Secretary Lawrence Summers in 2013.[24] According to Summers, only a new form of state interventionism can help capitalism out of its current morass. This would involve stimulating solvent demand, drastically reducing inequality, investing in infrastructure and waging a real fight against climate change.

Others go further. They argue that better-tuned economic policies have no chance of saving capitalism, since it is in any case about to run into 'insurmountable limits'.[25] These limits are not just external factors but ones immanent to capitalism itself. More particularly, they have to do with climate change, which threatens the survival of humanity. The

---

21 See Ernest Mandel, *Long Waves of Capitalist Development: A Marxist Interpretation*, London: Verso, 1995.
22 See David Harvey, *The Limits to Capital*, London: Verso, 2007 [1982].
23 In this heterodox monetary policy, a central bank buys debt securities en masse from actors on the financial markets, thus injecting liquidity to encourage banks to grant loans and thus boost economic activity.
24 Cédric Durand revisits this episode and discusses this idea in the article: 'L'économie à l'ère de la grande stagnation. Quand les capitalistes ne croient plus au capitalisme', *Revue du Crieur*, 2016, no. 5.
25 See Chesnais, *Finance Capital Today*.

responsibility for it lies not with 'humans' in general, but with capital and the way in which it has completely reorganised nature ('capitalocene').[26] The world-systems historian Immanuel Wallerstein and the sociologist Randall Collins likewise predict the end of capitalism. The former argues that it will not be able to cope with the social and environmental costs that it has generated, while the latter sees the explosion of technological unemployment, bound to hit ever larger sections of the population, as the main cause of a crisis that capitalism will be unable to overcome.[27]

In any case, global capitalism seems to be sinking into the impasse of a never-ending crisis. The reason for this lies not in the temporary jolts caused by the irrational mimesis of the financial markets, or by a simple lack of regulation, or even by the criminal madness of unscrupulous swindlers,[28] but in the neoliberal system of accumulation, which was created precisely in response to the crisis of the previous, so-called Fordist regime of accumulation.[29] However, capitalist decline surely does not amount to a triumphant march towards human emancipation. Firstly, because the processes involved are not necessarily synchronised: the temporality of capitalism reaching its limits is not the same as those of finance, of politics or of social struggles. As Cédric Durand writes, this 'structural blockage of the capitalist dynamic' could lead to a shift 'towards a stagnant post-capitalism, still dominated by market exchanges, but where a fully fledged authoritarianism would be required to contain intensifying socio-economic frustrations'.[30] The crisis of capitalism could

---

26 See Jason Moore, *Capitalism in the Web of Life: Ecology and the Accumulation of Capital*, London: Verso, 2015. For a strategic and programmatic reflection on the 'silent catastrophe in progress', see in particular: Andreas Malm, *Corona, Climate, Chronic Emergency: War Communism in the Twenty-First Century*, London: Verso, 2020; Daniel Tanuro, *Trop tard pour être pessimistes! Écosocialisme ou effondrement*, Paris: Textuel, 2020.

27 Immanuel Wallerstein, Randall Collins, Michael Mann, Georgi Derluguian and Craig Calhoun, *Does Capitalism Have a Future*, Oxford: Oxford University Press, 2013.

28 The 'exemplary' convictions of Jérôme Kerviel in France, and even more so that of Bernie Madoff in the United States, have thus served as useful smokescreens. They lent credibility to the moralistic account of the economic crisis and its genesis, which was adopted by all governments after the crisis first broke, in which they promised to 'clean up finance'. In the face of these attempts to use supposed moral failings to conceal the question of economic and social structures, and thus to shift blame for the crisis onto a few black sheep, we should remember that the devil lies at the heart of the system, in its logic of exploitation and dispossession.

29 On the regime of neoliberal accumulation, see in particular: Michel Husson, *Un pur capitalisme*, Geneva: Éditions Page-deux, 2008. On the crisis, see Isaac Johsua, *La Grande crise du XXIe siècle. Une analyse marxiste*, Paris: La Découverte, 2009.

30 Durand, 'L'économie à l'ère de la grande stagnation', p. 16.

well reopen the field of possibilities; but we must not forget that these possibilities also include a capitalist savagery pushed to its nadir.

This observation also needs making at a more specifically national level. While capitalism is a global system, it is more than ever before marked by the dynamics of unequal development. Claude Serfati has convincingly shown that, while France remains 'a major financial-rentier power' and 'one of the world's leading exporters' (in sectors such as aeronautics, telecoms, nuclear power and weapons), French capitalism is clearly on a path of decline. Indeed, its specialisation – linked to the central role of the state – has left it ill-equipped to respond to growing demand in sectors that are expanding rapidly worldwide (industrial capital goods and consumer goods for the middle classes).[31] The decline of French industry is especially profound, even in comparison with other European powers like Germany or Italy. Cédric Durand emphasises this desynchronisation of French and German capitalism, linked, in particular, to the conditions on which the European single currency was created.[32] France thus appears as a *dominated–dominant* power – dominant vis-à-vis the countries of the Global South (in particular its ex-colonies, although here too the trajectory of decline is clear, but also the overseas territories that are still under its rule like the French West Indies, Réunion, French Guiana or Kanaky-New Caledonia)[33] and the countries of Eastern and Southern Europe,[34] but dominated by Germany, undeniably Europe's hegemonic power, and even more so by the United States.

This is proving to be a politically dangerous cocktail, favouring a particular type of mass political subjectivation in which fascism is capable of sinking roots. This subjectivity is built on a nostalgia for French grandeur, as well as a certain superiority complex. This latter is linked to France's imperial history, but also to its enduring military-financial power and its real, though challenged, hold on its former colonial turf.

---

31   See 'L'insertion du capitalisme français dans l'économie mondiale', *La Brèche/Carré rouge*, April 2008, labreche.org. Empirical data supporting the thesis that French capitalism is in structural crisis, as well as an interpretation of this crisis, can also be found in the first chapter of Bruno Amable's latest book: *Structural Crisis and Institutional Change in Modern Capitalism: French Capitalism in Transition*, Oxford: Oxford University Press, 2017.

32   See Cédric Durand, 'Introduction: qu'est-ce que l'Europe?', in *En finir avec l'Europe*, Paris: La Fabrique, 2013.

33   Thomas Borrel, Amzat Boukari Yabara, Benoît Collombat and Thomas Deltombe, *L'Empire qui ne veut pas mourir*, Paris: Seuil, 2021.

34   See Cédric Hugrée, Étienne Penissat and Alexis Spire, *Les classes sociales en Europe. Tableau des nouvelles inégalités sur le continent*, Marseille: Agone, 2017.

But, decisively, it is also inflected by something quite different: a nagging and well-founded fear of national decline. In other words, what Daniel Bensaïd called the 'narcissistic wound of 'French greatness''.[35]

The Neoliberal Offensive and Class Polarisation

It may be surprising that in recent years even an institution like the IMF has expressed concern about rising global wealth inequalities.[36] But it surely demonstrates that a threshold has been crossed in terms of social injustice. Even in one of the institutions which has consistently pushed brutal neoliberal counter-reforms since the 1980s, questions are (belatedly) being raised over the viability of a regime of accumulation that creates such social polarisation. Who would have believed it, even just fifteen years ago?

In 2013, the IMF claimed – through the voice of its director general Christine Lagarde, now president of the European Central Bank – that 'widening income inequality is a growing concern for political leaders across the globe'. She even gestured towards an explanation for this trend, citing governments' tendency to slash welfare payments and cut taxes for the richest. She interpreted the wave of revolutionary uprisings in the Arab world and the Occupy Wall Street movement as reflections of exploding inequality. So, here, we have a former economy minister in Nicolas Sarkozy's government, voicing such concerns on behalf of an institution that has spared no effort in imposing policies on the peoples of the Global South, as well as on Greece and Portugal in the 2010s, that have been both devastating for workers and a blessing for capital.[37]

Wealth inequality has reached such obscene heights that it is difficult for national politicians and leaders of international organisations to deny the obvious. According to the NGO Oxfam's 2017 annual report,[38] the eight richest men in the world owned as much as that of half of humanity, in other words 3.6 billion human beings; the previous report also noted that the richest 1 percent of the world's population had more wealth

---

35   See *Fragments mécréants*, Paris, Lignes, 2005, p. 25.
36   See 'Le FMI s'inquiète que 0,5 % de la population détienne plus de 35 % des richesses', *Le Monde*, 15 May 2013.
37   Of course, grand claims are cheap, and they also serve to conceal the overwhelming responsibility of the IMF, the World Bank and the governments of the rich countries. Still, they signal a turning point in the zeitgeist and suggest an ideological space in which to wage a battle for hegemony.
38   Deborah Hardoon, 'An economy for the 99%', Oxfam International, 16 January 2017, oxfam.org.

than the remaining 99 percent combined. These inequalities are clearly growing, with the richest 1 percent having captured 27 percent of cumulative global growth since the early 1980s, compared with just 12 percent for the poorest 50 percent.[39] To look at an even more recent period, between 2020 and 2023, two-thirds of the global wealth produced was captured by the richest 1 percent.[40] In 2024, Oxfam estimated that the richest 1 percent worldwide owned 48 percent of all global financial assets.[41] These figures strikingly illustrate the – inevitable – effects of neoliberal policies over the last four decades. They also demonstrate the challenge faced by governments and international institutions in continuing to justify the implementation and even radicalisation of such policies.

Inequality has also been on the rise in France for several decades, especially as the mechanisms for redistributing wealth – partly a result of the gains of the postwar period – have gradually been dismantled. The growth in inequality appears particularly marked if we look at the wealthiest: the 500 largest business owners saw their cumulative wealth multiply by 2 between 2017 and 2023 (from $571 to $1,170 billion), and by 9.3 between 2003 and 2023. Moreover, as experts routinely point out, these inequalities are surely underestimated, seeing as (more or less legal) wealth concealment strategies make it hard to assess the numbers for the richest families.[42] But while inequalities are increasing mainly among the wealthiest segments of the population, they are not simply growing between bourgeois and proletarians, big capitalists and wage earners, the 1 percent and the 99 percent. Insofar as the dominant categories of the wage earners are in a position to acquire assets, particularly real estate, they have suffered less from the increase in rents and have also taken full advantage of the tax policies implemented by Macron's government. Wealth inequality has thus increased significantly in the most recent period, beyond the top fortunes: the richest 10 percent owned 47.3 percent of total wealth in France in 2021, compared with 41.3 percent in 2010.[43]

---

39   See Facundo Alvaredo, Lucas Chancel, Thomas Piketty, Emmanuel Saez and Gabriel Zucman, 'World Inequality Report 2018', wir2018.wid.world.
40   See the report: Martin-Brehm Christensen, Christian Hallum, Alex Maitland, Quentin Parrinello and Chiara Putaturo, 'Survival of the Richest', Oxfam International, 16 January 2024, oxfam.org.
41   See the report: Rebecca Riddell, Nabil Ahmed, Alex Maitland, Max Lawson and Anjela Taneja, 'Inequality Inc.', Oxfam International, 15 January 2024, oxfam.org.
42   See Alexis Spire, *Faibles et puissants face à l'impôt*, Paris: Raisons d'agir, 2012; Michel Pinçon and Monique Pinçon-Charlot, *Tentative d'évasion (fiscale)*, Paris: Zones, 2015.
43   See 'Les inégalités de patrimoine en France', Observatoire des inégalités, 11 July 2023, inegalites.fr.

The same trend can be seen in terms of income:[44] the inequality between the richest 10 percent and the poorest 50 percent has increased in the last period, rising from a ratio of 7.5 to almost 8.6 between 2014 and 2022. But within the top decile, it is mainly the incomes of the ultra-rich that have increased since the 2007–8 crisis, particularly under the reign of Emmanuel Macron, with the richest 5,000 people (0.01 percent) capturing a considerable share of productivity gains. Their incomes have thus grown by 50 percent since 2008 (while those of the poorest 40 percent have fallen in the same sequence), and the closer one gets to the richest fringe of the bourgeoisie, the greater the income growth: the 500 richest people saw their incomes triple between 2008 and 2022. There are therefore material grounds for the support of the richest for the Macronist option, particularly in terms of taxation, but also for a fringe of managers.[45] It is nevertheless important to note that, in the lower and intermediate fringes of the executive group, incomes have stagnated and their relative position – vis-à-vis the richest – has deteriorated. This undoubtedly helps us to understand both that the unions with the most managers mobilized against the pension reform in 2023, even if few managers – particularly from the private sector – demonstrated, but also the electoral transfer of some managers from Macronism to Le Penism (particularly visible during the 2024 elections).

As David Harvey has shown,[46] neoliberalism is a *class project* aimed at restoring the power of capital and raising the incomes of business owners, after the shocks of the 1970s and linked to the intense struggles led by workers in many countries. The experience of Augusto Pinochet's neoliberal-military dictatorship in Chile is a clear demonstration of this point. But the offensives against the workers' movement by Margaret Thatcher in Britain and Ronald Reagan in the United States point in the same direction. The implementation of this strategic project has not only resulted in bourgeois restoration and the concomitant increase in inequalities between the ultra-rich and the rest of the population. It has also fed rising inequalities within the 99 percent, a heightened dualisation

---

44   See 'Les inégalités de revenus en France 2024', *Elucid*, 26 November 2024, elucid.media.

45   A year after Emmanuel Macron came to power, a study had shown that 47 percent of private sector managers felt satisfied with Emmanuel Macron's action, compared with just 21 percent of unskilled workers. See L. Rouban, 'Qui est satisfait d'Emmanuel Macron?', *The Conversation*, 15 May 2018.

46   See 'Le néolibéralisme comme "projet de classe". Entretien avec David Harvey', *Contretemps*, 24 March 2013, contretemps.eu.

of the labour market[47] and increased differentiation of the workforce.[48] If the 99 percent are not the natural and obvious basis for mobilisation against the shameless looting of society by the 1 percent, this is not because of their supposed 'voluntary servitude'. It, first and foremost, reflects the reality that they are far from a homogenous group. Senior managers and the working classes do not have equivalent incomes, have greatly dissimilar positions of power (a factor which often makes the former faithful allies of the 1 percent), and develop widely varying forms of class consciousness based on their distinct positions in the relations of production.[49]

Bruno Amable and Stefano Palombarini point out that neoliberalism's success in imposing its agenda in politics and over society has relied on

> a growing segmentation – albeit one that varies depending on the country – between the core and the periphery of the workforce, with employment relations that conserve all or, most often, part of the 'good' properties of stability (job security, gradually rising wages), reserved to wage-earners useful to the stability and development of specific firm competences, whereas what is proposed for the others is a more precarious employment relationship.[50]

Champions of the liberalisation of the labour market make a big deal of the supposedly unfair 'privileges' enjoyed by certain categories of

---

[47] See Thomas Amossé, Corinne Perraudin and Héloïse Petit, 'Mobilité et segmentation du marché du travail: quel parcours professionnel après avoir perdu ou quitté son emploi?', *Économie et statistiques*, 2011, no. 450; Claude Picart, 'Trois segments pour mieux décrire le marché du travail', *Insee Références*, 2017 edition.

[48] This segmentation cuts across the popular classes but does not appear to have intensified over the last two decades. Rather, some studies show that as precarity spreads across broader layers of these classes and, given the growing (upwards and downwards) internal mobility within the subaltern workforce, this segmentation is tending to recede in favour of a general levelling-down of working-class living conditions. See Sophie Béroud, Paul Bouffartigue, Henri Eckert and Denis Merklen, *En quête des classes populaires. Un essai politique*, Paris: La Dispute, 2016. It should be noted, however, that the available data does not allow us to empirically test the hypothesis of increased ethno-racial segmentation of the popular classes. Such a claim would appear plausible, given the entrenchment of mass unemployment, which disproportionately affects immigrants and descendants of postcolonial immigrants. On this point, see Mirna Safi, *Les inégalités ethno-raciales*, Paris: La Découverte, 2013.

[49] See Erik Olin Wright, *Class Counts*, Cambridge: Cambridge University Press, 1997.

[50] Bruno Amable and Stefano Palombarini, *L'illusion du bloc bourgeois. Alliances sociales et avenir du modèle français*, Paris: Raisons d'agir, 2017, pp. 101–6. For an English translation, see *The Last Neoliberal: Macron and the Origins of France's Political Crisis*, London: Verso, 2021, pp. 94–5.

employees (protected 'insiders'). In reality, the blame lies with neoliberal policies themselves. By imposing insecurity on whole swathes of the workforce, they have transformed what were previously fundamental rights for all employees into 'privileges' for just a few. There is no telling how far job insecurity will spread. It depends not only on employers' needs for a skilled, stable workforce, but also on workers' ability to put up effective resistance against the erosion of their rights.

If some categories of workers can suddenly be thrown into precarious conditions, then, evidently, the boundary between stable and precarious workforces has become ever more fluid but undoubtedly generates all the more uncertainty and fear. Yet this boundary does really exist, and this has profound material and symbolic effects in driving competition and fragmentation within the working class, especially as it also partly overlaps with credentials, age, gender and ethno-racial divisions. Not everyone working for a wage has become precarious: the working class – and within it women, non-whites, the young and those with the least qualifications – are much more likely to suffer the now widespread ills of underemployment, chronic instability, involuntary part-time work, fragmented working hours and low pay,[51] not to mention occupational illness and suffering. This selective precarity has three positive effects from the ruling class's standpoint: (1) it obviously makes it very difficult for the most exploited workers to organise collectively, given how dominated their everyday lives are by social insecurity;[52] (2) it disciplines the stable workforce, by making them fear that they will lose their current, relatively better position; (3) it makes it unlikely that workers will mobilise in a united way at the firm, sectoral or, still less, national level.

This is what we are seeing today: while there surely are still labour conflicts in France – whether in informal and more discreet forms[53] or in the context of national movements over government plans for pensions, social security or labour law – the level of union membership and strike activity has fallen sharply over the last few decades.[54] This has left the labour movement unable to push through its demands. Of course,

---

51 One common ideological move to conceal these inequalities is the effort to highlight the individual cases where the children of workers, women or non-whites have achieved fame in sports or the arts, or else top positions as senior executives, elected representatives or company directors.
52 See in particular Robert Castel, *L'insécurité sociale. Qu'est-ce qu'être protégé*, Paris: Seuil, 2003; S. Paugam, *Le salarié de la précarité*, Paris: PUF, 2000.
53 See Béroud, Denis, Desage, Giraud and Pélisse, *La lutte continue?*
54 Pierre Blavier, Tristan Haute and Étienne Penissat, 'La grève, entre soubresauts et déclin', *Mouvements*, 2020, no. 103.

the national mobilisations against pension reforms (in 2003, 2010, 2019 and 2023) and against the Labour Law (in 2016) saw mass demonstrations with several million participants throughout France, and enjoyed broad popular support (around 80 percent, according to polls). Yet even this was not enough to defeat the government, especially because these mobilisations could not leverage sufficient strength at firm level (and more particularly in the private sector), that only a broad strike movement can impose.

So, the sharpening of class antagonisms contributes to the fascist dynamic only in combination with other factors. It has this effect insofar as it intersects with the heightening of the internal divides within the working class, the decline of collective solidarity built up in the labour movement over decades and the historic crisis of the left. Neoliberal policies have gradually undermined the bases on which most of the population could actively support the parties that have governed France since the 1980s. These parties are generally considered, *quite rightly*, to be responsible for the present situation. But these policies have also the effect of preventing, for the time being, the widespread disaffection with the dominant parties from developing into an active, collective opposition to the class whose interests these parties so staunchly defend. Rather, they orient this disaffection towards resentment and nostalgia for a largely imaginary France. Such a situation is more likely to spread the individual attitude of 'every person for themself' than collective action, and lends itself more to suspicion (especially of immigrants and minorities) than to (class and anti-racist) solidarity. The neoliberal utopias of generalised abundance (through the trickle down of wealth) and of liberalisation of the creative talents of individuals are now largely discredited. They are today rivalled by the retro-utopias of a return to past greatness ('Make America Great Again') or, less triumphantly, to the security of yesteryear, where everything and everyone seemed to be in their place. In this way, through its policies and the reaction to them, neoliberalism has produced affects that easily lend themselves to all kinds of exploitation by the far right, which aims to turn this resentment, despair and suspicion into an active force or, at the very least, to mobilise them at election time.

The Decline of the Main Parties and the Reordering of the Political Field

For the reasons I have outlined, it was surely inevitable that the major parties that have dominated French political life for nearly forty years would eventually meet with electoral collapse. If the traditional right (LR) fared better than the Socialist Party in the 2017 presidential election, this was not simply because its candidate – François Fillon – had the typical advantages of running from the opposition. The main factor was the reality that the right's record in office is much closer to its campaign rhetoric than the Socialists' is. When it is in government, the right continues to satisfy a significant share of the electorates most wedded to its camp (bosses, private sector executives, the liberal professions and small business owners). This remains true even if, in the most recent presidential election (in 2022), it was Emmanuel Macron who took most of the vote from this bourgeois and petty-bourgeois electorate (siphoning off a good part of LR's historic social base).

On the other hand, the defeat of the Socialist Party reflects forty years of betrayed promises and unremitting attacks on the achievements of the left and the workers' movement. These betrayals and attacks have ended up alienating the electorate who voted en masse for François Mitterrand in 1981 (blue- and white-collar workers, public sector employees, the intellectual professions) and whose living conditions often depended quite directly on these gains. Unable to convert the traditional left-wing electoral base to the virtues of neoliberalism – and even one that presents itself with a vague 'social' hue, reflecting the continued strength of social and especially trade union struggles in France – the Socialist Party has not managed to serenade this disillusioned electorate with the promise of a brighter tomorrow. It is not for lack of trying. In 2017, Socialist candidate Benoît Hamon's presidential campaign represented a desperate attempt to reorientate this party to the left (an ambition that the former candidate then himself gave up on, instead founding a new political movement and then leaving political life). It is worth noting that the opposite strategy used in the 2022 presidential election also failed totally: Paris mayor Anne Hidalgo adopted a right-wing line in order to win back the electorate lost to Macron in 2017; the result was easily the worst fiasco in the Socialist Party's history, scoring a paltry 1.7 percent of the vote.

This is because, from Mitterrand to Hollande, the Socialist Party has gone very far down the neoliberal road. It is the party that has imposed the most fundamental counter-reforms in France since the 1980s: the deregulation of financial markets, the free movement of capital and goods, the flexibilisation of the labour market and so on.[55] More than the right, it was in a position to gain the support or secure the passivity or active consent of certain trade union leaderships – in particular the Confédération française démocratique du travail (CFDT), which has recently become the country's leading trade union confederation – and thus to divide the social movement. From the viewpoint of the employers' federation, the MEDEF, the Socialist Party's Lionel Jospin and François Hollande – to name but two of its leaders to reach high office – have succeeded where right-wingers Alain Juppé and Nicolas Sarkozy at least partly failed. In government between 1997 and 2002, Jospin managed to push through not only far more privatisations than the right-wing governments before him, but also the flexibilisation/ annualisation of working hours demanded by the employers. As for Hollande, he considerably increased the public funds made available to businesses, particularly in the form of tax credits or lowered contributions; the total amount of aid to businesses has increased in recent years to reach the exorbitant sum of €160 billion per year (according to a recent report) making it the largest single item of public spending.[56] Moreover, Hollande introduced a series of laws[57] that constitute real turning points in French labour history, completely reorganising labour law and structurally shifting the balance of power in favour of employers, in particular by decentralising collective bargaining to the company level.

In the name of the 'competitiveness' of French capitalism and the 'need to restore corporate profits', from 2012 to 2017, François Hollande, Manuel Valls and Emmanuel Macron devoted themselves body and soul to employers' interests. In pursuing this neoliberal agenda, they had few

---

55 On the crucial role played by the French Socialists, including at the international level (especially via Jacques Delors and Pascal Lamy), see Serge Halimi, *Le Grand bond en arrière*, Marseille: Agone, 2012 [2004]; Rawi Abdelal, *Capital Rules: The Construction of Global Finance*, Cambridge, MA: Harvard University Press, 2007; Bruno Amable, *La résistible ascension du néolibéralisme. Modernisation capitaliste et crise politique en France 1980–2020*, Paris: La Découverte, 2021.

56 See Aïmane Abdelsalam, Florian Botte, Laurent Cordonnier, Thomas Dallery, Vincent Duwicquet, Jordan Melmies, Simon Nadel, Franck Van De Velde and Loïck Tange, 'Un capitalisme sous perfusion: Mesure, théories et effets macroéconomiques des aides publiques aux entreprises françaises', CGT – IRES, May 2022, ires.fr.

57 The Accord national interprofessionnel (2013), then the Macron (2015) and El-Khomri (2016) laws. See Gaëlle d'Amicelli, Pierre Khalfa and Willy Pelletier, *Un président ne devrait pas faire ça! Inventaire d'un quinquennat de droite*, Paris: Syllepse, Notes de la fondation Copernic, 2017.

qualms about leading the Socialist Party to a historic (and predictable) electoral rout, reducing it to a mere prop for a policy such as had never been discussed or agreed within the party's own democratic structures. The Socialist Party has been embourgeoisified, depoliticised and bureaucratised,[58] and, throughout, Hollande's five-year term proved incapable of making its own voice heard. Indeed, Hollande can hardly be accused of electoral opportunism, given that the Socialist Party's debacle in the 2017 presidential elections was preceded by a series of warning signs. We had already seen all its electoral defeats between 2012 and 2017, its inability to organise any public event without risking major protest (its traditional summer university in 2016 had to be cancelled outright), and, of course, the president's own enormous unpopularity. There was such visible anger at Hollande that he had to give up the idea of standing for re-election; he was forced to hand over the reins not to his prime minister or even to a less compromised figure in his party, but to the investment banker-turned-politician Macron.[59] The Socialist Party was thus effectively liquidated in favour of a new Macronite party, initially known as En Marche, whose claims to break with the past soon failed the test of power insofar as it merely recycled old ideas and stale politicians. This reordering of the party system was the price that had to be paid for the employers to secure an accelerated neoliberal overhaul of French capitalism.

The decline of the Socialist Party marked the end of a long process of decomposition which has affected all of Europe's centre-left parties, albeit unevenly. All of them have, to one degree or another, converted to neoliberalism.[60] The expansionary long wave of the postwar decades had

---

58 See Rémi Lefebvre, '"Dépassement" ou effacement du Parti socialiste (2012–2017)?', *Mouvements*, 2017, no. 89. See also: Rémi Lefebvre and Frédéric Sawicki, *La société des socialistes. Le PS aujourd'hui*, Bellecombe-en-Bauge: Le Croquant, 2006.

59 See François Denord and Paul Lagneau-Ymonnet, 'New man Macron's old-style expertise', *Le Monde diplomatique*, March 2017; Christakis Georgiou, 'La candidature de Macron et la recomposition politique à l'œuvre', *Contretemps*, 14 March 2017, contretemps.eu.

60 The transformation of France's Socialist Party cannot therefore be explained by national-level factors, or even factors purely internal to this party. Yet this is what Bruno Amable and Stefano Palombarini do by focusing on the ideological and political victory of the so-called Second Left. This merely poses another set of questions at the next level of explanation: how come this neoliberal current succeeded when, as the authors themselves note, the positions it defended represented only one-third of the members of the Socialist Party at the Metz congress in 1979, and its most eminent representatives did not occupy the top jobs when the Socialists reached government in 1981? If Mitterrand came to adopt the neoliberal austerity policies advocated by a minority around Jacques Delors, then this was surely not just a matter of Delors's ability to persuade him,

given governments room to pursue policies favourable to certain parts of the workforce even within a capitalist framework. Yet this long wave is now exhausted, drastically reducing their margins of manoeuvre. The stagnation of capitalism since the onset of crisis in the 1970s has increased the political cost of such measures, which were previously implemented even by right-wing governments. Thus, the policy of serving capital while granting concessions to workers (or simply reversing some of the worst setbacks of recent decades) has become increasingly impractical. It would require a break not only with the employers and the European institutions, as we saw in 2015 when Syriza took office in Greece – and therefore not only a determination that almost all the left-wing parties and their current leaders lack – but, above all, a kind of social pressure, reliant on intense popular mobilisation, that far exceeds what we have seen in recent years, including in France.

The centre-left parties long ago made their choice between the promised 'break with capitalism' (which Mitterrand vigorously advocated at the Épinay Congress in 1971, organically linking this to Socialist identity), or else leading the neoliberal offensive. Contrary to what so many short-sighted and rather forgetful pundits (blaming the French left for its alleged 'paleo-Marxism') constantly harp on about, France's Socialist Party was, in fact, among the earliest turncoats, convincing itself of the virtues of the market and of globalised finance.[61] Already with the 'austerity turn' in 1983, its choice had been made; and it was never subsequently put into doubt by the party's main leaders.[62] It is true, however, that the neoliberal option has long been cloaked in more popular ideals (especially 'social Europe' but also the idea of a 'happy globalisation'[63]), or

---

nor of Mitterrand having long previously planned to betray the promises he had made at founding congress of the Socialist Party at Épinay-sur-Seine in 1971. The decisive consideration is that – given the new situation of capitalism, faced with a structural crisis – refusing austerity would not have meant a return to Keynesian policies within a stable capitalist framework, but, instead, a confrontation with French and international capital, such as neither Mitterrand nor the Socialist Party were ready to enter into.
61   R. Abdelal, *Capital Rules: The Construction of Global Finance*, Harvard University Press, 2007.
62   This was set in stone by the Socialist Party's new statement of principles in 2008. It celebrated capitalism, modestly renamed the 'social and ecological market economy', while expunging all references to 'classes' and above all to class struggles. These latter had become embarrassing for a party that is a world away from the one founded by Jean Jaurès, whose historic 1905 declaration presented it as 'a class party whose aim is to socialise the means of production and exchange'. See Daniel Bensaïd and Samuel Johsua, 'Requiem pour un socialisme défunt', *Le Monde*, 7 May 2008.
63   See: A. Dianara Andry, *Social Europe, The Road Not Taken. The Left and European Integration in the Long 1970s*, Oxford, Oxford University Press, 2022.

hidden behind a denunciation of finance (Hollande), the 'market society' (Jospin) or, even further back, the 'social fracture' (Chirac). Today, the neoliberal camp feels sufficiently sure of itself that for the most part it no longer needs to be so coy: while he may have changed positions considerably on other subjects, Macron has done little to mask his choices in terms of economic and social policy.

The weakening of the left (in the conventional sense of the term, that is, including the Socialist Party) over the last two decades, as seen in the fall from a total 44 percent vote in the first round of the presidential election in 2012 to 31 percent in 2022, is not just the result of the Socialist Party's betrayals. It also reflects the work done by Nicolas Sarkozy in the 2000s and 2010s, which shifted the overall political field to the right by reordering it around a securitarian and Islamophobic consensus.[64] Although Macron did not play this card during his first presidential campaign, he certainly did take advantage of this shift. It has, after all, constantly weakened the left – a political camp much too divided on these issues to unite the working classes around a consistent anti-neoliberal and anti-racist project. And, in fact, as soon as the effects of the Macron administration's socially destructive policies became obvious, it adopted – first through different ministers: Gérard Collomb and then Gérald Darmanin or Jean-Michel Blanquer and now Bruno Retailleau – a more clearly xenophobic, Islamophobic and neo-conservative rhetoric to appeal to parts of the right-wing and far-right electorate. It has undeniably succeeded to a certain extent: despite disappointment among some of its original base, the Macron camp has apparently managed to win over significant sections of the traditional right-wing electorate (LR shrinking from 20 percent in 2017 to 4.8 percent in 2022).[65]

If Macron's victory was unexpected even a few months before the first round of the 2017 presidential election, it reordered the entire French political field. It did not *only* shatter the Socialist Party, which had been so politically dominant just five years previously. Rather, Macron's breakthrough reconfigured the French political system, exploding the fragile balances that had structured its two main pillars since the early 1980s. Looking at the Socialist Party more specifically, five years in power under François Hollande virtually wiped the Socialist Party off the political map, while also sweeping away the possibility of coexistence between the two politico-strategic lines embodied by Hamon and Valls respectively.

---

64   See Chapters 3 and 4 of this book.
65   See Julia Cagé and Thomas Piketty, *Une histoire du conflit politique*, Paris: Seuil, 2023.

They represented, in Hamon's case, a renewed social democracy re-anchored to the left; and, in Valls's case, an authoritarian neoliberalism with a racist bent. While the new leader of the Socialist Party, Olivier Faure, has managed to ensure the survival of a very thin political apparatus with no militant roots, at the cost of a temporary leftward drift of the line and a left-wing alliance under LFI domination, the return in force of the party's right-wing sectors around François Hollande and Raphaël Glucksmann suggests the same impasses and endless betrayals. For its part, the traditional right (LR) faced a highly perilous situation, and indeed emerged from it in tatters. Macron managed to force through at least part of the planned neoliberal purge of French society, while putting down social protest and also pushing some of the bourgeoisie's historic demands (notably the de facto abolition of the wealth tax). This has allowed his camp not only to attract segments of the traditional right-wing electorate that he failed to win over in the first round of the 2017 presidential election, but also to attract a growing number of its top personnel (Édouard Philippe, Gérald Darmanin and, more recently, Rachida Dati).

To exist independently in this reconfigured political field, those on the right unwilling to fall in behind Macron have opted for a race to the bottom on racism, authoritarianism and nationalism. This can be combined with a neoliberal discourse radicalised by competition with Macron's party (an orientation clearly embodied by Laurent Wauquiez and Éric Ciotti, the latter backing an alliance with Le Pen in the 2024 parliamentary elections), or with a 'social' discourse with certain Gaullist overtones (Nicolas Dupont-Aignan and Henri Guaino have been trying this for years, without much success). These two options also had their equivalents within the FN in the 2012–17 period, through the split between the line defended by Marion Maréchal-Le Pen (granddaughter of the historic leader Jean-Marie Le Pen) and that of Florian Philippot, before they each left the party. Chirac's success in uniting the right-wing camp at the end of the rather strange 2002 presidential election cycle left it with a series of nagging strategic debates. How could it accelerate the neoliberal offensive while at the same time winning the support of at least part of the workforce? Should it deepen European integration or, on the contrary, press for a restored national sovereignty? What role for the state in the age of capitalist globalisation? The new political situation has forced the right to confront these questions and clarify its positions. But it has surely not done so successfully – and it currently finds itself at an impasse, hesitating between the neoliberal-authoritarian bloc (around Emmanuel Macron) and the nationalist-identitarian bloc (around Marine Le Pen).

This creates possibilities for – and imposes responsibilities upon – the radical left: both to build a social opposition and to represent a political alternative to neoliberalism, nationalism and racism. This realignment of the political field around the 'extreme centre' is less the upsurge of a classic centrism than an elite radicalisation, cohering it around a neoliberal matrix that is also authoritarian, imperialist and xenophobic in character. This could also prepare the ground for another convergence, between a right radicalised by Sarkozyism and fired up by its recent defeats (2012, 2017, 2022),[66] and a far right which, since the 1980s, has dreamt of capturing not only the traditional right's networks of support, but also its social base and political legitimacy.[67] From this point of view, the movement against the extension of marriage rights to same-sex couples (known as the 'Manif pour tous') was surely not just an anachronistic remnant of a Catholic France doomed to die out with the inexorable march of 'progress' and 'tolerance'. This reactionary mass mobilisation could draw on considerable energies over an extended period of time,[68] and clearly demonstrated the mobilising power of networks linked to the Church, Christian private schooling and so on. But by creating or strengthening political and activist links between the younger generations of the right and the far right, it also had the effect of radicalising significant sections of the right-wing base, in opposition to equality and minorities. This is creating the conditions for a cultural convergence and a political alliance between the right and the far right. However, what unites this camp, making it possible to overcome the differences that doubtless do exist, is the desire to build a new hegemony based on trampled-on traditional values and, most importantly, a threatened national identity. There is no doubt that the rise of Éric Zemmour, who managed to win over the most radicalised wing of the conservative right's electorate during the 2022 presidential election, expresses this new situation.

---

66   For an analysis of Sarkozysm and the transformation of the right, see Florence Haegel, *Les droites en fusion. Transformations de l'UMP*, Paris: Presses de Sciences Po, 2012.

67   See Luc Boltanski and Arnaud Esquerre, *Vers l'extrême. Extension des domaines de la droite*, Paris: Dehors, 2014.

68   See Gaël Brustier, *Le mai 68 conservateur. Que restera-t-il de la Manif pour tous*, Paris: Éditions du Cerf, 2015.

The Coronation of the Extreme Centre: The Last Stop Before the Fork in the Road?

Macron's rise to the presidency is itself symptomatic of the weak bases on which neoliberalism's triumph rests. After all, his election relied on broad swathes of the political field having to drop their separate party affiliations and close ranks around the extreme centre. Given the polarisation of political life, but also the characteristics of the Fifth Republic (in particular, the dominance of the executive and, more specifically, of the president, further intensified with Macron's rule), it was difficult for any 'grand coalition' to emerge. So, one man had to rise above the parties that had ruled over the last thirty years and set himself up – or, rather, be set up by all the neoliberal ideologues in the media bubble – as the saviour, the only one capable of finally carrying out the neoliberal counter-reforms deemed 'necessary' for France.

Of course, this new kind of transformism was bound to delight those who have, since the 1970s, relentlessly called for the overcoming of the left/right divide, desperately awaiting the arrival of the messiah who can fulfil their dreams of the neoliberal modernisation of French capitalism. For decades, a whole string of politicians associated with either left or right were the subject of enamoured editorials and impassioned columns in a French media system widely devoted to the virtues of the 'free market'. Their number has included everyone from Jacques Delors and Dominique Strauss-Kahn to Édouard Balladur, Michel Rocard and François Bayrou. But none of these figures managed to unite the neoliberal right and left under a single banner and win the presidential election. Popularised in the 1980s by the intellectuals of the Fondation Saint-Simon, and supported in countless reports by generations of technocrats, the aim of this project was – to use an expression beloved of Alain Minc, the organic ideologue of this bourgeoisie spanning both sides of the political divide – to win political dominance for the 'circle of reason'. The aim was to subject French society to the inflexible 'laws' of the market economy (that is, the neoliberal diktats) by freeing it from its 'bad old habits': not only social struggles and the gains resulting from them, but also the opposition between left and right and, with it, politics itself.[69] Macron is thus little more than the private name of a collective

---

69   As Luc Boltanski and Pierre Bourdieu wrote,

the most directly political effect of the cardinal opposition [between the 'past' and the 'future', the 'archaic' and the 'modern'] is revealed when, applying the new classification system to the opposition between Right and Left, it is claimed that this fundamental

dream: that of a 'Republic of the Centre' championed as early as 1988 by François Furet, Jacques Julliard and Pierre Rosanvallon, in what appears, in retrospect, to be the manifesto of the French extreme centre.[70]

Only exceptional circumstances have made it possible to realise this 'dream', which had, until now, been held back by the structure of the French political field. Macron was doubtless a deft politician who grasped the opportunities that opened up before him; he also had the advantage of embodying, to the point of caricature, the 'converted conservatism' whose rhetoric Bourdieu and Boltanski had analysed already back in 1975.[71] But, above all, Macron benefited from a deepening political crisis. There was, of course, the collapse of a Socialist Party that had entirely devoted itself to the employers' cause during François Hollande's presidency. The rout of this party was compounded by the burial of the traditional right's candidate François Fillon, whose campaign was overwhelmed by accusations of embezzling public funds – and, it should be remembered, opinion polls right after the primaries had widely predicted a Fillon presidency. The fact that, despite his many 'scandals', Fillon's score in the first round was only just behind Marine Le Pen (who in late 2024 was the target of similar accusations, which could make her ineligible for the presidency) was a sign of the solidity of the neoliberal-conservative political bloc.

Macron's election was both an expression and a product of the hegemonic crisis, and a factor in accentuating it yet further. This was only to be predicted: indeed, capital had little to gain from the political clarification that Macron offered. All things considered, the regulated exchange of power between a neoliberalised Socialist Party and the liberal-conservative right, between rigorous austerity and austerian rigour, provided a much more comfortable means of rolling back social

---

opposition in the political arena is 'outdated', and with it politics itself. From the viewpoint of a taxonomy which indifferently classifies farmers and trade unionists, the bureaucracies of parties and the state itself, and 'Poujadism' and 'communism', in one same 'backward-looking' camp, there is no more decisive testimony to a 'backward-looking mentality' than the fact of refusing to dispatch to the most radically outmoded past the opposition between Right and Left and everything that might resemble something like classes and the class struggle.
In *La production de l'idéologie dominante*, Paris: Demopolis/Raisons d'agir, 2008, pp. 58–60.
  70   François Furet, Jacques Julliard and Pierre Rosanvallon, *La République du centre: la fin de l'exception française*, Paris: Calmann-Lévy, 1988. It should be noted that, from the 2000s onwards, Rosanvallon made a turn to the left. He came to deplore the consequences of neoliberalism, albeit without putting forward an alternative to neoliberal capitalism or making any criticism of his activity over the previous two decades.
  71   See Denord and Lagneau-Ymonnet, 'New man Macron's old-style expertise'.

rights while maintaining the illusion of possible change. It is doubtful that, from the employers' point of view, the sham novelty of Macron and his party is really a good enough substitute for the benefits of the previous system, in which the reins of government could be handed back and forth without any real alternative ever actually coming along to trouble them. After Macron's election it quickly became apparent to a large section of the population that, behind the change of costumes, the same play was being performed, once again at their expense. The advent of a *single party of the neoliberal counter-revolution* – translating at the political level the unification of the senior public administration and private managers around the neoliberal project – immediately offered a logical and obvious target to all those suffering the effects of the policies that have been implemented since the early 1980s. A sizeable share of the discontent thus rapidly found its expression not only outside Parliament and the dominant parties but also the trade unions that usually voice – and channel – grievances in society. This is precisely what the Gilets jaunes movement did in 2018–19, only a year and a half after Macron's election.

Some members of Macron's party were also aware of this, such as the MP who said before the second round of the 2017 parliamentary elections: 'We will have to find a way of staging a certain pluralism within our ranks, so that there is some semblance of debate. The streets should not be the only outlet for ideas.'[72] A 'semblance of debate' and the attempt to write a pluralist 'script' were the rather meagre expedient that, it was imagined, could find a way around the looming political turbulence. This was an even thornier problem given that – contrary to what the 'mainstream' media kept telling us, in a fine example of elite unanimity – no 'Macron wave' swept across France. This did not happen in 2017, and still less so in 2022. Even if we stick to the 2017 parliamentary elections (which went a lot better for the Macron camp than the 2022 contest), never has a party that won the presidential election obtained such a meagre score in the first round of the parliamentary elections that followed (in percentage terms and even more so in votes, given the abstention rate which reached an unprecedented 51.3 percent). Macron's party, LREM, took 28.2 percent of the first-round vote in 2017 (32.3 percent if we add in its ally MoDem), compared with 39.9 percent for the Socialists in 2012, 45.6 percent for the right-wing UMP in 2007 and 43.3 percent for this same party in

---

72   Laure Bretton and Gilles Gendron, 'L'Assemblée se prépare au parti unique', *Libération*, 16 June 2017.

2002 (to take just these examples). Taking abstention into account, only 13.4 percent of registered voters gave their vote to Macron's movement (15.4 including MoDem): if we take into account non-registered voters (11.4 percent of the potential electorate, and 28 percent of 18–24 year-olds without qualifications),[73] this brings the proportion of Macron voters in the 2017 parliamentary elections down to just *one in eleven* of the eligible electorate. And this just a few weeks after his election – presented by all the media as 'triumphant' – as president of the Republic.

Alain Badiou has referred to this as a 'democratic coup d'état':[74] a rather nice turn of phrase, though it does a poor job of capturing the processes that are really happening. A coup d'état? There has been no overthrow of power or any shift of power within the state in favour of a fraction of the ruling class that has established itself as a new hegemonic player. That is, unless we imagine that big business – in industry, in finance – was not already dictating its policies to successive governments even before Macron's victory. Democratic? That would be to give the current government a legitimacy in the name of which it has constantly forced through the destruction of hard-won social gains – using expedients that are, in reality, highly undemocratic, even in the minimally liberal sense of the term, since they involve bypassing Parliament (through decrees, constitutional Article 49.3[75] and so on). Having garnered just 24 percent of the vote in the first round of the 2017 presidential election, and won the second round essentially by default,[76] Macron nevertheless had an absolute majority in the National Assembly for the first five years of his reign. This alone demonstrates the minority support for Macron's project and the extent of the anti-democratic swindle enabled by the institutions of the Fifth Republic. This allows for the creation of parliamentary

---

73   See Xavier Molénat, 'Elections: participation inégale', *Alternatives Economiques*, 19 April 2017, alternatives-economiques.fr.

74   See his interview on Public Sénat: 'Pour Alain Badiou: "Emmanuel Macron est l'auteur d'un coup d'État démocratique"', Public Sénat, 22 June 2017, publicsenat.fr.

75   This article allows a government to avoid a vote in the National Assembly on a bill, which will be automatically adopted unless the government loses a vote of no confidence.

76   His 66 percent score – a far cry from Chirac's 82 percent against Jean-Marie Le Pen in 2002 – masks not only the high abstention rate (25.4 percent) and the record number of blank and invalid votes (8.6 percent of voters), but also the high proportion of voters (43 percent according to one poll) who only voted for him to block Le Pen's path. See Alice Bardo, 'Sondage: 43% des électeurs de Macron ont voté en opposition à Le Pen', Public Sénat, 7 May 2017, publicsenat.fr. It should be added that in the first round of the presidential election, 45 percent of Macron voters said they voted for him in order to avoid a Fillon/Le Pen run-off. See Alexandre Rousset, 'Le 'vote utile' a joué à plein pour le leader d'En marche', *Les Echos*, 25 April 2017.

majorities but does nothing to guarantee their legitimacy or stability. This trend has become even more pronounced since 2022, as Macron no longer has an absolute majority in the National Assembly, and even more clearly since the dissolution of the National Assembly and the snap elections in June–July 2024. After two striking electoral defeats (in the European elections and parliamentary elections), he decided not to ask the left-wing coalition – which had won a relative majority of seats – to form a government. Instead, breaking with an unwritten convention, he appointed a premier – Michel Barnier – from a now-shrunken party (the right-wing LR), whose success in pursuing the same policies would depend on Marine Le Pen's willingness to tolerate him.

Such a coalition did not survive more than a few weeks after attempting to impose a particularly austere budget and refusing, in typical Macronist fashion, to make any kind of social compromise. Michel Barnier's government was therefore censured by a de facto coalition between the New Popular Front and the far right, forcing Macron to once again play out the charade of negotiations, including with the left (except for La France insoumise, which refused to play along). He then appointed one of his long-standing allies, François Bayrou, himself one of the political figures who claimed to be a Macronist before Macron; that is, to overcome the right-left divide on a . . . right-wing basis.

The propertied classes in France are thus again posed with the same unresolved problem they have faced across the last four decades: how can they build a social and political bloc capable of fully carrying through the neoliberal agenda? They do, however, have one advantage, in this regard. Through Macron and his party – which gives pride of place to bosses, professionals and other senior executives, and whose top-down structure would surely be the envy of the Stalinist leaders of yesteryear (who, after all, still had to grapple with a politicised activist base)[77] – they have managed to overcome their internal differences like never before. At the same time, they have won the support of the most privileged elements of the workforce (private and public sector managers), previously divided between the right and the Socialist Party.[78] The victories achieved by

---

77   It is undoubtedly another symptom of the political crisis to see so many political professionals and party figures announcing the end of political parties, praising 'horizontality' and creating movements in which they ensure themselves a close, purely top-down control of all important decisions and appointments.

78   According to an Ipsos/Sopra Steria poll, in the first round of the presidential election Macron received 33 percent of the vote among *cadres* or managers (Fillon 'only' got 20 percent) and only 16 percent among *ouvriers* or blue-collar workers (compared with 24 percent for Mélenchon and 37 percent for Le Pen in this same socio-professional

Macron and his party in both the western and eastern arrondissements of Paris, at least in 2017, showed this political homogenisation of the most privileged social circles, under the thumb of a delighted employer class. We have not seen a democratic coup d'état, but a (limited) bleeding out of the bourgeoisie's political personnel, and its (partial) unification under a single banner. And we now live the last moments of this project.

The rise of Macron and his movement thus proves how right Antonio Gramsci was to say that in a situation of political crisis, 'The traditional ruling class, which has numerous trained cadres, changes men and programmes and, with greater speed than is achieved by the subordinate classes, reabsorbs the control that was slipping from its grasp.' It should be noted, however, that, in this case, no change of programme was necessary. The Italian communist thinker and activist added:

> The passage of the troops of many different parties under the banner of a single party, which better represents and resumes the needs of the entire class is an organic and normal phenomenon, even if its rhythm is very swift – indeed almost like lightning in comparison with periods of calm. It represents the fusion of an entire social class under a single leadership, which alone is held to be capable of solving an overriding problem of its existence and of fending off a mortal danger.[79]

Although a 'bourgeois bloc'[80] was fused together in 2017 (with large sections of the traditional right staying outside it), its social and political foundations remained narrow. It was unlikely to become hegemonic, and it should be recognised that Macron only managed to expand his electoral bloc by eating into part of the traditional right-wing electorate. This has, moreover, added to the bourgeois character of his base, to such an extent that Julia Cagé and Thomas Piketty spoke in a recent book – the fruit of a monumental collection of electoral and socio-economic data since 1789 – of the 'most bourgeois vote' in French political history.[81]

---

category). See '1er tour présidentielle 2017: sociologie de l'électorat', Ipsos, 23 April 2017, ipsos.fr. In the second round, Macron won 82 percent of the managerial vote but was beaten among blue-collar workers, 56 percent of whom voted for Le Pen. See '2nd tour présidentielle 2017: sociologie des électorats et profil des abstentionnistes', Ipsos, 7 May 2017, ipsos.fr.

79   Antonio Gramsci, 'Observations on Certain Aspects of the Structure of Political Parties in Periods of Organic Crisis', in David Forgacs (ed.) *The Gramsci Reader: Selected Writings, 1916–1935*, New York: New York University Press, 2000, pp. 218–19.

80   Amable and Palombarini, *The Last Neoliberal*.

81   See Cagé and Piketty, *Une histoire du conflit politique*.

Macron has stirred mass movements against him almost every year in his presidency so far and fuelled a grinding atmosphere of anger against him in the country at large. This forces him, for instance, to travel only under heavy escort, generally without prior announcement and using all means at hand to prevent him from ever meeting an audience that has not been pre-selected. This was, once again, surely, easy to predict. How could Macron's camp ever have enlisted and integrated large segments of the workforce – beyond just senior executives – when his entire political project amounts to undermining millions of workers' employment and living conditions? It took all the arrogance of the current president and all the blind confidence of the neoliberal media elites to imagine that he could have squared the circle. How do you break up the 'French social model' – trampling on the gains of past struggles and crushing the fighting spirit which is today on display – while, at the same time, broadening the social base of the neoliberal project? The experience of the previous two presidents had already shown that it is not enough to push back the social movements, which have been particularly vigorous in France since 1995, to remove any hope of a political alternative to neoliberalism, and even less to win the support of a majority of the population for the undermining of past social gains. Moreover, even when they have not succeeded, the mass social movements that France has seen over the last decade have shown that neither Sarkozy, Hollande nor Macron had overcome this readiness to struggle, notwithstanding the defeats inflicted on the trade unions.[82] Macron's first term as president provided further evidence of this; as soon as he was re-elected, he had to confront the biggest mass movement for some fifteen years (and widely supported by the population), in opposition to his reform of the pension system.

One of the keys to grasping the contemporary French political situation lies in its being caught between two stools. On the one hand, governments are imposing a series of regressive social measures without being able to carry out their neoliberal reordering of France in full. On the other, the radical left and social movements, while strong enough to delay the implementation of this project, are not powerful enough to create a real political alternative in the land. This unresolved conflict is surely part of the basis of the FN/RN success. To this, we can add the fact that its presence in the second rounds of three of the last five presidential elections has given it credibility as the main opposition force.

---

82   See Sophie Béroud and Karel Yon, 'Automne 2010: anatomie d'un grand mouvement social', *Contretemps*, 2 December 2010, contretemps.eu.

This helps to make it a receptacle not only of active support, that is, the votes that express a genuine ideological affinity with it, but also of protest votes from less politicised parts of the population who are looking for change from whoever is able to defeat the ruling party's candidate. While some workers may be more attracted by the RN's 'neither right nor left' rhetoric[83] than by Jean-Luc Mélenchon's left-wing approach, this is not primarily because of its programme – which is far less favourable to workers than the left's, particularly La France insoumise's. It is, rather, more an effect of the build-up of both defeats for the unions and political failures on the left. The latter's policy proposals on wages, the cost of living, public services and so on, may well have majority support. But, at this stage, it does not appear to be in a position to win elections (let alone to implement these measures once in power).

Does this mean that Macron's victories in 2017 and 2022 necessarily point towards a Le Pen victory in 2027? The processes of political history are never quite so automatic as that, and prophecies of this kind often lend themselves to despair or cynicism rather than to collective action. It is more useful to observe that the coronation of the extreme centre has stabilised the political situation in France only in a temporary, and indeed illusory sense. While it was previously concealed, there is a now overt convergence and open collaboration of the political elite around the same objective of freeing capital from all fetters, discipline the working class and of beating down the social movements. Yet this development could instead lead to a radical change of direction. There surely is a real risk that this will favour the far right, which has a strong electoral and ideological advantage which we will go on to explain in the next chapters. But there is nothing to rule out a priori that a force or a coalition on the left might be able to popularise an alternative, emancipatory perspective and make it into a credible option.[84] Jean-Luc Mélenchon's good score in the first round of the 2022 presidential election, based on his broad success among the working classes in major cities and among young people, is a good indicator of this kind of potential. This dynamic, confirmed by the Nouveau Front Populaire's victory in the parliamentary elections in

---

83   This was not always the case, however. The FN long presented itself as the party of the 'national, social and popular right' or the 'true right'; in this era, it defended an even more aggressively neoliberal policy than the Gaullist right did. With this approach, it targeted the latter's traditional electorate – small businessmen, managers and the 'middling' strata of the private sector – rather than the popular classes and people disappointed with the left. On this point, see Chapter 5.
84   On this point, see the conclusion.

July 2024, indicates a clear basis for a left that wants to confront both the neoliberal extreme centre and the neofascist extreme right.

Even faced with crises, the ruling classes have continued to push ever further with the neoliberal configuration of capitalism that has prevailed since the 1980s. For them and their appointed ideologues, there is always just one solution: if austerity, privatisations and the destruction of social rights are not enough to reinvigorate the (national or global) economy, that must be because it has not yet gone far enough. At different speeds in different countries – linked, in particular, to the unequal levels of popular resistance – the great neoliberal transformation aimed to contain the fall in profit rates, which began in the United States at the end of the 1960s. It also sought to deal with the scale and radicalism of the struggles – by workers in particular, but also students, racialised minorities, feminists and so on – at the heart of the capitalist world economy. But the so-called neoliberal solution went into crisis in 2007–8. With no alternative recipes or political project that would be able to mobilise people, bourgeoisies instead chose to force through an extended array of the same policies: privatisations, wage compression, tax cuts for the rich and corporations and so on.

Their aim is to restructure all aspects of the economic and social system, of production and reproduction, in order to subject them, as far as possible, to the logic of capitalist valorisation and accumulation. For this reason, this accelerated imposition of neoliberal agenda demands the smashing of all the gains made by the left, the workers' movement and emancipatory struggles. This is also what makes it a difficult task, since these gains have crystallised over a long period of time in law (the Labour Code in particular), in institutions (social security, public services), in organisations (trade unions in particular), but also in the assumptions individuals make about their own lives. You cannot convert people at the click of a finger to the idea that they will have to pay for healthcare, education and so on, for instance. Hence the need for the ruling classes both to conceal their destructive efforts in the short term, but also to work in the long term to transform subjectivities themselves.

What is more, it was precisely these achievements that cushioned the 2008 crisis and ensured that French society could withstand it, even despite unemployment peaking at unprecedented levels.[85] It has rightly

---

85   There are over five million unemployed people in France – around 15 percent of the active population – if we take into account all categories of unemployed people.

been argued that, in the twentieth century, it was paradoxically the workers' movement that saved capitalism. This was not due to a simple 'betrayal' by its leaders but was the effect of (partial) victories which constituted so many factors for social and political stability, softening the effects of the crises which capitalism routinely produces, or even limiting – at least temporarily – the occurrence of these crises themselves. To do away with these achievements is to do away with these stabilisers and run the risk of the situation becoming politically uncontrollable. In any case, it would make it even more difficult for the ruling class to establish any kind of hegemony. Yet, for want of a lasting hegemony, and faced with constant opposition, capitalist politics imperceptibly veers towards becoming a pure and simple policing operation, as we shall show in the next chapter.

At this stage, even if class conflict remains contained in most capitalist countries, the ruling classes' ability to obtain the active consent of a majority of the population is already under threat. Much has been said about Donald Trump's recent success, but not enough about the fact that his gain in votes is actually small, and that his victory is linked first and foremost to a massive demobilisation of the Democratic electorate, due specifically to Joe Biden's record in office. This won't prevent Trump from implementing his project, if mobilisations don't force him to back down, but at this stage the Trumpist movement is far from having created the conditions for a new hegemony. In the United States, as elsewhere, the capitalist class is still in control of the situation, because of the exorbitant power it wields, but the regressions imposed over the last few decades have weakened the foundations of their political domination: the mediations on which they rely in civil society (in particular, the integration of the working class via social democracy, unions and welfare states),[86] or the concessions that used to allow a significant part of the social body to adhere to even a socially unjust order.[87]

The number would be even higher if we included those who are not counted because they have been struck off the Pôle emploi register or have given up active job seeking.

86 In France, certain trade union confederations – in particular the leadership of the CFDT, but also segments of the FO, CFTC and UNSA – are nonetheless effectively compensating for the decline of social democracy, at least for the time being. Still, Macron's extremely aggressive social policies have in the most recent period pushed even these unions to mobilise their bases in the streets, in the movement against the pension reform in 2023.

87 Neil Davidson aptly speaks of neoliberalism as the 'agent of capitalist self-destruction'. See 'Neoliberalism as the Agent of Capitalist Self-Destruction', *Salvage*, 1 May 2017, salvage.zone.

Our contention is that neoliberalism makes fascism possible, because it engages capitalist societies in an infernal cycle of rising (and already monstrous) inequalities, authoritarian tendencies[88] and upsurges of nationalism and racism.[89] Moreover, in particular political circumstances, made exceptionally inflammatory by the policies pursued by the ruling class, certain sectors of the latter are already being led to support – or ally themselves with – parties and ideologues proposing to overcome the crisis through solutions that are unthinkable within an ordinary rule-of-law framework. The twentieth century has given plenty of examples of such excesses by the ruling classes, which are by no means accidental. This fact alone demands greater caution from those who insist that fascism – understood here not simply as a political movement but as a specific form of the state of exception[90] – belongs to the past or is reserved for 'backward' societies.

Various transformations have made capitalism far more complex and resilient than it was a century ago. Yet – to use an image offered by Walter Benjamin at a time when the world was plunging into an apocalyptic imperialist war – capitalism can still be compared to that train that heads straight for disaster when humanity proves incapable of pulling the emergency brake.[91] Fascism, with its changing forms and the meandering paths it follows, is one of the faces of this disaster. Some observers still have their eyes stuck on its old forms of appearance or perhaps got too accustomed to the political stability of a now-bygone era. But, contrary to what they claim, fascism did not disappear under the rubble of a bunker in 1945.

---

88 See Chapter 3.
89 See Chapter 4.
90 See Nicos Poulantzas, *Fascism and Dictatorship*, London: Verso, 2019.
91 The exact quote is as follows: 'Marx says that revolutions are the locomotive of world history. But perhaps it is quite otherwise. Perhaps revolutions are an attempt by the passengers on this train – namely, the human race – to pull the emergency brake.'

3
The Neoliberal-Authoritarian State and Fascisation

Doubtless one of the main political facts of our time is the hardening of authoritarian tendencies in the dominant capitalist powers. We could hardly explain this development by citing purely national factors, and still less by looking to the personality of any individual leader. Rather, this trend began with the neoliberal turn pioneered by Margaret Thatcher in Britain and Ronald Reagan in the United States, after its brutal anticipation under the Pinochet regime in Chile. This key characteristic of the current domestic, European and global political landscape has also been keenly noted by contemporary social movements. Many of these movements, in France and elsewhere, have closely connected their denunciation of growing inequality, imperial wars or ecological destruction with criticism of the capture of political power by an oligarchy which pays no heed to social needs or concerns. But this, in turn, poses the need to understand the origins of this phenomenon – and to examine what links it really has with the danger of fascism.

The current surge in authoritarianism may seem paradoxical, when we consider that 'capitalism has never been so little confronted with the theoretical and practical challenge of a powerful antithesis'.[1] Indeed, while some popular mobilisations have returned to more radical practices, and rebellion against capitalism does again seem audible among some parts of the population (particularly young people), anti-capitalist movements remain politically weak. If we can today see heightened

---

1   Ellen Meiksins Wood, 'Redéfinir la démocratie', *Contretemps*, September 2009, no. 4.

repression, this does not reflect a vital necessity on the part of the ruling classes, as if compelled to face down and crush revolutionary uprisings. What we are seeing is not so much a short-term response, as if preceding a return to a normal parliamentary democracy that cherishes public freedoms, as a lasting transformation of the political forms under which capitalist domination is reproduced. Such a transformation, which has become more or less necessary according to the level of popular resistance to the bourgeois offensive,[2] should, then, properly be understood as a corollary of the neoliberal project. This latter is both a product of capitalism's crisis and a factor which is itself making this crisis more intense.[3] Insofar as the dominant classes do not, at this stage, have an alternative hegemonic project, they are driven to subvert the political and institutional mediations through which the consent of the working classes had been peacefully obtained in the previous historical period. The existing order is kept alive by increasingly brutal means, and these undermine the conditions for its reproduction in the long and even medium term.

In particular, this authoritarian hardening involves the use of political and legal forms that conform ever less with parliamentary-democratic principles.[4] The less of a solid social base and consistent political legitimacy that the dominant classes have, the more they will resort to improvised legislative procedures, bypass the intermediary bodies in society (civil society, 'social partnership'), and resort to increased police and judicial repression. There are many examples of this at work in France. We could mention the increasing use of constitutional Article 49.3 to impose unpopular reforms when the government does not have a clear parliamentary majority. We could likewise cite the contempt that France's political authorities showed towards all trade unions – including the most moderate and willing to negotiate – during the mobilisation against the pension reform in 2023, or the decrees that Macron has issued since the beginning of his first term, not in spite of but because of his (weak) electoral legitimacy. This ruling-class tendency towards abandoning liberal-democratic forms thus points to a situation of *domination without hegemony*.[5] This is true in two senses, for it is a product

---

2 This undoubtedly explains the intensity of the hardening authoritarianism in France, where, since the mid-1990s, popular struggles have had far more energy behind them than is true of most European countries, first and foremost Germany and Italy.

3 See previous chapter.

4 Pierre Dardot and Christian Laval, 'La sortie de la démocratie est engagée', *Contretemps*, September 2016, no. 31.

5 This formula was used by the Indian historian Ranajit Guha to describe a very

of the crisis of hegemony but also forbids the rebuilding of a genuine hegemony. By relying ever more on force rather than consent, and by refusing any real negotiation (which would require retreats and compromises), the political authorities isolate themselves and enter into a spiral of radicalisation, which thus also becomes difficult to reverse.

Thus, the hegemonic instability does not simply upset the balances established in the political field over the last several decades and, by extension, the conditions under which stable and lasting majorities are possible. It implies a transformation of states themselves or, more precisely, an increasingly authoritarian reorganisation of the centres of power and command. In a historical era marked by the sharpening of the contradictions of capitalism, which gives rise to sometimes explosive popular mobilisations – even if they struggle to leave a lasting impression on the political scene – the dominant classes choose the path of increased authoritarianism. In many countries, this means significantly undermining democratic rights and, more fundamentally, peoples' ability to exercise real control over their representatives and to influence which policies are implemented. In particular, we are seeing democracy ever-more hollowed out through the marginalisation of national political institutions, which were, in any case, rather remote from the popular classes, in favour of unelected and out-of-reach supranational bodies. The parliamentary vessel remains but it is voided of any content; it is literally running on empty.[6] This process has reached its most complete expression in the European Union, with its rump parliament and its power captured by the Commission, the European Central Bank (ECB) and the European Court of Justice.

It is true that capitalism is not *inherently* democratic, even in the truncated and hypocritical sense of liberal democracy.[7] Nothing in its fundamental structures requires the existence of representative

---

different situation, namely that created by British colonialism in India. See R. Guha, *Dominance Without Hegemony: History and Power in Colonial India*, Cambridge, MA: Harvard University Press, 1998.

6   This certainly does not mean that nation-states are obsolete: as we saw during the 2007–8 crisis, it was through the intermediary of these states that the bourgeoisie managed to plug the gaps and defer the destructive effects of the anarchic operation of the financial markets.

7   It takes all the blindness connected to obsessive anti-communism to imagine – as does the French 'anti-totalitarian' current (even in Claude Lefort's intellectually most demanding version of it) – an organic link between capitalism and democracy. On this current, which left a considerable mark on the French intellectual and political field from the 1970s onwards, see Michael Scott Christofferson, *French Intellectuals Against the Left*, New York: Berghahn Books, 2004.

government, universal suffrage and civil liberties, let alone social rights that even somewhat rein in exploitation; still less does it imply democracy etymologically conceived as *popular power*, which is, in fact, unthinkable in a capitalist regime.[8] On the contrary, over the last two centuries, capitalism has constantly produced an authoritarian spiral, and has even installed or maintained regimes that were fulsomely anti-democratic. Major industrialists have generally had no qualms about finding beneficial compromises with dictatorships, from Mussolini's Italy to Pinochet's Chile, via Nazi Germany and Salazar's Portugal, and have even directly financed fascist organisations and anti-union militias, hand-picking small far-right groups to serve as their goons. Even the initial advent of capitalism was bound up with the enslavement of millions of Africans. Closer to home, the construction of liberal democracy, particularly in France, was paid for by colonial subjugation and all the crimes associated with it. It was based on a national-racial pact that denied colonised peoples all political rights and condemned them to exceptional treatment. This exclusion persists, albeit in less visible forms, even for their descendants living in today's France, whose independent political initiative is permanently and deliberately crushed. It likewise continues to affect the so-called 'overseas' territories still under French colonial domination (as is particularly visible in Kanaky).[9]

Beyond that, the invention of democracy in the modern sense – and especially the mechanisms of parliamentary representation – objectively enabled the dominant classes to cope with the threat posed by the subaltern classes' tumultuous appearance on the public stage that was then still being constituted. In particular, it served to renew social domination by other means, as it helped to win the consent of new social strata, the so-called 'middle classes', by integrating them into the systems of power.[10]

---

8   This distance between capitalism and democracy, which renders obsolete the identification of 'democratic revolutions' with simple 'bourgeois revolutions', is visible from the French example from 1789 onward. The sans-culottes attempted to achieve a real democracy and a 'right to an existence', while the bourgeoisie was already trying to limit democracy to its strictly representative dimension and repress the revolutionary movement. See in particular: Florence Gauthier, 'Critique du concept de "révolution bourgeoise" appliqué aux Révolutions des droits de l'homme et du citoyen du XVIIIe siècle', *Raison Présente*, 1997, no. 123, p. 59–72. See also Marc Belissa and Yannick Bosc, *Le Directoire. La République sans la démocratie*, Paris: La Fabrique, 2018.

9   On these aspects, see in particular: Sadri Khiari, *La Contre-révolution coloniale en France. De Gaulle à Sarkozy*, Paris: La Fabrique, 2009; and Mathieu Rigouste, *L'ennemi intérieur. La généalogie coloniale et militaire de l'ordre sécuritaire dans la France contemporaine*, Paris: La Fabrique, 2011.

10 On this point, see Ellen Meiksins Wood, *Democracy Against Capitalism*, London: Verso, 2016 [1995], pp. 204–37.

Whether in terms of political and legal equality, or labour law, popular conquests have limited the arbitrariness and violence at the very heart of the capitalist mode of production, particularly in the workplace, where the fight for democracy has always been a pipe dream.[11] What has varied throughout capitalism's history is the *degree* of state arbitrariness and violence, not the fact that it existed. The Western imperialist powers have ever been ready to use any means necessary to open up new markets, subjugate recalcitrant trading partners or force large sectors of the population – particularly poor peasants – into wage labour. It has often shown its willingness to dispossess them, forcibly if necessary, of their means of subsistence and production.[12]

So, here, we are not trying to point to a risk of capitalism *becoming* authoritarian. Rather, this economic system is based on an authoritarian structure, at the level of production but also at the level of the state; this structure will come to the fore whenever the subaltern classes act against the interests of those who dominate over them. Furthermore, while it is surely true that liberal democracy provides the best political framework for capitalists, allowing them to disguise an oligarchy as a political regime that belongs to its citizens, the creation of police states and various forms of regimes of exception is a possibility ever-present at the heart of capitalism, because of its structural contradictions and the political crises that it inevitably produces. While fascism cannot be reduced to a simple stepping up of repression,[13] it certainly does feed on liberal democracies' own slide towards authoritarianism. When the centres of political command gradually free themselves from (even a very limited parliamentary form of) popular control and trample on counter-powers (trade unions, human-rights associations and so on), when there is a mounting criminalisation of social protest or even the raising of demands and when the public space is hemmed in by the submission of the news media to private capital or governmental demands, then, even if democratic appearances are maintained, there is no doubt that the fascist counter-revolution is gaining ground.

Historically, the fascists developed an opportunistic critique of these obvious anti-democratic trends – even while proposing to remedy them

---

11   Marx used the term 'factory despotism' to refer to the system of subordination of workers to capitalist owners; such a system extends far beyond factories themselves and concerns workplaces in general.

12   Here, it may be worth rereading the pages which Marx devoted to primitive accumulation in *Capital*, Volume I. See also: Karl Polanyi, *The Great Transformation*, New York: Farrar & Rinehart, 2004.

13   See Chapter 1.

by establishing an authority even more brutal than the current strong state but closer to deep popular aspirations (in particular, through the repeated use of referendums, which would make it possible to ignore the Constitution, notably in matters of foreigners' rights or public freedoms). It should be remembered that referendums are not in themselves a guarantee of democracy: in a situation in which the means of information and communication are increasingly subservient to a clique of billionaires, and political pluralism is extremely weak, they appear more like a plebiscite for political power than a genuine means of popular expression. They claimed that this would allow national regeneration through a fantasised fusion between this authority and a 'people' reduced to a passive and subordinate role of offering its plebiscitary acclamation for the leader.

This purely instrumental relationship with democracy is a central feature of fascism, which uses democratic means while fundamentally despising democracy and wishing to free itself from it. Presenting *The Doctrine of Fascism*, Mussolini could thus assert that 'fascism . . . is the purest form of democracy' and, a few pages later, express his disgust for the 'manifestations which are [according to Mussolini] the hallmark of the democratic spirit': 'carelessness, improvisation, the absence of any sense of personal responsibility, the exaltation of numbers and of that mysterious divinity called "the people"'.[14] The same opportunism can also be found among the Nazis, who sing the praises of 'the people' but despise democracy. In his Düsseldorf speech of January 1932, in which Hitler sought to seduce Germany's big bosses, he asserted that democracy, equality and popular sovereignty were absurd in both the economic and political spheres:

> There are two closely related manifestations of the degeneration of nations. The first replaces the value of the individual with the levelling, purely quantitative concept of democracy. The second denies the intrinsic value of each people, nor the differences in the biological dispositions and achievements of different peoples . . . Internationalism and democracy are two inseparable concepts . . . It is absurd to base economic life on the principle of performance, on the value of the individual, and therefore on the authority of the person, but to deny the authority of the individual in politics, and to substitute the law of the greatest number for it.[15]

---

14 See Benito Mussolini, *The Doctrine of Fascism*, 1932, translation at sjsu.edu.
15 Karl Polanyi, 'The Essence of Fascism', in Karl Polanyi, John Lewis, and Donald

A Rising Authoritarianism in France: From Nicolas Sarkozy to François Hollande

The 'question of democracy' has once again become central in France. This has happened because of a powerful intensification, throughout the last fifteen years, of the authoritarian tendencies intrinsic to capitalism. This authoritarian hardening builds on political institutions and a way of exercising power which surely make France one of the Western countries furthest from minimum democratic standards. Since de Gaulle's institutional coup d'état in 1958,[16] French society has lived under a regime that can best be described as a *strong state*.[17] This is a set-up in which parliamentary structures are marginalised. The president of the Republic has overweening powers (further strengthened by the fact that since 1962 he has been directly elected, and since 2001 the inversion of the electoral calendar has heightened his pre-eminence over the prime minister), and has the prerogative to declare war without any real control by Parliament, to dissolve the National Assembly and so on. Added to that, exceptional procedures feature prominently in the constitution (with the 'state of siege' and assumption of 'full powers'), and a state of emergency can be introduced by simple decree.

However, while this authoritarian drive can surely find a base of support in the existing institutions of the Fifth Republic, the parties and leaders in power over the past two decades have radicalised these traits. The 2000s were marked by Nicolas Sarkozy's hyperactive securitarian push, first as Jacques Chirac's interior minister from 2002 to 2007, before he himself became president from 2007 to 2012. As part of his strategy to win over the FN electorate, Sarkozy pushed a law and order populism to extremes, regularly whipping up anti-immigrant xenophobia. He devoted great energy to stepping up the criminalisation of poverty and young people. He did this, in particular, through the introduction of minimum sentences and the extension of summary trials to minors, as well as hunting down undocumented immigrants (through the policy of constantly raising the number of deportations). He built up the forces responsible for the most brutal repressive efforts

---

K. Kitchin (eds), *Christianity and the Social Revolution*, New York: Charles Scribner's Sons, 1936, pp. 392 ff.

16   See Grey Anderson, *La guerre civile en France, 1958–1962. Du coup d'État gaulliste à la fin de l'OAS*, Paris: La Fabrique, 2018.

17   See Jean-Marie Brohm, Daniel Bensaïd, Gérard Filoche, Pierre Franck, Jean-Pierre Martin, Jean-Yves Touvais, Jean-François Godchau and Edgardo Pellegrini, *Le gaullisme, et après? État fort et fascisation*, Paris: Maspéro, 1974.

in working-class, ethnic-minority and immigrant neighbourhoods (in particular, the Anti-Criminality Brigades, BAC)[18] and vaunted his unyielding and unconditional support for the police. In autumn 2005, when many of these neighbourhoods rioted following the deaths of two teenagers – Zyed Benna (aged seventeen) and Bouna Traoré (fifteen) – who had taken refuge in an electricity transformer after being chased by the police for no reason, Sarkozy backed the police officers in question to the hilt, and the government declared a state of emergency.[19] Tellingly, this repressive procedure, which originated in French colonialism's exceptional regime (it had only previously been used during the Algerian War and then in Kanaky in 1985), now turned to metropolitan France to target neighbourhoods where the descendants of colonised people are over-represented, before then being applied to everyone, across France's territory, following the 2015 terrorist attacks.

In 2010, by which point he was president, Sarkozy pushed through a law proposed by right-wingers Christian Estrosi and Éric Ciotti (a figure today allied with the RN) which created an 'offence of being in a grouping'.[20] The law was presented as meaning to prevent youths from working-class neighbourhoods from breaking into schools and to stop football supporters' groups ('ultras') from committing acts of violence in stadiums. Described as the 'anti-*casseurs*' law, in reference to another law passed in 1970 specifically targeting the far-left movements of the post-1968 period (and repealed by the Socialist-Communist government in 1981), it set a grave and dangerous precedent. This legislation allowed the charging of individuals who had not committed any recorded offence, on the pretext that they belonged to a group – even a temporary one – and that they were preparing to commit violence. However, as left-wing critics feared when the law was passed, its scope would be considerably expanded over time. In particular, it was used against social mobilisations to pre-emptively arrest hundreds of demonstrators (Gilets jaunes, trade unionists, environmentalists and so on). It was reminiscent of the

---

18 For an ethnography of the BAC, see Didier Fassin, *La force de l'ordre: une anthropologie de la police des quartiers*, Paris: Seuil, 2011.

19 The revolt also erupted because of the (false) allegations made by Sarkozy and the prime minister of the day, Dominique de Villepin, that the victims were in the process of committing a burglary. These remarks sounded like a provocation at a time when emotions were running high.

20 This was defined more precisely as 'the fact of a person knowingly participating in a grouping, even one formed on a temporary basis, with a view to the preparation, characterised by one or more material acts, of deliberate violence against persons or destruction or damage to property'.

so-called 'villainous laws' (*lois scélérates*) of the late nineteenth century, passed in the name of tackling anarchist movements.[21]

Another element of Sarkozy's authoritarian repertoire directly targeted workers and trade unions. As soon as he came to power in 2007, he used his post-election political capital to challenge the right to strike. He did this by introducing a minimum service law for passenger land transport (metros, buses, trains), which was extended the following year to national education and then in 2011 to passenger air transport. These provisions moreover demanded that workers declare themselves on strike at least forty-eight hours before they do take any industrial action. This limits the possibilities for collectively and spontaneously building the strike by way of general assemblies, of the kind that unions have traditionally organised on the morning of strike days, thus making it possible to rally more workers' support. Under the Sarkozyan regime, going on strike became an individual decision – and thus a more difficult one – often before any collective deliberation has taken place. To this should be added the practice of requisitioning strikers, which Sarkozy and his government introduced during the 2010 movement against the pension reform (undoubtedly the largest in numerical terms since May–June 1968).[22] This was specifically done in order to break the mobilisation of workers in the refinery and fuel-depot sector, whose strike threatened to bring the country to a standstill within just days (indeed, half of France's service stations had run dry as of 18 October 2010). Seeing as this decision was then approved by the Conseil d'État, notwithstanding the fact that it contravenes the fundamental right to strike (France was reprimanded by the International Labour Organisation), Emmanuel Macron was also able to requisition strikers. He did this once to avoid a petrol shortage caused by a strike in the refinery sector in autumn 2022, but also during the movement against a further pension reform in spring 2023, as the government sought to kill off a strike by refuse collectors.

Although François Hollande was elected as a result of Sarkozy's unpopularity, and, indeed, in the name of breaking with his policies, in reality his economic and social policies continued in line with the previous right-wing administration. In particular, this meant increasing state support for private companies,[23] without any strings attached,

---

21 See Raphaël Kempf, *Ennemis d'Etat*, Paris: La Fabrique, 2019.
22 Between spring and autumn 2010, the unions united to organise nearly fifteen days of action, eight of which mobilised between 1 and 3.5 million demonstrators (according to union figures), or around 1 million if we believe the police's numbers.
23 See Chapter 2.

but it also meant a continued offensive against civil liberties. Hollande studiedly avoided reversing his predecessor's repressive measures and restrictions on the right to strike. As for his way of exercising power, since there was no parliamentary majority for certain bills (notably the 2016 Labour Law), Manuel Valls – Hollande's prime minister from 2014 to 2016 – resorted no less than six times to constitutional Article 49.3. This procedure marginalises parliamentary democracy by allowing a bill to be passed without a vote in the National Assembly. Moreover, in the name of combatting the terrorist threat, Hollande and Valls imposed a state of emergency from November 2015, before extending it again for three months after the Nice massacre in July 2016 – which we learned, some time later, was not in fact a terrorist attack planned and prepared by the Islamic State, as was claimed at the time in order to justify extending the state of emergency. What we also now know is that, from late 2015 to 2017, the state of emergency meant hundreds of house arrests and thousands of brutal searches (of which only 1 percent resulted in terrorism-related charges being brought).[24] Bypassing the judiciary, these procedures have targeted Muslims on a massive scale, in an almost totally arbitrary fashion. More generally, they have targeted the residents of working-class, ethnic-minority and immigrant neighbourhoods, as well as the activists of the radical left (ZADists, environmentalists, trade unionists, anti-racists, anti-fascists and anti-capitalists).[25]

This worrying increase in arbitrary state power has also been reflected in the brutality of the unending police crackdown on refugees and their makeshift dwellings (tents ripped open, belongings scattered and so on), generally without this raising an eyebrow in mainstream media. This repression has likewise struck against popular mobilisations. It is impossible to understand why so many protestors are increasingly hostile towards so-called law enforcement – clearly shown by the popularisation of the slogan 'Everyone hates the police!' – without taking seriously the increased repression that the police use. This includes the systematic use of baton charges and the widespread use of 'kettling' (although this practice of encircling or rather 'encaging' demonstrators rides roughshod over the freedom to protest); punitive interventions by units specifically set up for the purpose of brutal repression, especially the club-wielding motorbike division known as the BRAV-M; but also the mobilisation of brigades previously used only in working-class, ethnic-minority and

---

[24] In the period between November 2015 and February 2016. See 'Les victimes de l'état d'urgence en France', Amnesty International, 17 January 2017, amnesty.fr.

[25] See Kempf, *Ennemis d'État*.

immigrant neighbourhoods (the anti-criminality brigades)[26] on demonstrations in general. Added to this is the media indifference and judicial impunity that almost systematically encourage police violence, particularly against young Arab or Black men, notwithstanding the wide documentation of said violence.[27]

The crisis of liberal democracy has also been expressed in recent years through the repeated suspension of the freedom to protest. Indeed, it is all too often forgotten that the first demonstrations to be banned, even before the state of emergency, were the summer 2014 protests in solidarity with Gazans, as they suffered yet another murderous Israeli assault. On 19 July 2014, one of the forbidden demonstrations was held in Barbès, a historically immigrant and especially Algerian neighbourhood in northern Paris, despite the ban. Thousands of people – mostly from postcolonial immigrant backgrounds – came to show their solidarity with the Palestinian people and their disgust at French government complicity. They were subjected to staggeringly violent police repression. These bans were part of the international criminalisation (which has since harshened much further) of the Palestine solidarity movement, in particular the Boycott-Divestment-Sanctions civil disobedience movement, and, more broadly, of all forms of politicisation of the descendants of colonised peoples, often at the forefront of demonstrations in solidarity with the Palestinians.

In the period that followed, in the span of just one and a half years the public authorities – taking advantage of the state of emergency introduced in November 2015 – banned 155 demonstrations and forbade 639 individuals from joining demonstrations.[28] In particular, in autumn 2015, this allowed the government to rein in the mass mobilisation for climate justice that was expected to take place during the Paris COP21 summit.[29] While the state of emergency has not prevented terrorist

---

26   On the history of these units, see Mathieu Rigouste, *La Domination policière*, Paris: La Fabrique, 2012.

27   An investigation by Ivan du Roy and Ludo Simbille for the newspaper *Basta* showed that between 1977 and 2022, some 861 people died as a result of police action, with a peak in 2021 and a vast over-representation of young men of African origin among those killed across this more than four decade period. On the connection between racism and police violence, see in particular: Rachida Brahim, *La Race tue deux fois*, Paris: Syllepse, 2021.

28   These figures come from the survey by Amnesty International published in May 2017. See 'France. Le droit de manifester menacé', Amnesty International, 31 May 2017, amnesty.fr.

29   A few months later, the same government again tried to ban a demonstration, in this case a mobilisation by trade unions against the Labour Law. No trade union

attacks in France, it has proved effective in containing and repressing social protest. Hollande himself said:

> It's true that the state of emergency was used to secure COP21, which we couldn't have done otherwise ... Imagine if there hadn't been the terrorist attacks, we wouldn't have been able to arrest the ZADists to prevent them from coming and demonstrating. This was made easier by the state of emergency, not in order to fight against terrorism, but in order to prevent skirmishes taking place.[30]

The state of emergency was thus opportunistically used to neutralise climate justice activists through house arrests and bans on demonstrations. Still, it would be mistaken to see it only in terms of its opportunistic and short-term uses. Rather, it is the culmination of a process through which political elites have converged around a new security doxa, with the left aligning itself with the positions of the right ever since the late 1990s.[31] In the context of the terrorist attacks of November 2015, and the constant attempts by the right and far right to outbid each other in their responses, the Hollande-Valls government pushed forward this authoritarian agenda on which the main French parties have converged for three decades. All the so-called 'parties of government' have done so, from the Socialist Party to LR (formerly the RPR, then the UMP) and, since 2017, the Macron camp (En Marche, or LREM, today rebadged as Renaissance). And this is not to mention the RN, whose well-known ultra-securitarian agenda plays the role of a bogeyman, making the measures pushed through by the ruling parties seem reasonable, even as they hack away at our freedoms.

Macronism, the Highest Stage of Authoritarian Neoliberalism

Since 2015, the shock effect of terrorist attacks has been systematically used to strengthen the repressive state apparatus's capacity for reactive

---

demonstration has been banned in France since the 1962 protest against the Algerian War, during which nine demonstrators, including eight CGT activists, were killed by the police.

30 See Gérard Davet and Fabrice Lhomme, *Un président ne devrait pas dire ça. Les secrets d'un quinquennat*, Paris: Stock, 2016.

31 On this point, see in particular: Laurent Mucchielli, *La Frénésie sécuritaire: retour à l'ordre et nouveau contrôle social*, Paris: La Découverte, 2008; Laurent Bonelli, *La France a peur. Une histoire sociale de l'insécurité*, Paris: La Découverte, 2008; Vincent Sizaire, *Sortir de l'imposture sécuritaire*, Paris: La Dispute, 2016.

but also preventive action. It has also been used to increase the degree of autonomy (and therefore arbitrariness) that these apparatuses enjoy. This was already apparent in the Urvoas law passed in June 2016 (under François Hollande's presidency). In the name of the fight against terrorism, it gave (even off-duty) police officers new freedoms to use their weapons, bordering on an outright licence to kill, and handed new powers to the administrative authorities. Emmanuel Macron has completed efforts that had already been intensely pursued under Sarkozy or Hollande (and the presidents who went before), in particular by piling up anti-terrorism laws – no less than fifteen were passed between 1986 and 2015[32] – and imposing a series of measures destroying civil liberties.[33] But, if Macron has drawn particular criticism on this question, it is because he has satisfied himself with just continuing the authoritarian trajectory of the French ruling class, indeed in blatant contradiction with the 'progressive' electoral promises made in 2017. President Macron has, in fact, greatly amplified the securitarian and authoritarian legacy of the Sarkozy (2007–12) and Hollande (2012–17) presidencies, to such an extent that it is fair to speak of a *fascisation* process at work, as an effect of his policies.[34] The authoritarian tumour was growing in the French body politic even a few months after Macron's first election in 2017. For he had already decided to pass a new anti-terrorism law (which had not been mentioned in his election programme),[35] allowing the state of emergency to be lifted but integrating some of its essential provisions (house arrests, administrative raids without judicial review and so on) into ordinary law. In this way, he transformed a set of freedom-destroying measures, previously justified in the name of an *exceptional* situation, into an ordinary, 'normal' repertoire for state intervention.[36]

---

32   See the list published in Le *Monde diplomatique* in February 2015: 'L'empilement des lois antiterroristes', *Le Monde diplomatique*, February 2020.

33   Just think of the law on intelligence enacted in July 2015, which strengthens the existing surveillance apparatus; an amendment was also passed allowing 'surveillance of all communications data', not just of the 11,700 people on the 'S' list, but also of their 'entourage', potentially implicating hundreds of thousands of people. See the analysis by La Quadrature du Net: 'État d'urgence: surenchère dans la surveillance de masse', La Quadrature du Net, 21 July 2016, laquadrature.net.

34   For more on this point, see Ludivine Bantigny and Ugo Palheta, *Face à la menace fasciste. Sortir de l'autoritarisme*, Paris: Textuel, 2021.

35   Jean-Baptiste Jacquin, 'Antiterrorisme: le gouvernement veut mettre l'état d'urgence dans le droit commun', *Le Monde*, 7 June 2017.

36   In a rather telling slip of the tongue, both Macron and his interior minister Gérard Collomb confused 'rule-of-law state' and 'state of emergency' within just a few weeks of each other. See 'État d'urgence et État de droit: le lapsus d'Emmanuel Macron', *Le Point*, 20 September 2017.

In yet another example of the shock doctrine,[37] Emmanuel Macron and his interior minister Gérald Darmanin then took advantage of the grim decapitation of the teacher Samuel Paty on 16 October 2020 to beef up two related laws attacking freedom of association (known as the 'global security' and 'separatism' bills) that were already being prepared, and pushed them through in spring 2021. When the first of these bills stirred a considerable counter-mobilisation, a great deal of emphasis was placed on the government's intention to ban the video recording and broadcasting of police actions (Article 24, which was ultimately censured by the Constitutional Council). But this law, above all, made it possible to legalise techno-policing measures (notably through the use of drones), increase the powers of private security agencies, extend the right of law enforcement to carry weapons, and increase surveillance of the public space in general. The second bill, supposed to 'strengthen respect for the principles of the Republic', in fact called into question a number of fundamental freedoms. In particular, it raised doubts over the freedoms of association and religion, by forcing all associations who sought public subsidies (crucial for them to be able to eke out an existence) to sign up to a 'contract of republican allegiance'. The seven pledges set out in this contract are vague in the extreme, in turn providing the state with the tools to exert an essentially arbitrary control over associations (particularly Muslim ones). More broadly, the 'separatism' law allowed interior minister Darmanin to launch an outright witch hunt where, in the name of the fight against terrorism (and often enough, on the mere *suspicion* of apology for terrorism), Muslim mosques and denominational schools are closed, public funding withdrawn, imams deported or forced to resign and so on.

This authoritarian offensive thus targeted Muslims in particular, and it had even graver consequences given that in this same moment the main associations standing up for Muslims' rights were broken up by the state. Especially important in this sense was the dissolution of the Collective Against Islamophobia in France (CCIF), an association that became crucial during the state of emergency following the 2015 attacks. The CCIF worked both in the legal defence of Muslims who had suffered discrimination because of their religion, and in keeping an annual database of Islamophobic acts. The CCIF also played a major role in organising the largest street demonstration against Islamophobia in French history, on 10 November 2019, which, for the first time, mobilised almost all

---

37 Naomi Klein, *The Shock Doctrine*, London: Penguin, 2007.

the forces of the political left, as well as trade unions and human rights associations, alongside Muslims. The march followed an upsurge in Islamophobic interventions in the political and media sphere, but also the terrorist attack on the Bayonne mosque on 28 October 2019, in which two Muslims were seriously injured by the bullets fired by a former FN activist (and FN candidate in the 2015 departmental elections). This anti-racist demonstration was vilified by the whole arc of Islamophobic forces, from Macron's camp to the far right, including Gaullists as well as small circles eventuating from the Socialist Party's milieu, such as Printemps républicain. It also marked the start of an all-out campaign against the threat of 'Islamo-leftism'. This slogan has since been taken up by the Macronist ministers of national education (Jean-Michel Blanquer) and higher education (Frédérique Vidal) in an attempt to silence anyone who might challenge the securitarian-Islamophobic consensus.

The sharp emotions sparked by the teacher's murder thus provided the authorities with the pretext for the first ever administrative dissolution of an anti-racist association. A procedure originally devised by the Popular Front in 1936 to tackle fascist leagues, dissolution had also been used against movements denouncing French colonialism and demanding independence for the colonies.[38] Turning things on their head, the government and the Conseil d'État reckoned that the CCIF's denunciation of Islamophobia – and of state Islamophobia in particular – could 'give credence to a permanent suspicion of religious persecution in public opinion, liable to stir up hatred, violence or discrimination'. Denouncing discrimination was thus said to be tantamount to stirring up discrimination, without specifying which ethnic, national, racial or religious group the CCIF was supposedly targeting when denouncing Islamophobia. Macron's camp found a fig leaf of legitimacy for this move by pointing to the other (violent, far-right) groups that had also been dissolved. Yet there is no comparison between dissolving racist groupuscules of a few dozen or a few hundred members (which, sometimes, have no legal existence anyhow, and which then instantly re-form under other names), and an anti-racist association with several thousand members and an essentially institutional role.

This government decision and then its rubber-stamping by the Conseil d'État set a dangerous precedent, which then allowed for the dissolution of another anti-racist collective (the Collective Against Racism

---

38 See Abdellali Hajjat, 'Le grand retournement du droit antiraciste : la dissolution paradoxale du Collectif contre l'islamophobie en France', *La Revue des droits de l'homme*, 2024, no. 25.

and Islamophobia) in October 2021, and very recently the activist collective Palestine Vaincra. This fed a climate of intimidation for anyone who might think of openly denouncing Islamophobia, in what amounted to a severe infringement of freedom of expression. As these dissolutions and the 'separatism' law show, the acceleration of authoritarianism in France, as in most Western countries, is inextricably linked to the rise of Islamophobia. Since 11 September 2001 – and in redoubled form in France since the 2015 attacks – this has made it possible to construct an 'enemy within', without which figure it would surely have been hard to justify such challenges to basic democratic rights and public freedoms.[39] It should also be noted that the threats initially directed against Muslims and the organisations defending them were soon turned against left-wing and social movements. Thus, adding his voice to the slanderous accusations that have constantly targeted La France insoumise since the start of Israel's genocidal war on Gaza, the then-president of LR (the historic party of the bourgeois right) Éric Ciotti, proposed in spring 2024 that there needed to be a discussion of dissolving La France insoumise, the main left-wing force in the National Assembly. This proposal was even taken up by some Macronist MPs. A few years earlier, in 2021, a number of right-wing MPs had called for the dissolution of the historic students' union associated with the left (the UNEF), on the grounds that it had organised non-racially mixed meetings to discuss issues of racism in universities; the then minister of national education, Jean-Michel Blanquer, went so far as to speak of UNEF's 'fascist' turn.

We can also see this accelerating authoritarianism in the heightened repression of popular mobilisations, which sociologists call a 'brutalisation of policing'.[40] This process had begun under Hollande, as early as 2014. But it reached its climax thanks to Macronism, during the Gilets jaunes movement (whose Act I took place on 17 November 2018). Here, the powers that be were clearly intent on raising the level of physical violence against demonstrators.[41] The first Gilets jaunes protests came from parts of French society little-familiar with social mobilisations

---

39 See Didier Bigo, Laurent Bonelli and Thomas Deltombe, *Au nom du 11 septembre . . . Les démocraties à l'épreuve du totalitarisme*, Paris: La Découverte, 2008; Rigouste, *L'ennemi intérieur*; Claude Serfati, *L'Etat radicalisé*, Paris: La Fabrique, 2022. We will return more specifically to the racist dimension, and Islamophobia in particular, in the next chapter.

40 See Olivier Fillieule and Fabien Jobard, *Politiques du désordre*, Paris: Seuil, 2020.

41 See in particular: Yann Bouchez, Samuel Laurent and Nicolas Chapuis, '"Allez-y franchement, n'hésitez pas à percuter. Ça fera réfléchir les suivants": le jour où la doctrine du maintien de l'ordre a basculé', *Le Monde*, 7 December 2019.

and unwilling to submit to the usual rituals of conflict (even if that just meant reporting the planned route of their march to the local police authorities). Driven by radical hostility to Emmanuel Macron and enjoying wide popular support, the first such demonstrations evidently caused a form of panic at the top of the government, among the most bourgeois parts of its electorate (particularly in the upmarket areas of Paris where some of the protests were taking place), and among certain pundits who called, like former Sarkozy minister Luc Ferry, for the army 'to use their weapons once and for all'. Leaving aside the French state's crimes in the context of the Algerian War, and in the territories still under colonial rule (Guadeloupe in 1967, Kanaky-New Caledonia from 1984 to 1988), during the Gilets jaunes crisis the use of force and state repression reached a level unseen in France since the immediate postwar period.

This repression first and foremost meant police repression, with the systematic use of violent techniques (baton charges, kettling, gassing and so on) and so-called 'non-lethal' weapons that are known to injure, mutilate and even kill, in particular blast balls (in French known as LBDs) and sting-ball grenades (which are classified as weapons of war and which no other police force in Europe uses). We should not forget that, during the Gilets jaunes movement, some twenty-four people lost an eye to blast-ball shots, five people lost a hand, a woman (Zineb Redouane) was killed in December 2018 during Act III of the Gilets jaunes by an (illegal) tear gas grenade shot into her flat on the fourth floor while she was closing her blinds, or that a demonstrator (Rémi Fraisse) had been killed a few years earlier, in 2014, by an offensive grenade shot during an environmentalist demonstration in Sivens. It is also worth noting that not a single police officer has been convicted of firing blast balls or grenades, often as a result of botched investigations. In his work on the police's use of so-called 'non-lethal' weapons, Paul Rocher offers some staggering figures: until 2014, only a few dozen rubber bullets had been fired each year (14 in 2010, 145 in 2014), compared with 19,071 in 2018. The same applies to sting-ball grenades, which were used 67 times in 2010, 266 times in 2014 and 5,420 times in 2018. Finally, the number of tear gas shots rose from 929 in 2010 to 3,092 in 2014 and 7,940 in 2018.[42] But the repression also involved a judicial crackdown: and in this sense, too, the Gilets jaunes protests marked a turning point in terms of the repressive management of social movements. More than 1,000 people were

---

42 See Paul Rocher, *Gazer, mutiler, soumettre*, Paris: La Fabrique, 2020.

sentenced to jail time, along with more than 1,200 suspended sentences, and the more than 12,000 people remanded in police custody.

Although the two movements resisting pension reforms (in 2019–20 and 2023) met with less severe repression, it is not as if the Macron camp had reverted to previous policing strategies. 'De-escalation' is just a myth. There are several pieces of evidence for this: according to a report by the Cour des comptes published in February 2024, while, in 2019, there had already been 75 orders banning demonstrations (compared with 6 in 2016 and 2 in 2017) from the Paris Prefecture of Police, the figure would rise to 370 in 2022. In addition, the number of mobile police forces increased over this whole period, as well as the frequency of their deployment. Another example: the number of grenades fired by mobile forces rose from around 14,000 in 2020 to 23,000 in 2022, exceeding the peak reached in 2019 (around 22,000).[43] Speaking at a more qualitative level, we might mention the handling of the Sainte-Soline demonstration against a proposed mega-basin in spring 2023. This saw the deployment of a real war arsenal by the police, a move justified by Interior Minister Darmanin in the name of fighting 'eco-terrorists'. The result was two people left fighting for their lives, who will suffer lifelong after-effects; but also a much larger number of demonstrators left traumatised by the police crackdown. There was similar treatment of the revolt that broke out in many working-class and immigrant neighbourhoods after the killing of seventeen-year-old Nahel Merzouk, who was shot dead by a police officer at point-blank range on 27 June 2023 during a road stop in Nanterre. This met with an outburst of police violence: in the space of a few weeks, several young men lost an eye (again because of blast balls being fired), some had their skulls smashed with truncheons (like Hedi in Marseille), and another – Mohamed Bendriss – was killed, again almost certainly by a blast ball.

The picture would be incomplete without noting that the authoritarian push has decisive implications also in the workplace. Back in the late 1990s, drawing on a long-term study of the transformations of the working class, Stéphane Beaud and Michel Pialoux pointed to the specific forms of this offensive at the level of production.[44] In particular, they showed that the upheavals spurred on by the bosses – cascading subcontracting, more aggressive management doctrines, precarious

---

43 The report can be read here: 'Observations définitives: Les forces mobiles', S2024-0185, ccomptes.fr.
44 Stéphane Beaud and Michel Pialoux, *Retour sur la condition ouvrière*, Paris: Fayard, 1999.

employment status and so on – but also by the state (New Public Management), were essentially aimed at curbing all forms of insubordination, dissent and counter-power, such as had been generalised and strengthened in workplaces in the post-1968 period.[45] These transformations extend well beyond the factory itself.[46] They reflect a whole range of employer tactics: from discrimination against trade unionists to the rise of mechanisms for enlisting employees themselves, and their organisations, in new ways of managing the workforce. This is also premised on the domestication of protest activity in the name of 'social dialogue', the blackmail of raising doubts over workers' future employment, and, of course, intensified forms of anti-union repression.[47] In December 2023, the newspaper *L'Humanité* revealed that more than 1,000 members of the Confédération Générale du travail (CGT) trade union confederation were the subject of disciplinary or legal proceedings. There had indeed been a radicalisation of the ruling class in this regard following the 2023 movement over pensions, with even national CGT leaders harried by the courts. From this point of view, the Labour Laws imposed in France in spring 2016 and autumn 2017 are but the most recent stages – if certainly not the last – in a process of destroying social rights. But the aim is also to establish an undivided employer power and total subordination of employees, by eroding all the spaces for intervention, organisation and autonomy that these latter have conquered in decades past. So, the anti-democratic dynamics of our present moment are not playing out only at the level of fundamental freedoms, respect for universal suffrage or the

---

45 For a description of these forms of counter-power, see Marcel Durand, *Grains de sable sous le capot. Résistance & contre-culture ouvrière: les chaînes de montage de Peugeot (1972–2003)*, Marseille: Agone, 2006; Xavier Vigna, *L'insubordination ouvrière dans les années 68. Essai d'histoire politique des usines*, Rennes: PUR, 2007; Christian Corrouge and Michel Pialoux, *Résister à la chaîne. Dialogue entre un ouvrier de Peugeot et un sociologue*, Marseille: Agone, 2011; Fanny Gallot, *En découdre. Comment les ouvrières ont révolutionné le travail et la société*, Paris: La Découverte, 2015; Ludivine Bantigny, *1968. De grands soirs en petits matins*, Paris: Seuil, 2018.

46 See in particular: Christophe Brochier, 'Des jeunes corvéables. L'organisation du travail et la gestion du personnel dans un fast-food', *Actes de la recherche en sciences sociales*, 2001, no. 138, pp. 73–83; Marie Buscatto, 'Les centres d'appels, usines modernes? Les rationalisations paradoxales de la relation téléphonique', *Sociologie du travail*, 2002, vol. 44, no. 1, pp. 99–117; Sarah Abdelnour, *Les nouveaux prolétaires*, Paris: Textuel, 2012; Marlène Benquet, *Encaisser. Enquête en immersion dans la grande distribution*, Paris: La Découverte, 2013.

47 Étienne Pénissat (ed.), 'Réprimer et domestiquer. Stratégies patronales', *Revue Agone*, 2013, no. 50. See also 'Rapport 2014 de l'observatoire de la répression et de la discrimination syndicale first report by the Observatoire de la discrimination et de la répression syndicale', Observatoire de la discrimination et de la répression syndicale, 2014.

place given to parliamentary representation, but also at the heart of the relations of production.

Finally, it is worth noting the rise of a penal state built on the ashes of the welfare state.[48] This has its most visible symptom in the boom, over the last forty years, in the number of people imprisoned – rising from 36,913 in 1980 to 91,647 in 2024 – but more widely in the number of people in the grip of the justice system – rising from 77,336 in 1982 to 272,619 in 2024.[49] This trend is all the more striking given that it has taken place at a time when politicians and pseudo-experts (who are nonetheless very real entrepreneurs) in the security business[50] are constantly accusing the justice system of being 'lax' and the left of being 'a soft touch', and when crime rates have generally remained stable (or even fallen, in the case of the most serious physical violence, notably homicides).[51] Finally, it should be pointed out that this is not simply a question – as per Pierre Bourdieu's metaphor[52] – of the capitalist authorities organising the expansion of the 'right hand' of the state (the repressive apparatus) and getting rid of its 'left hand' (the education, health and 'social' services). Rather, this is making the welfare state function on the model of the penal state, that is, according to the logic of surveillance and punishment rather than public service and the common good.[53]

---

48 See Loïc Wacquant, *Les prisons de la misère*, Paris: Raisons d'agir 1999 (*Prisons of Poverty*, Minneapolis: University of Minnesota Press, 2009); and his *Punir les pauvres. Le nouveau gouvernement de l'insécurité sociale*, Marseille: Agone, 2004 (*Punishing the Poor: The Neoliberal Government of Social Insecurity*, Durham, NC: Duke University Press, 2009).

49 See the report produced in May 2014 by the French prison administration: 'Séries statistiques des personnes placées sous main de justice, 1980–2024', La direction de l'administration pénitentiaire, 9 January 2023, justice.gouv.fr.

50 On the example of two of the most high-profile such experts, Alain Bauer and Xavier Raufer (the latter, whose real name is Christian de Bongain, was also an activist in the neofascist groupuscule Occident), see Laurent Mucchielli, *Violences et insécurité. Fantasmes et réalités dans le débat français*, Paris: La Découverte, 2007.

51 See for example: Didier Fassin, *Punir. Une passion contemporaine*, Paris: Seuil, 2020 (*The Will to Punish*, Oxford: Oxford University Press, 2018).

52 See in particular: Pierre Bourdieu, 'La démission de l'Etat', in *La misère du monde*, Paris: Seuil, Points, 1998, pp. 337–49 ('The Abdication of the State', in *The Weight of the World: Social Suffering in Contemporary Society*, Cambridge: Polity Press, 2000). For an analysis which revisits this point, see Christian Laval, *Foucault, Bourdieu et la question néolibérale*, Paris: La Découverte, 2018, pp. 221–5.

53 Think of the handling of unemployment, which is increasingly being transformed into an apparatus for monitoring and coercing the jobless, who are constantly threatened with being stripped of their rights and subjected to the form of social death known as 'deregistration'. See in particular: Emmanuel Pierru, *Guerre aux chômeurs ou guerre au chômage*, Bellecombe-en-Bauges: Le Croquant, 2005. See also: Pierre Martin, *Les métamorphoses de l'assurance maladie. Conversion managériale et nouveau gouvernement des pauvres*, Rennes: Presses universitaires de Rennes, 2016.

When the Bourgeoisie Dismantles Bourgeois Democracy[54]

What has happened over the last two decades reflects a crisis of liberal democracy, that is, the main means by which the ruling class has organised its political domination since the end of the nineteenth century. This model has been pitched into crisis by the popular struggles of the post-1968 years but also, in reaction, by governments themselves. The latter have preferred to gradually chip away at the (parliamentary) political forms, democratic rights and social achievements on which states rebuilt their legitimacy after World War II, and which have become increasingly cumbersome as the crisis of capitalism has deepened.

Back in the 1970s, the Trilateral Commission – one of the many international think-tanks useful to the bourgeoisie in consolidating its political and ideological homogeneity and elaborating a common orientation[55] – turned to address the issue of democracy, albeit very much in its own way. Its authors were Samuel Huntington (later world-famous for his 'clash of civilisations' thesis, which legitimised imperial intervention after 11 September 2001), Michel Crozier (a French sociologist beloved of neoliberal elites, particularly for his pamphlet *La Société bloquée*) and Joji Watanuki. In their report published in 1975,[56] they expressed concern about democracy's 'excesses' and its conflict with 'governability'. To deal with this problem, the report argued that political institutions should be placed as far as possible from any form of popular control. The people and universal suffrage, seen as volatile and too insensitive to so-called economic 'necessities', were to be framed by new institutions devoted

---

54 As mentioned above, the expression 'bourgeois democracy' is itself highly questionable. It bundles together rights and freedoms that really were won by the bourgeoisie when it was a 'rising class' challenging the power of the traditional ruling classes, with others that were instead won by the working classes and progressive – feminist, anti-racist, LGBT – movements, often against fierce resistance from the bourgeoisie. These include everything from universal suffrage to freedom of organisation, assembly and demonstration, the right to strike, the right to abortion, the decriminalisation of homosexuality and so on.

55 Historian Dylan Riley uses the concept 'intra-class hegemony' to designate the processes by which certain fractions of the dominant class draw allied groups within a social bloc behind them, but this could be extended to the domination that the dominant fractions of international capital assert over capital or blocs of capital belonging to second-tier powers or dominated countries. See *The Civic Foundations of Fascism in Europe. Italy, Spain, and Romania, 1870–1945*, Baltimore, MD: Johns Hopkins University Press, 2010, p. 15.

56 Michel J. Crozier, Samuel P. Huntington and Joji Watanuki, 'Crisis of Democracy: Report on the Governability of Democracies to the Trilateral Commission', New York: New York University Press, 1975. For an analysis of this report, see Grégoire Chamayou, *La société ingouvernable*, Paris: La Fabrique, 2018 (*The Ungovernable Society: A Genealogy of Authoritarian Liberalism*, Cambridge: Polity Press, 2021).

entirely to the accumulation of capital and the maintenance of the existing order. This report gives both an explicit and exhaustive picture of what is generally presented in euphemistic and fragmented terms, namely the 'de-democratisation' agenda[57] pursued by the ruling classes ever since the late 1970s. The rise of authoritarianism has not simply been the product of piecemeal, ad hoc adjustments; it is the result of intellectual reflection within the political and economic elites, and of decisions taken by governments (of both right and centre-left). Reflecting the concerns among ruling circles (particularly employers), this programme sought to rein in potentially disruptive liberation movements and reduce social conflict, which had been on the rise since the late 1960s. In particular, it sought to overcome an apparently irresolvable problem: how to restore capitalist power, which was being undermined by popular struggles, even while maintaining the formal structures of democracy (free elections, political pluralism and so on)? The ruling-class response was based on three series of structural transformations.

The first is neoliberal globalisation which, by giving ever greater power to a specific actor – capitalist finance – has altered the balance of power between classes, but also between the ruling classes' internal fractions. One of the central characteristics of deregulated and globalised finance is its tendency to free itself of even minimal political control, because of its ability to detach itself from any territorial base. Finance has become so powerful that it is able, through ventriloquist institutions – the ECB, but also the IMF, the WTO and the World Bank, which are all centres of capitalist power – to directly impose public policies favourable to capital. In particular, this is done by blackmailing investment (with the interventions by rating agencies, for example) or, as in Greece, by blackmailing the financing of states deliberately kept on the brink of default. In truth, this is nothing new: this type of pressure has always been one of the capitalist class's most important weapons. But we too often forget that it was identifiable political players and specific decisions that freed finance from the constraints that had shackled it since the postwar period. In the case of France, we need only think of the 1984 banking deregulation law and the 1986 Bérégovoy law on financial deregulation – both initiated by a government dominated by the Socialist Party.[58] It was government decisions that unleashed the free movement

---

57 See Wendy Brown, *Undoing the Demos: Neoliberalism's Stealth Revolution*, New York: Zone Books, 2015.

58 See Bruno Amable, *La Résistible ascension du néolibéralisme*, Paris: La Découverte, 2021.

of capital, both in Europe and around the world. This has dramatically stepped up the competition between workers and between countries, encouraging unlimited social and fiscal dumping. The financial crisis of 2007–8 did nothing to change the situation from this standpoint, simply because there is no middle way: either we confront capitalist finance, which presupposes breaking down its fundamental structures (in particular, by socialising the banking system and closing down the stock market)[59] or, sooner or later, we are bound to end up complying with all its dictates. Governments have unanimously chosen the second option, once they have got past the indignation that must be expressed faced with each financial hurricane.

The second transformation is linked to the first, but it also has a relative autonomy and a historical trajectory of its own. It proceeds via the regional integration of capitalist economies, in particular through the most advanced such project, the European Union. Since the 1980s, the EU has not been constructed simply as a free market in which 'free and undistorted competition' must reign. It has also been built as a proto-state dominated by unelected bodies (the European Commission and the ECB, but also a wide variety of lobbies).[60] This does not *replace* nation-states – although, in the case of Greece, the EU's emissaries have played the role of a shadow government – but is bound up with them.[61] Drawing on the powers transferred upwards by national governments, the EU proto-state has gained binding force, including through its courts of justice but, above all, through its single currency – what we might call its monetary tools. The Greek example in the first half of 2015 showed that an elected government in an EU member state could not apply an economic policy without the agreement of the governments of the main European powers (mainly Germany and secondarily France), or, indeed, that of the European Commission, the ECB and the IMF, that is, institutions organically linked to (and subordinate to) financial capital. In January 2015, following Syriza's election victory built on the promise to break with austerity, Commission president Jean-Claude Juncker declared: 'There can be no democratic choice against the European treaties.' We should also remember how the French and Dutch popular votes against the European Constitutional Treaty (ECT) in 2005 were erased by the

---

59 See Frédéric Lordon, 'Et si l'on fermait la Bourse', *Le Monde diplomatique*, February 2010.
60 On the role of lobbyists within the EU, See Sylvain Laurens, *Les Courtiers du capitalisme*, Marseille: Agone, 2015.
61 See Cédric Durand (ed.), *En finir avec l'Europe*, Paris: La Fabrique, 2013.

stroke of a pen. The Lisbon Treaty – a document which differed from the planned constitution only in terms of its internal order, according to the admission of the ECT's main designer Valéry Giscard d'Estaing – was ratified by parliament with no further popular vote, also with the complicity of most Socialist Party MPs and senators. We might add that, when the Irish people voted against this second treaty, the entire EU oligarchy balked and forced them to vote again until they got an answer that better suited their interests.

The third structural factor involves a long-term transformation process in capitalist states themselves, which consists of a rise in 'authoritarian statism' and marks the 'decline of democracy'.[62] The traditional mechanisms of liberal parliamentarianism in fact began to be marginalised well before the construction of the EU and capitalist globalisation. In France, Gaullism and the Fifth Republic constituted a new way of organising the political domination of the bourgeoisie and building its hegemony, marginalising parliamentary organs in favour of other bodies, elected or otherwise. The executive and the state administration, controlled by the tops of the main parties, themselves organically integrated into *both* state institutions *and* business circles. On the Gaullist and liberal-free marketeer right, the links with the latter have always been obvious, but in the case of the Socialist Party, they needed to be proactively cultivated, particularly from the 1980s onwards. This is well illustrated by the creation of the Cercle de l'Industrie in the early 1990s. Co-founded by Dominique Strauss-Kahn, long a prominent Socialist leader who went on to become economy minister and then director of the IMF, this employers' lobby deliberately included as many leaders from the Socialist Party as from the right – in addition to the presidents of France's biggest companies.

It would be wrong to imagine that the election of Emmanuel Macron, who has the distinction of not having had his political training within one of the two parties that have exchanged the reins of government since 1981, would change anything in this regard. On the contrary, Macron has followed in the footsteps of previous governments, radicalising the two-sided authoritarian tendency highlighted by Poulantzas: the fusion of parties and the state administration, and the domination of the executive over the latter. It should also be noted that, while the Socialist Party may have shown a few rare signs of independence under Hollande, which were quickly either repressed or suppressed, Macron's own vehicle (En

---

62   See Nicos Poulantzas, *State, Power, Socialism*, London: Verso, 2014.

Marche) was created solely as a means of gaining power and has absolutely no depth of its own (even compared to the parties of the traditional right). It has no activists, no cadres (apart from its elected representatives) and no internal democracy. En Marche was designed to remain under the tight control of its president and to act as a pool of 'expertise' – essentially from the world of business, finance, consultants, management and so on – for the purpose of gaining power. What is more, Macron's way of exercising power has proven hyper-centralised, even by the Fifth Republic's standards: the entire decision-making machinery has been concentrated around the president and his close entourage, and he has studiedly bypassed all of those many civil society forces, associations and institutions that the French call 'intermediary bodies'. Even the trade unions most favourable to a social-liberal line and to negotiations with employers, such as the CFDT or the CGC, have expressed very harsh criticism of Macron and joined the general mobilisation against the pension reform in 2023. This says a lot about the isolation of the political powers that be, the weakness of their base and their ability to find transmission belts for their message within civil society.

It is as if Macron imagined that he could build a hegemony without any mediations, by sheer force of his own word. Hence, during the political crisis prompted by the Gilets jaunes movement, the president thought he could respond not only by repression, but also by holding meetings throughout France with elected representatives and (often hand-picked) citizens, the so-called *grand débat*. This added up to over ninety-two hours of discussions that amounted to a 'great debate' more akin to a long presidential monologue. Add to this the constant marginalisation of the National Assembly (not only during the pandemic), the absence of autonomy granted to Macronist MPs and, more generally, the contempt that the president has shown towards parliamentarians. This was particularly stark during his second term as president, when Prime Minister Élisabeth Borne (in office from May 2022 to January 2024) used Article 49.3 to bypass parliament twenty-three times in just eighteen months. Most importantly, she did this to force through a pension reform that was drastically unpopular among the general population (93 percent of the working-age population opposed the reform),[63] rejected across almost all socio-professional groups (particularly the working classes, but even small business owners), and for which the Macron government

---

63 See Catherine Gasté, 'Réforme des retraites: seuls 7% des actifs favorables à une augmentation de l'âge légal de depart', *Le Parisien*, 12 January 2023.

did not have a majority of MPs in the National Assembly. The decision to dissolve parliament and head to snap elections in June 2024, in the wake of a crushing defeat in the European elections, again illustrated Macron's solitary and authoritarian practice of power, since he did not even see fit to inform his prime minister, Gabriel Attal, let alone consult him or his own MPs.[64]

Macron, in continuity with Sarkozy and Hollande before him, thus openly stands as a harshened embodiment not only of the Fifth Republic and its top-down order, but also of the neoliberal-authoritarian state – that particular modality of the capitalist state meant to be built entirely on the model of company management. Much like the pseudo-consultations known as 'company referendums', in which employees are asked to choose between the devil (working more to earn the same or even less) and the deep blue sea (job cuts), in this model, democratic debate has no purpose other than to rubber-stamp and legitimise a posteriori the decisions already taken by a tiny minority in the name of considerations far removed from the interests of the vast majority. This model dispenses with the whole issue of making the concessions that will allow social alliances to be forged, in order to build a stable power bloc. Rather, it's all about 'teaching us what is best' and, failing to convince, imposing neoliberal counter-reforms by forceps through forcing parliamentary procedures and deploying repression in the streets.

Capitalism and Democracy in the Neoliberal Era

If we take these three structural transformations seriously, it is easy to understand that the main threat facing democracy is not 'jihadism' or 'Islamism', as the ruling classes have got used to telling us since the beginning of the 'war on terror'. Terrorism endangers civilian populations, but it is governments' responses to it that pose a real threat to democracy, whenever the rule of law and public freedoms are attacked in the name of the 'global war on terror'. This is particularly the case when the Muslim minority is subjected to exceptional treatment in the name of the dynamics of 'radicalisation' or 'rising fanaticism' that governments more or less explicitly identify with Islam. Despite what many conservative intellectuals claim, the anti-democratic threat does not lie in the plague of 'individualism' – itself the product of competitive individualisation

---

64   Solenne de Royer, 'Emmanuel Macron, Alexis Kohler, Ismaël Emelien: ce trio qui dirige la France', *Le Monde*, 7 August 2017.

driven by state and employer coercion – or in the supposed passivity of the population. Citizens who feel that they are stripped of all real power may indeed become passive. But the public authorities have stubbornly constructed this passivity. They have done this, in part, through rhetoric (Thatcher's famous 'there is no alternative', repeated over and over again for thirty years by the chorus of pundits, media intellectuals and mainstream journalists). But, most of all, this has been achieved through the construction of institutions that make decision-making increasingly opaque, and through the disappearance of any significant difference between 'right-wing' and 'left-wing' governments.

The main danger for democracy is the radicalisation of a bourgeoisie that would love to shake off the burden of this demos and the social and democratic rights that it has won. We find a fine illustration of this from one of its most assiduous spokespersons in the mainstream media, who could unironically comment in March 2016:

> How nice governing would be if it weren't for the bloody French people! Without them, our country would long have been a land of milk and honey, with a dynamic economy and an unemployment rate close to zero, just like our neighbours . . . France doesn't get any help, but it doesn't help itself either. If its people are not up to the job, can it at least change?[65]

His claims chimed with a message we had already heard in *The Class Struggles in France*, when Karl Marx reminded us that the bourgeoisie relies on universal suffrage and the constitutional regime only insofar as they allow it to peacefully ensure the reproduction of the capitalist order:

> Bourgeois rule as the outcome and result of universal suffrage, as the express act of the sovereign will of the people – that is the meaning of the bourgeois constitution. But has the constitution any further meaning from the moment that the content of this suffrage, of this sovereign will, is no longer bourgeois rule? Is it not the duty of the bourgeoisie so to regulate the suffrage that it wills the reasonable, its rule?[66]

In other words, as soon as democracy – even when corseted by capitalist domination, limited by the reality of inequality and impoverished

---

65 Franz-Olivier Giesbert, 'Le cauchemar de Tocqueville', *Le Point*, 10 March 2016.
66 Karl Marx, *The Class Struggles in France*, marxists.org.

by the weakness of political and media pluralism – becomes an obstacle on the road to capital accumulation or the stabilisation of the political order, the bourgeoisie will readily cast it aside. At least it will do so if the benefits outweigh the costs of some other form of political domination. Wherever the left and popular movements have challenged the interests of the property-owning classes, even partially and through institutional means, these classes and their political representatives have never been afraid to do away with liberal democracy altogether, even using the most criminal means to maintain or consolidate their power. For evidence of this, we need only look to the many episodes of ferocious repression (of popular uprisings, workers' mobilisations, racial and national minorities and so on), coups d'état and military dictatorships (from Franco's Spain to Pinochet's Chile or the colonels' Greece), support for fascist movements (as in interwar Italy and Germany; and we too often forget that it was the parties of the bourgeois right that handed power to forces who had only a minority of the electorate behind them).[67] Then there are the thousand and one times that the imperialist powers have organised the slaughter of populations in the Global South: in the French case, we need only mention the massacres of 8 May 1945 in Algeria or 1947 in Madagascar, or 17 October 1961, when the French police murdered hundreds of peaceful Algerian demonstrators in the middle of Paris (the deadliest act of repression in Western Europe since 1945, according to the historian Emmanuel Blanchard).

In the current period, it is increasingly clear that capitalism has no 'natural' need for democracy. Instead, we are seeing an authoritarian wave spread over the world. If we take this line of reasoning further, we could even argue that the Chinese model is no exception in the contemporary capitalist world, any more than it is a simple throwback to the era of primitive accumulation and the first industrial revolution. As Slavoj Žižek puts it, the Chinese case could even be 'a sign of the future':[68] not so much in terms of single party rule and the absence of free elections or universal suffrage, as the drastic curtailment of political and trade union rights, the radical reduction of the freedoms of organisation and expression, and the preventive surveillance of the population. Among the EU's own member states, Viktor Orban's Hungary already provides an image

---

67 See the preface to this book.
68 Giorgio Agamben, Alain Badiou, Daniel Bensaïd, Wendy Brown, Jean-Luc Nancy, Jacques Rancière, Kristin Ross and Slavoj Žižek, *Démocratie, dans quel état*, Paris: La Fabrique, 2009, p. 131 (*Democracy in What State?* New York: Columbia University Press, 2011).

of the type of democracy that neoliberal capitalism can support: one where the right to strike no longer exists or hardly exists in reality, where public debate is atrophied by the suffocation of independent media, where critical journalists and researchers are harassed, where universities are privatised and handed over to the ruling clique, where teaching programmes on inequality and discrimination disappear, and where the rights of foreigners and minorities are whittled down to nothing.

One of the main weaknesses of the approaches of Alain Badiou and the Invisible Committee, among others, is that they simply dismiss the contradictions between capitalism and democracy. Badiou dissolves democracy into capitalism (hence his expression 'capitalo-parliamentarism'), and 'reduces all political equality to a simple inverted reflection or a deceptive instrument of the domination of Capital';[69] the Invisible Committee, following Giorgio Agamben, tends to collapse democracy into a simple technique of government.[70] At the root of these approaches is an aristocratic critique of 'democratic man', which Alain Badiou owes essentially to Plato and Giorgio Agamben to Heidegger.[71] Their positions lead to the postulate that universal suffrage, civil liberties and even social rights would have no other function and effect than to subjugate and deceive the populations by lulling them into the illusion of having 'rights', and cannot pose any threat to the capitalist order. The Invisible Committee goes so far as to present the trade union movement and the political left, including the radical left, as docile organs of an omniscient and omnipresent Power (the 'Empire').[72]

Such approaches reduce democracy to an essence frozen in procedures and institutions; in these accounts, the history of class struggles seems to have no place and to have left no trace. Any social or democratic gain that has been won is reduced to just another mechanism for enlisting the subalterns in the 'capitalo-parliamentary' machinery or in 'Empire'. All this makes the bourgeoisie's current policies rather puzzling. Why would the ruling classes go to such lengths to undermine

---

69   Jacques Rancière, *En quel temps vivons-nous? Conversation avec Eric Hazan*, Paris: La Fabrique, 2017, p. 13 (*What Times Are We Living In? A Conversation with Eric Hazan*, Cambridge: Polity Press, 2020).

70   Jacques Rancière writes: 'We have seen a resurgence of the old rhetoric, with Cohn-Bendit at the forefront saying that it was democracy that brought about Hitler, and so on. These positions can be found from the right to the far left, from Finkielkraut to *Tiqqun*', ibid., p. 96.

71   In both cases, this criticism is pulled apart by the devastating counter-critique proposed by Jacques Rancière in his *Hatred of Democracy*.

72   See Ugo Palheta, 'Les influences visibles du Comité invisible', *La Revue du Crieur*, June 2016, no. 4.

subaltern movements (by alternately playing on repression and domestication, the stick and the carrot), limit public liberties (by imposing the various forms of regression documented in this chapter) or circumvent universal suffrage (several recent examples of which have shown that it cannot be bent to the bourgeoisie's wishes), if all these elements of democracy as we know it – that is, in an extremely limited form – were pure cogs in capitalist domination, or a mere veil masking reality? This is a puzzle only for a 'pure' politics, which can easily degenerate into an anti-politics, since it sees no contradiction in capitalist domination that subalterns could base their struggles on, and it imagines no opposition to this system other than one standing totally and impossibly external to the economy and politics.

Against this tendency to dodge around the analysis of contradictions, we should realise that it is only by tracking the historical trajectory of social and political struggles that we can understand what is at stake today. In particular, doing this allows us to understand the neoliberal offensive as a ruling-class response to the wave of popular struggles and widespread insubordination that marked the post-1968 years. Neoliberalism, conceived as a class project and implemented since the end of the 1970s, has had several combined aims: the destruction of all social rights and the drastic reduction of the political freedoms won by the workers' movement in the nineteenth and twentieth centuries, as well as the crushing of the slightest space for autonomy won by the exploited classes and oppressed groups. But what are these social rights (the right to health and education, for example), what are these freedoms and these margins of autonomy, if not the lasting imprint of the struggles waged by the dispossessed in the past? What are they, if not the sites of an embryonic but real popular counter-power, and sometimes even 'deposits of communism'[73] – signs of another possible world?

Have advanced capitalist societies entered the era of 'post-democracy'?[74] Stimulating as this hypothesis is, it nevertheless has the flaw of being based on a fetishised vision of the period prior to the neoliberal offensive: the misnamed 'Thirty Glorious Years', seen as a kind of golden age of social and democratic capitalism. But this period was just a parenthesis in the long history of capitalism.[75] And who would dare

---

73 See Isaac Johsua, *La révolution selon Karl Marx*, Lausanne: Editions Page-deux, 2012.
74 Colin Crouch, *Post-Democracy*, London: Wiley & Sons, 2004.
75 See Wolfgang Streeck, 'The crisis of democratic capitalism', *New Left Review*, September/October 2011, no. 71.

tell the men and women who toiled in factories and on building sites, the farm labourers and immigrant workers, the trade unionists and anti-colonial activists, that, in those years, exploitation was gentler, employer power less arbitrary and the state more sympathetic to the struggles of the exploited and oppressed? This also applies to the French case. Apart from the authoritarianism of the Gaullist regime and the violence of the employers' goon squads (which recycled many far-right militants), this is to forget that, as the economist Thomas Piketty recently pointed out, 'the period 1945–1967 was characterised in France by . . . a movement of reconstruction of inequalities' (in terms of class and gender); it was, in fact, the movement of May–June 1968 that began a process of reducing inequalities (lasting up until 1983).[76] To speak of a 'divorce' between capitalism and democracy, as some authors do,[77] seems to miss the mark. Unless we consider that their union in times past was a marriage of convenience alone and forget that capitalism constantly indulged in authoritarian adventures. Was not the era of so-called 'democratic capitalism' in the United States the age of McCarthyism and the federal state's low-intensity war against the civil rights movement and, more generally, Black movements? Was not this period in France the years of the colonial wars in Indochina and Algeria, with their trail of repression, torture and massacres?

But can we simply assert that behind the veneer of liberal democracy, the political structures of capitalism invariably remain authoritarian? Is there really nothing new under the sun? This is far from the case. But the transformations of these structures correspond to the balance of power between classes and between nations. Ultimately, this depends on the willingness of the subalterns to fight, and on the ability of the dominant classes to politically integrate significant layers of the populations into hegemonic power blocs. It also crucially depends on their ability to quell the resistance of the peoples of the Global South, whether directly or – more often than not – with the help of co-opted elites. The transition that Colin Crouch describes as a shift from democracy to 'postdemocracy' is better understood as a transformation of the political forms of social domination, under the effect of a vast, worldwide defeat of the working class[78] and of most oppressed nations faced with the offensive

---

76   Thomas Piketty, 'Mai 68 et les inégalités', *Le Monde*, 5 May 2018.
77   See in particular the column by the influential British columnist Martin Wolf: 'Capitalism and democracy: the strain is showing', *Financial Times*, 30 August 2016.
78   In each country, the labour movement has suffered emblematic defeats, which have had major political effects. Among these we could cite the US air traffic controllers'

waged by Western bourgeoisies ever since the mid-1970s. The European and international institutions have been key players in this authoritarian offensive, with the complicity of national governments.

The Neoliberal-Authoritarian State and Fascism

As we have said, the authoritarian counter-revolution that began in the late 1970s was initially a response to the rise of mass anti-capitalist consciousness, which in turn was a result of social struggles: workers' mobilisations, but also anti-racist, anti-imperialist, feminist and, albeit secondarily, environmentalist struggles. Even so, the constant extension of this counter-revolution in the present moment ought not be mistaken for the negative proof of a revolutionary threat to the ruling classes of the dominant capitalist powers. Indeed, notwithstanding the scale of the setbacks that populations have suffered and the brutal methods that have become increasingly commonplace, levels of class struggles in these countries still remain relatively low for the time being, and undeniably less intense than they were in the interwar period. The high level of social and political conflict in today's France is the exception rather than the rule in Western Europe, particularly compared with Germany and Italy. What we are currently seeing is a gradual breakdown of previously established political balances (with unpredictable medium and long-term effects) and a pre-emptive authoritarian offensive. It is not that there is a sudden breakthrough by the dispossessed, turning the tables on the existing order and forcing the bourgeoisies to abandon all semblance of democracy in response. That said, there is nothing to stop us from considering that, in the years to come, there will indeed be a deepening political crisis, large-scale radical politicisation and a more marked authoritarian shift on the part of the ruling classes.

We have spoken of capitalist democracies sliding towards authoritarian models that generally respect formal legality while marginalising, strictly containing or even crushing direct forms of democratic intervention. As we have said, in the French case this shift did not start only with the introduction of the state of emergency in 2015. It began in the late 1970s and since then has been the expression of a latent crisis in capitalist states as they were constructed in the nineteenth and twentieth

---

strike broken by Ronald Reagan in 1981, the British miners' strike in 1984–5 in the face of Thatcher's intransigence and repressive violence, and the strikes by steel and car industry workers in France in the early 1980s.

centuries. The current political challenge that the ruling classes face thus lies in the very structures of these states: their concern is to kickstart capitalist accumulation while ensuring the reproduction of social relations and the continued legitimacy of bourgeois domination. This demands not the simple repression of protest movements, but their domestication and the political integration of large segments of the wage-earning population into the dominant order. In France, however, this dimension has proved to be a stumbling block for the neoliberal-authoritarian state, particularly in view of the scale of popular struggles ever since the strikes of winter 1995.

If we face such an authoritarian offensive, then where should we locate the fascist threat in relation to change taking place already? First of all, we should remember that the rise of authoritarianism is not necessarily synonymous with fascism and is not always a sign of a fascisation process (of society, the elites and/or the state). A government that bans demonstrations, governs by decree, marginalises parliament, cracks down on the populations of poor neighbourhoods and so on, cannot *ipso facto* be equated with a fascist government. The fascist state does not mean a government a certain degree more repressive than ordinary ones, but a regime of exception in which the rule-of-law state, such as we know it, no longer exists, almost every civil organization is destroyed and a high level of ideological and political control is exerted over the population.[79] Individual and collective freedoms, fundamental democratic rights and legal defences against arbitrary state power are already highly differentiated according to citizenship status, if we consider the situation of postcolonial immigrants, ethnic minorities and residents of urban working-class neighbourhoods with large non-white populations. Under a fascist state, these protections are simply abolished. Such an exceptional regime can only be imposed in an extraordinary situation, at the end of a succession of political crises, while also taking advantage of the absence of a viable left-wing alternative. It cannot be the result of a step-by-step, linear evolution: a state does not gradually become more and more authoritarian until, one fine (or rather, sinister) morning, it discovers itself to be fascist. Fascism is not the final stage in a slow process that inevitably leads capitalist democracies to totalitarianism, passing through all the many degrees of authoritarianism.

Only situations that have become ungovernable can allow for a radical transformation of the state by those who only a few years before

---

79 See Nicos Poulantzas, *Fascism and Dictatorship*, London: Verso, 1974.

had appeared as grotesque rabble-rousers surrounded by their hate-filled followers and gangs operating in the shadows. Fascism is neither the inevitable endpoint of capitalist democracies, nor some project secretly but unyieldingly pursued by the ruling classes. The transition from liberal or authoritarian states to exceptional regimes (military or fascist dictatorships) has historically been quite rare. This is not because the ruling class is attached *in principle* to liberal democracy, but because its components generally consider that this type of political regime gives them more legitimacy – and therefore stability – than a dictatorship would. The danger is not that the ruling classes will lose everything (indeed, they generally manage to reach an accommodation with any regime). Rather, the risk is that they will have to give up control of the political situation, as handled by their traditional political representatives, and that eventually social and political polarisation will grow. This is why fascists, while they have historically benefited from the *indulgence* and even the *direct aid* of the ruling class, have never been their *first* option. The majority of the ruling class only resigns itself to fascist rule in the absence of some better alternative (from the point of view of its own interests). Even then, it does so with the (pathetically illusory) claim of being able to keep the fascists on a leash.

Nevertheless, for a number of reasons, historically, the ground has been prepared for fascist triumph by a previous authoritarian hardening of the capitalist state, driven by bourgeois governments.[80] It is worth shedding light on these factors. First of all, authoritarianism tended to accustom the traditional political elites to increasing recourse to exceptional procedures and intensified (sometimes extra-legal) forms of repression. This generalised use of force necessarily brings them closer to the far right, by legitimising the 'solutions' which the latter proposes. It also leads the right, or at least segments of it, to take a different view of fascists and to consider the possibility of alliances with them, at all levels of politics. It also has the effect of getting people used to seeing their fundamental political rights restricted, often making them less inclined to revolt than to apathy or passivity (in the face of the increased costs or risks of mobilisation: injuries, arrests, punishments and so on).

---

80   We need only think of the cabinets led by Giovanni Giolitti in Italy or the governments led by Brüning and then Von Papen in Germany, before the coming to power of Mussolini and Hitler respectively. On the relationship between these authoritarian bourgeois governments and the fascist dynamic, see Leon Trotsky's magisterial text: 'Democracy and Fascism', in *Germany, What Next? Vital Questions for the German Proletariat*, New York: Pioneer Publishers, 1939.

This authoritarian hardening also helps strengthen and empower the repressive state apparatus, in which the far right generally finds solid points of support, useful for future battles against popular movements but also conflicts internal to the state.[81] Finally, authoritarianism implies the establishment of an institutional base and a legal arsenal which give the far right, immediately upon its arrival in power, the means to build an authority which is difficult to challenge, to legally establish its domination, to isolate organisations hostile to the new government, and to deploy a potentially unlimited repression against any form of opposition.[82] It should be remembered in passing that both the Mussolini and Hitler regimes, as well as the Pétainist regime in France, came to power and imposed their dictatorship not through coups d'état, but by means that formally and superficially respected the law (although they did not win a majority in democratic elections).

There is also a more indirect, but crucial, link between authoritarian tendencies and the fascist threat. The emergence of a powerful fascist movement, capable of conquering and exercising political power, is only possible in the context of a crisis of hegemony of the dominant classes. The authoritarian transformation of contemporary capitalist states derives, at least in part, from the weak political legitimacy of successive ruling parties and their declining roots in society. However, it is doubtful whether the neoliberal state – which has little to do with liberal democracy and is more of an updated version of the authoritarian statism described by Nicos Poulantzas[83] – can be sustained in a stable form. Even apart from the fact that fast-track means of governing without popular consent – ordinances, decrees, '49.3' and so on – can only partially and temporarily plug the holes in the ship, the neoliberal-authoritarian state is both a product of the crisis of hegemony *and* a factor in heightening that crisis. The deeper the crisis gets, the more governments are led to rule in an authoritarian manner, thereby intensifying

---

81   The FN/RN's huge support among the personnel of the repressive apparatus (in both the police and armed forces) is well-known and seems to have stabilised at over 50 percent since the mid-2010s. See in particular: '2012–2017: une radicalisation du vote des membres des forces de sécurité', IFOP Focus, March 2017, no. 151. A more recent study by Luc Rouban estimated that 58 percent of police and military personnel intended to vote for a far-right party (the FN/RN or some other) in the 2024 European elections.

82   For an attempt to anticipate how the RN might use the institutions of the Fifth Republic once in power, see Carine Fouteau and Michaël Hajdenberg, 'Si Marine Le Pen était présidente', *Mediapart*, 14 March 2017, mediapart.fr.

83   See Nicos Poulantzas, *State, Power and Socialism*, London and New York: Verso, 2014 [1978].

the mistrust of large sectors of the population and thus sharpening the crisis of hegemony.[84] Beyond parliamentary organs themselves – which increasingly appear a mere shadow theatre that lays on a tragi-comic play with no grip on the real world – this self-destructive dimension of the neoliberal-authoritarian state is particularly evident in its modes and capacities of intervention.

This state is built on the ashes of the capitalist state of the previous period, in which the democratic and social conquests of the working class made their mark on the dominant institutions. By progressively undoing these gains, the dominant classes deprived themselves of the instruments they needed to manage politically the crises inherent in the capitalist economy and to cushion their social fallout. Subjected to the joint injunctions of capital (which is increasingly deterritorialised under the rule of market finance) and international or supranational institutions, the neoliberal-authoritarian state is becoming increasingly incapable of 'managing the common affairs of the entire bourgeoisie'.[85] Under these conditions, how can we imagine the development of a unifying political project, one that could take over from neoliberalism as the hegemonic axis around which the dominant classes are able to build inter-class alliances? By seeking to transform the nature of the state – by imposing new modes of operation and intervention based essentially on standards imported from private enterprise, by substituting the imperatives of profitability for a logic of public good and by vastly expanding the apparatus of repression – successive governments have weakened what was formerly a decisive element in stabilising and legitimising capitalist domination.

One of the particular features of the neoliberal-authoritarian state is the gradual but considerable reduction of its autonomy from the ruling class, if not the complete abolition of this distinction. It is becoming increasingly difficult for the state to embody a supposed 'general interest' – in other words, to cast the self-interest of the ruling class as a

---

84 The whole of the present phase is characterised by a particular accentuation of the generic elements of political crisis and crisis of the state, an accentuation which is itself linked to the economic crisis of capitalism. It is this accentuation ... which constitutes a structural and permanent feature of the present phase. Authoritarian statism is also a result of, and a response to, the accentuation of these elements of crisis.

In Nicos Poulantzas, *L'État, le pouvoir et le socialisme*, Paris: Éditions Amsterdam, 2013 p. 291 (Poulantzas, *State, Power and Socialism*).

85 Karl Marx and Friedrich Engels, 'Manifesto of the Communist Party', in *MECW*, vol. 6, p. 483.

universal interest. In France, each of the last three presidents – Sarkozy, Hollande and Macron – soon became known to a large part of the population as a 'president of the rich'. Yet capitalist hegemony requires a political state which is capable of enacting this mystification/abstraction of the purely economic interests of the bourgeoisie, by holding them up as the interests of society as a whole – a *national interest*. Politics itself is devalued and tends to wither away, under the impact not only of this reduction in the relative autonomy of the state but also of a 'depoliticized politics'[86] or more precisely a 'politics of depoliticization'.[87] As a result, a growing section of the population feels contempt not only for professional politicians, but for politics as such. This feeling feeds both abstention and the far-right vote (the latter skilfully playing on the idea of widespread corruption: 'they're all as rotten as each other!'). Left-wing mobilisation is not the same, for it presupposes some form of hope in viable political solutions.

The ideological crisis facing the ruling class, a particular dimension of the crisis of hegemony, is not just a crisis of the institutions that disseminate the dominant ideology (the education system, mainstream media or the churches). It is primarily a product of the growing inability of the state and its representatives to give substance to the fiction that there exists an autonomous public power that stands above the classes and is able to transcend their particular interests (especially the interests of the powerful). At a deeper level, the really crucial factor is the decline of mass parties. Nothing has been able to replace them in fulfilling the hegemonic function they once performed, and the dominant media have been unable to plug the gaps. Nicos Poulantzas pointed out in his day that the senior state administration was tending to become the 'real party of the whole bourgeoise'. But he added that this did not make it any less essential to have a dominant party of government, embedded in the state and with mass roots in society. This party had to be capable of coordinating and driving activity at all levels of the state, but also of weaving links between the heights of the state apparatus and the population, through a whole web of civil organisations, local institutions and organic intellectuals (particularly local elected representatives).

---

86   Wang Hui, 'Depoliticized Politics. From East to West', *New Left Review*, September/October 2006, no. 41.
87   Pierre Bourdieu, 'Contre la politique de dépolitisation', in *Contre-feux 2*, Paris: Raisons d'agir, 2000 (*Firing Back: Against the Tyranny of the Market 2*, London: Verso, 2003).

The fact that parties frantically seek out 'civil society figures' to support them and even boast of their presence on their electoral lists, should not mislead us. It is precisely because these links are extremely weakened, to the point of non-existence, that they need to put forward 'personalities' who are not professional politicians but are overwhelmingly recruited from the ranks of bosses (large or small), the professions or senior executives (and possibly a few more or less famous artists or sportsmen). The only organic relationships that seem to exist today are between the top business spheres, the top echelons of executive power and political parties (themselves increasingly reduced to mere stables of supporters of the president), and the senior civil service. These links are not new: they were, indeed, already the subject of the classic works on the capitalist state by Charles Wright Mills and Ralph Miliband.[88] But these ties have become extremely close. They encourage a constant revolving door between government ministries and the boards of large companies and, above all, a way of managing the state that is modelled on and in service of capitalist companies.

From One Stage of Fascisation to Another?

Finally, let us return to the links between the authoritarian hardening of capitalist democracies and the fascist dynamic. Our description of the authoritarian trend in France shows how this dynamic cannot be reduced to the electoral rise of the far right, or, for that matter, as the effect of its rise on the policies actually pursued (a simple question of political influence). The rise of fascism should not be understood simply as the development of a party capable, at a certain stage, of 'taking over' an unchanged democratic state and transforming it – more or less quickly and easily – into a fascist one. This common way of representing the problem is well-designed to absolve the ruling classes and liberal democracies of their responsibility for the fascists' rise. And, yet, fascist movements do not conquer political power like an armed force seizes a citadel, through a purely external action of capture (a military assault).

---

88   C. Wright Mills, *The Power Elite*, Oxford: Oxford University Press, 1956; Ralph Miliband, *The State in Capitalist Society*, London: Merlin Press, 2009 [1969]. See also the debate between Poulantzas and Miliband over the theory of the capitalist state: Nikos Poulantzas, 'Le problème de l'État capitaliste', *Contretemps*, 22 September 2015, contretemps.eu. On the French case, see François Denord, Paul Lagneau-Ymonnet and Sylvain Thine: 'Le champ du pouvoir en France', *Actes de la recherche en sciences sociales*, 2011, vol. 5, no. 190.

If they have generally succeeded in gaining power by legal means (which does not mean without bloodshed) it is because this conquest is prepared by a whole historical period that can be described as a process of fascisation. The victory of fascism is the combined product of the radicalisation of whole sections of the ruling class, out of fear that the political situation will get out of hand, and the social entrenchment of the fascist movement, its ideas and affects.

The fascisation of the state must not be reduced, then, especially in the first phase preceding the fascists' conquest of political power, to a promotion or integration of recognised fascist elements into the apparatuses for maintaining order (police, army, justice system, prisons). It operates, rather, more as a dialectic between the endogenous transformations of these apparatuses, as a result of the political choices made by the bourgeois parties over nearly three decades, and the rise in the organised far right's political power, at this stage mainly at the electoral and ideological levels. To take the case of the police, its fascisation is not primarily expressed or well-explained in terms of the presence of fascist militants in the ranks, or by the fact that the police vote massively for the far right (in France and elsewhere). Rather more decisive is the reinforcement and increasing autonomy of police power (in particular, of the units assigned to the most brutal tasks of maintaining order, in working-class and immigrant neighbourhoods, against migrants and social mobilisations). In other words, the police are increasingly becoming unbound by political authority and the law, that is, from any form of external control (not to mention popular control, which would surely be hard to find).

So, the police are not undergoing fascisation because fascist organisations are gradually eating away at it. On the contrary, it is because the whole police operation is in a process of fascisation – obviously to varying degrees depending on the forces concerned – that it is so easy for the far right to spread its ideas within the police and to gain a foothold therein.[89] In this process, we must not forget the primary responsibility of political leaders, from Sarkozy through Hollande to Macron. And, if police violence is part of the long history of the state and the police, it is

---

89 This is particularly evident in the fact that in recent years the police union most directly linked to the organised far right (France Police-Policiers en colère) has not gained extra weight. Instead, we have seen a dual process: the rise of factious mobilisations from below (but covered up by the top brass, in the sense that these have not been subject to any administrative sanctions); and the right-wing radicalisation of the mainstream police unions (Alliance and Unité SGP-FO).

indeed the crisis of hegemony, in particular the political weakening of the bourgeoisie, which makes it increasingly dependent on its police and increases the strength, but also the autonomy, of the latter: the interior minister's function is no longer to direct (and control or even repress) the police but to defend them at all costs, to increase their resources and so on.

It is only at the end of this first stage of fascisation that fascism can appear both as a (false) alternative for various sectors of the population and as a (real) solution for a politically desperate ruling class. Given the near-universal shame which has surrounded the words 'fascist' or 'fascism' since 1945, it evidently does this without saying its name and while taking care to disguise its project. It is then that, from being an essentially petty-bourgeois movement, it can become a cross-class movement with a mass influence (mainly electoral or more militant), even if its sociological core, which provides its cadres, remains the petty bourgeoisie: the self-employed, independent professions and middle-management.

Of course, a fascist state does not emerge fully armed from the current capitalist state. Fascism can only be put on the agenda in a situation in which the hegemonic crisis turns into a regime crisis and a neofascist (or protofascist) movement proves sufficiently skilful to impose itself as a credible alternative, without having to confront a unified reaction from the left and social movements. Nevertheless, the authoritarian transformation of the state does, however imperceptibly, favour the fascists. It creates the conditions, in such a situation of crisis, instability and uncertainty, for a second stage of *fascisation* of the elites, of the state and of society. Today, as in the interwar period, this proceeds through a series of ruptures, both within and outside the state proper. It was at this stage that the fascists really succeeded in establishing their power over society as a whole, by adopting and amplifying the tendencies already present at the heart of the capitalist state. This means strengthening the executive power, marginalising elected organs, imposing command over intermediary bodies and, of course, intensifying repression. With the new political situation that has opened up following the snap elections in summer 2024, marked by a rise in the RN and increasing ungovernability, France could well be at the tipping point between the first stage of fascisation and the second.

4
The Nationalist and Racist Offensive

Having made it this far, there may be a strong temptation for the reader to imagine that power and order in France are maintained through brute force. To use Antonio Gramsci's categories, it would seem that we have already moved from *hegemony* – which combines coercion and consent, repression and integration, force and trickery – to *domination*, based on intensified state violence alone. But we are not there yet. It seems obvious that neoliberalism brings with it a hardening of authoritarianism, that it drastically curtails the previously existing social compromises (though these are necessary for the ruling class to obtain the long-term consent of a majority of the population) and that it tends to domesticate all counter-powers and forms of popular intervention – and failing that, it resorts to fierce repression. Yet if this is a clear *trend*, it is not a *complete* process.

Governments, including those spearheaded by the most zealous proponents of neoliberal reform, know that it is dangerous to base their rule on repression alone. So, they also have to fight on a more directly ideological level: to win the support of at least a substantial number of workers, but also to hamper the subaltern classes' capacity for invention and political intervention by sowing a widespread feeling of powerlessness. Margaret Thatcher and Nicolas Sarkozy were exemplary in this regard. They are often seen on the left as leaders who brutally imposed their will. Yet they should instead be counted among the leaders who most consistently and resolutely battled over ideas in order to justify or camouflage the dismantling of welfare, the commodification of social relations, tax cuts for corporations and the richest and so on. They strove to build a political camp which reached beyond the actual material beneficiaries of their policies, that is, the propertied classes, but also beyond the traditional right-wing electorate as such.[1]

One first means they used was to disguise their political intentions – a necessary move whenever popular opposition to neoliberal counter-reforms is too strong. Those who want to scrap France's social security system (or Britain's National Health Service) almost never express this desire openly, seeing as voters remain attached to these services. The more effective way to destroy France's so-called 'Sécu' is not to challenge it on principle, but rather to claim to save it from 'abuses', by deliberately worsening the service provided (notably by shutting off funds) and by gradually marginalising it in favour of private insurance. However, the major focus of the political and cultural struggle waged by the French ruling class over the last thirty years, and particularly by Sarkozy in the 2000s, lay elsewhere. Indeed, it was rather more ambitious. In seeking to build a socially diverse political coalition, divide the opposition and isolate the most oppressed sectors of the population, Sarkozy's strategy sought to shift the fears, tensions and conflicts that inevitably develop as a result of the neoliberal offensive onto some other level. This has primarily meant the terrain of xenophobia and racism, but also that of values (meritocracy, the family and so on). More specifically, Sarkozy did this by popularising a series of talking points likely to win the sympathies of large sections of the population, including the working classes. He thus posed as a champion of the 'work ethic' (said to be undermined in favour of 'handout culture') or the 'right to security' (presented as the 'first of all freedoms'). But above all he sought to condense all these claims into the defence of a 'national identity' which, he said, was under threat from 'mass immigration', 'Islamic terrorism' or 'Muslim communalism'. Through this double operation of displacing the issue and condensing different threats,[2] uncertainties about the future, day-to-day difficulties and social injustices no longer appear as reflections of the power relations between classes. Rather, they are cast as the product of left-wing policies (Sarkozy promised in 2007 to 'liquidate once and for all the legacy of May '68'), of immigration (or what the conservative president then called 'the failure of integration', which

---

1 Stuart Hall highlighted this dimension of the Thatcherite project. See *The Hard Road to Renewal: Thatcherism and the Crisis of the Left*, London: Verso, 2021 [1988].

2 We are borrowing these Freudian categories, which Daniel Bensaïd has shown to be useful for thinking about politics as an instance of the translation/deformation of latent social tensions and conflicts. See for example: Daniel Bensaïd, '"Leaps, Leaps, Leaps": Lenin and Politics', *International Socialism*, July 2002, vol. 2, no. 95.

he wanted to replace with an imperative of assimilation); and of the Muslim presence in France.

These last two dimensions gained increasing importance in Sarkozy's discourse, as he emerged as a French political hegemon over the 2002–12 period. His strategy was hegemonic, in the sense that he succeeded in imposing the terrain on which the wider political battle was fought out – indeed, with lasting effects. The main weakness of Bruno Amable and Stefano Palombarini's analysis is that it underestimates this dimension of political struggle in France.[3] Posing the question of hegemony solely in terms of the economic strategies which the main parties put forward for overcoming French capitalism's crisis allows them to show the neoliberal impasse which the Socialist Party has run into, as well as the difficulties that the right has in broadening its social base in any sustainable way. The pair also show how far European integration has become a major cleavage in French politics, dividing and reconfiguring both the right- and left-wing space. But this approach leads them to overlook the rise of immigration and Islam – and the often-denied (at least in the colour-blind French republicanism) *race question* – as one of the most important structuring axes of current French politics and, more broadly, of the fight for hegemony.[4] The constant public disputes – and the divisions they create and maintain – around everything with even a remote relationship to immigration or Islam can, in their model, only be reduced to a series of incidents with no major consequences or overall logic. In other words, these issues appear as an epiphenomenon or a mask.

But if we fail to take these controversies and these divisions seriously, we can offer only a very partial understanding of the French political situation. They are not simply a battle between open-mindedness and intolerance, and still less between 'the Republic' and 'communalism'. Rather, they are at the heart of a long-term battle to build a new hegemony. From alternative menus in school canteens to veiled mothers on school outings; the building of mosques and minarets; the ritual slaughter of animals; the 'burkini' on beaches; cafés said to be off-limits to women in towns or neighbourhoods with high levels of immigration; runners in hijabs and, more broadly, the wearing of headscarves in sport; the wearing of long dresses (known as the 'abaya') in schools and so on – all these recurring debates are only apparently trivial. They both

---

3   See Bruno Amable and Stefano Palombarini, *The Last Neoliberal: Macron and the Origins of France's Political Crisis*, London: Verso, 2021.
4   See Didier Fassin and Éric Fassin, *De la question sociale à la question raciale? Représenter la société française*, Paris: La Découverte, 2009 [2006].

reflect the panic whipped up over a supposedly besieged French identity[5] and serve as the vehicle for a neocolonial strategy which ultimately amounts to questioning the presence of Islam and Muslims in French society. Such a strategy is not simply a diversionary tactic, although that intention surely is always there. It has the dual aim of politically subjugating the non-white elements of the working classes – the same ones who suffer disproportionately from underemployment, job insecurity and low wages, added to racist discrimination and police harassment – but also, by fashioning the figure of an enemy within,[6] of building a broad coalition of oppositional interests on a national-racial basis. In Gramscian terms, the aim is to nurture the formation of a 'historic bloc',[7] in this case a *white bloc under bourgeois domination*, in which the white working classes serve only as a pool of votes.[8]

This building of a white bloc makes it possible to strengthen bourgeois domination by slowing – or altogether strangling – the emergence of a *subaltern bloc* which would overcome the internal divisions of the working classes through a joint struggle against capitalist exploitation and all forms of oppression. Particularly important in this sense is the fight against *structural* racism: not simply racism at the level of personal prejudice but a set of systemic discriminations inscribed in institutions – the state and the labour market in particular – and particularly targeting non-European immigrants and their descendants.[9]

---

5   In each case, these panics are the product of a media-political operation, based on politicians' tactical ventures to grab public attention, but also from more impersonal mechanisms (media outlets' bid for ratings, for example). See in particular Laurence De Cock and Régis Meyran, *Paniques identitaires. Identité(s) et idéologie(s) au prisme des sciences sociales*, Bellecombe-en-Bauges: Le Croquant, 2017.

6   See Mathieu Rigouste, *L'ennemi intérieur. La généalogie coloniale et militaire de l'ordre sécuritaire dans la France contemporaine*, Paris: La Fabrique, 2011.

7   Gramsci's concept of the 'historic bloc' refers both to the alliance between heterogeneous classes or fractions of classes and to 'the dialectical unity of material tendencies and ideological representations'. See Panagiotis Sotiris, 'Gramsci and the Challenges for the Left: The Historical Bloc as a Strategic Concept', *Science and Society*, 2018, vol. 82, no. 1, pp. 94–119.

8   We take up Sadri Khiari's argument here: 'It is not just a question of "dividing" the working class or turning French workers against the apparent immigrant "scapegoat". More than that, at a time when the dismantling of the welfare state continues apace and French nationalism coincides less and less with the interests of the dominant classes, the aim is to *unite* whites, beyond their social contradictions, as part of a republican pact recomposed around its racial dimension.' See *La contre-révolution coloniale en France. De Gaulle à Sarkozy*, Paris: La Fabrique, 2009, p. 192.

9   For a summary of racial inequalities and segregation in French society, see Mirna Safi, *Les inégalités ethno-raciales*, Paris: La Découverte, 2013. See also: Cris Beauchemin, Christelle Hamel and Patrick Simon, *Trajectories and Origins: Survey on the Diversity of the French Population*, London: Springer, 2018; Mathieu Ichou and Ugo Palheta, 'Un

The formation of this national-racial bloc is far from complete, however, given the extremely divergent material interests of those who are called upon to make up and defend such an 'imagined community'.[10] This is particularly true in a period of structural capitalist crisis, in which the bourgeoisie has few material benefits to offer to white proletarians. Nevertheless, we can hardly ignore the fact that, in times of mass unemployment and housing crisis, whites benefit from some privilege, in the form of priority access to the labour and rental markets. Similarly, faced with hardening authoritarianism, it becomes all the more important if one can be near assured of not being arbitrarily spot-checked by the police, or even harassed and abused by them. Finally, at a time when Emmanuel Macron has shown such constant contempt for the working classes and has so systematically ignored trade unions in general, racism also serves the purpose of at least minimally re-establishing a form of (negative) dignity. This is especially true of the sense of being 'at home' or the 'true French' – a feeling unknown to those who are perceived as eternal 'guests' because they are constructed as such by so much public discourse and state policy. Still more important is the pride, and often the status-arrogance, of being part of a white community considered culturally superior and morally more enlightened.

It is not the case that a social crisis will level out everyone's situation – as if reducing everyone to the same state of dispossession, and thus erasing any privilege associated with whiteness (and likewise, nor does it remove inequalities of gender). In the absence of a vigorous antiracist movement and the credible prospect of far-reaching social change, we can even suggest that the opposite is true: such a crisis will tend to enhance the importance of the material, psychological and symbolic advantages that racism grants to whites.[11] Understanding the racist offensive and its effects demands that we do not consider nationalist and racist ideologies as a mere collection of illusions, clichés or lies. They cannot be dismissed as an archaic remnant, operating outside of all logic and content to mystify our thinking or to divert our attention.[12] Far from a

---

salaire de la blanchité en France? Les revenus salariaux, une dimension sous-estimée des inégalités ethno-raciales', *Revue française de sociologie*, 2023/4.

10   See Benedict Anderson, *Imagined Communities: Reflections on the Origin and Spread of Nationalism*, London: Verso, 2016 [1983].

11   On this point, see in particular: W. E. B. Du Bois, *Black Reconstruction in America*, New York: Free Press, 1999 [1935]; David Roediger, *The Wages of Whiteness*, London: Verso, 2007.

12   On this point, and for an in-depth discussion of the concept of ideology, see Isabelle Garo, *L'idéologie ou la pensée embarquée*, Paris: La Fabrique, 2009.

mere veil over reality, ideology consists of a set of 'principles of vision and division of the social world', of 'schemes of perception, appreciation and interpretation',[13] connected to the divisions that objectively organise social life, giving them a visible and sayable form, though without being a mere reflection of them. A powerful ideology thus has social foundations (real divisions that it will allow to be named and described, often in a distorted way), satisfies material interests and produces concrete effects (since it leads people to see reality in a certain way rather than another, and therefore to adopt certain behaviours rather than others). Ideology is, then, neither a direct translation of reality (ideology-reflection), nor a simple diversionary manoeuvre (ideology-dissimulation), nor a pure manipulation tactic (ideology-trickery). It is, at once, a weapon, a product of the social world and a focus of the struggle for hegemony, and, as such, refers to a field of struggle connected to social and political power relations.

While racist ideology often has delusional aspects, it is based on social divisions that are anything but fantastical, from educational and occupational inequalities to racial segregation in the workplace[14] and schools.[15] It provides an interpretation that tends to endorse and entrench racism as a system of inequalities, in particular by concealing or legitimising the systemic discrimination suffered by racial minorities. Developed in large part by intellectuals,[16] reworked and popularised by a range of

---

13 We take these expressions from Pierre Bourdieu, who did much to question the genesis and influence of the categories through which we understand the society in which we live and our place within it. In particular, he emphasised the enormous work involved in imposing the categories of the dominant ideology, which is not simply a matter of indoctrination but of appropriation and incorporation (thus highlighting what he called 'bodily learning'). See in particular Pierre Bourdieu, *Practical Reason*, Stanford, CA: Stanford University Press, 1998.

14 See in particular Mirna Safi, 'La dimension spatiale de l'intégration : évolution de la ségrégation des populations immigrées en France entre 1968 et 1999', *Revue française de sociologie*, 2009, vol. 50, no. 3.

15 On the specific case of segregation and racial inequalities in schools, see Georges Felouzis, Françoise Liot and Joëlle Perroton, *L'Apartheid scolaire*, Paris: Seuil, 2005; Fabrice Dhume, Suzana Dukic, Séverine Chauvel and Philippe Perrot, *Orientation scolaire et discrimination. De l'(in)égalité de traitement selon 'l'origine'*, Paris: La Documentation française, 2011.

16 On the genealogy of racism in its intellectual and scholarly forms in France, see in particular Pierre-André Taguieff, *The Force of Prejudice: On Racism and Its Doubles*, Minneapolis, MN: University of Minnesota Press, 2001. On the emergence of Islamophobia and the role of intellectuals, see Vincent Geisser, *La nouvelle islamophobie*, Paris: La Découverte, 2003. It is not the least paradoxical to find Pierre-André Taguieff, who was one of the analysts of the genesis and transformations of racist ideology, has since the early 2000s counted among the propagators of Islamophobia.

political leaders, racist ideology is not static but dynamic. As such, it is liable to major changes in the way it appears, and tends to adapt to the context in which it is used, to the resistance it faces and in particular to the struggles waged by those who suffer the many forms of racism. What nonetheless always remains is its core element: the stigmatisation, essentialisation, otherising and inferiorisation of minority groups in the name of the threat they supposedly pose to the identity and integrity of a mythical community (whether that community is conceived of as a 'nation', a 'civilisation' or a 'race', according to a principle of political, cultural or biological unity).[17]

As for the actors involved, here our analysis will concentrate on properly political forces, particularly those that have governed in France over the last half-century. It does so for two reasons. Firstly, the sociologist Pierre Bourdieu convincingly showed that, in addition to the state's role in exercising physical coercion (as emphasised by both Friedrich Engels and Max Weber), it has a 'monopoly of legitimate symbolic violence'. This more particularly allows it – more than any other actor – to initiate and legitimise campaigns to denigrate entire groups. Secondly, Islamophobia in France is quite clearly distinguished by the fact that it has been a top-down construct, and more precisely a state ideological formation, via a series of laws, decrees and circulars imposed by various forces in government over the last twenty years, added to constant discourse justifying this permanent state activity of control and repression. We will return to this. It is also important to discuss the specific role played by the mainstream media in this regard, although that is beyond the scope of this book. Most of all, the media have acted more as amplifiers and transmission belts for the policies pursued at the highest levels of government, rather than as driving forces in the strict sense. Even this consideration should not lead us to minimise the complicity of the media and media ideologues in promoting far-right ideological focuses (the 'explosion of insecurity', the 'flood of immigrants', the 'threat of Islam' and so on).

---

17 See the seminal book by Colette Guillaumin: *L'idéologie raciste. Genèse et langage actuel*, The Hague: Mouton, 1972. We can recognise that the – political, cultural and especially biological – homogeneity of the groups targeted by racist ideology is always exaggerated, even invented; that their supposed group existence is often itself questionable; and that they sometimes include people who do not consider themselves to be members. Yet, this does not change the reality: it is even in the nature of this ideology that it creates for itself, by pure collective invention, opponents who are powerful, united and likewise imaginary.

The Transformation and Spread of Racism

Racism and xenophobia have long been central to the *frontiste* project and remain so today. The rise of this party, and at a deeper level the fascist dynamic in France, cannot be understood without taking the nationalist and racist offensive seriously. This offensive, combined with the dismantling of the welfare state and a hardening of authoritarianism, have enabled the far right to make electoral inroads, to take root in the political arena, before expanding its audience from the mid-2010s onwards. The far right as a whole won around 37 percent of the vote in the first round of the snap parliamentary elections in June 2024.

Of course, the Le Pen party has played an active part in this offensive, in particular, by giving a pervasive but diffuse xenophobia and racism an explicit and mobilised political form. By *organising* the resentment towards postcolonial immigrants and their children, sharpened by the social crisis, and raising it to the level of a systematic ideology, the FN/RN has fed the emergence of a new consensus. Thus, immigration and Islam, immigrants and Muslims, are seen above all as problems to be solved, threats to be repelled, undesirables to be expelled or even enemies to be annihilated. For a time, it was imagined that this racism was limited to those nostalgic for French rule in Algeria, or even Nazism, and was little more than the shameful remnants of a bygone era, that is, the days of the Vichy regime and/or colonisation. But this reading was illusory and overlooked the changes that have been taking place since the 1970s.

By gradually abandoning the trappings of pseudo-biological racism – in other words, the old language of racial inequality, untenable since the Nazi genocide – racism has spread by way of a much more presentable rhetoric. It instead takes up the banner of defending French identity and, more broadly, European (or Western) civilisation, threatened by groups deemed hostile or unassimilable because of their 'culture', particularly Muslims. The Le Pen party has played a hardly negligible role in this process of transforming and disseminating racist ideology. But, most importantly, it has benefited from the choices made by the dominant parties – both the Gaullist right and the Socialist Party – and by a range of media and ideologists who have worked to promote a new xenophobic and racist common sense. Finally, it took advantage of the prevalence of anti-Muslim prejudice within parties to the left of the Socialist Party (even if the latter were divided), generally in the name of secularism or women's rights. This ubiquity of Islamophobia in the political field has prevented any serious response to Islamophobic policies and discourse when these began to develop in the 1980s and especially 2000s, leaving the Muslim minority without any strong allies in the political arena. It took the radicalisation of Islamophobia, notably with the attack on the Bayonne mosque in 2019, for a change in attitude to be observed among left-wing forces and even a turning point for La France insoumise, which is paying the political price for this, as its leaders – especially Jean-Luc Mélenchon – have been constantly attacked since then for their alleged 'clientelism' or 'communitarianism' and even their antisemitism and complicity with Islamism.

An example of the penetration of racist discourse can also be found in the rhetoric of 'anti-white racism', a claim that has become widespread in the French media-political sphere over the last two decades. In the 1980s and 1990s, only the far right had made routine use of this idea, through the euphemistic expression 'anti-French racism'. Since, for the far right, 'real French people' were necessarily white, there was no doubt that 'anti-French racism' was simply a code name for 'anti-white racism'. In 1998, Jean-Marie Le Pen claimed that 'anti-racism, the political tool used today, like anti-fascism was before the war, is not non-racism. It is an inverted racism, an anti-French, anti-white, anti-Christian racism.'[18] This rhetoric was taken up in the 2000s by right-wing politicians and then by leaders of the Socialist Party, as well as by intellectuals formerly associated with the Left (Alain Finkielkraut, Pierre-André Taguieff, Jacques Julliard and so on). During the students' and high-schoolers' protests against the Contrat première embauche (CPE) youth employment reform in 2006,[19] these intellectuals went so far as to use the term 'anti-white bashing' to describe the assaults that took place on demonstrations.[20] There is a devastating logic at work here, which renders incomprehensible the discourse and behaviour that may in fact express hostility towards whites. This is what the great anti-racist and anti-colonialist thinker Albert Memmi called a 'toothless racism':[21] a reaction to the structural racism

---

18   Speech of 15 August 1998 given at the closing of the FN summer university, http://theses.univ-lyon2.fr/documents/getpart.php?id=lyon2.2009.fontana_a&part=344461.

19   The CPE was supposed to be a specific precarious labour contract for people below the age of twenty-five. The movement against this project was the largest students' mobilisation in the last forty years in France: huge street demonstrations were organised twice a week and most universities were shut down for at least two months.

20   See Laetitia Van Eeckhout, 'Un appel est lancé contre les 'ratonnades anti-Blancs'', *Le Monde*, 25 March 2005.

21   See Albert Memmi, *Le racisme*, Paris: Gallimard, 1994 [1982]. See also the comments on this point by Sadri Khiari in *Pour une politique de la racaille. Indigènes, immigré-e-s, jeunes de banlieue*, Paris: Textuel, 2006.

suffered by the descendants of colonised people, which can be all the more violent precisely because it is fundamentally *powerless* to change the unequal power relations between groups. The claim that 'anti-white racism' not only exists but is even the main form of racism in France today (Marine Le Pen claimed in November 2021, during her presidential campaign, that 'state racism and systemic racism exist . . . but against the French')[22] seeks to delegitimise in advance any consequential political struggle against the systemic discrimination suffered by non-whites in French society. But, more strongly and implicitly, it calls for a policy of *asserting a white interest*. To speak of racism is to point to oppressors (in this case, non-whites), and the need to fight against them.

Clearly, when we say that today there is a racist offensive, this is by no means to deny that racism has deep roots in French history. This is, indeed, inscribed into state policies[23] – in particular, in the operation of its apparatus of repression and coercion (police, the justice system, prisons)[24] – as well as structures of the labour market, of space and of educational institutions. Still less would we claim that public discourse was formerly immune to racism: we know what a hold colonial racism and antisemitism had over French politics under the Third Republic (1870–1940).[25] The fact remains that, after the end of the Algerian War in 1962, the racial issue took a back seat in France's domestic political arena. At the time, employers had a pressing need for immigrant labour, particularly from the former colonies, and hence bourgeois politicians avoided heading too deep into xenophobia. What is more, because of the power of the labour movement (and, in particular, the French Communist Party), the opposition between employers and workers tended to marginalise all other political cleavages. The situation began to change in the

---

22   Even more clearly, in June 2020, Michel Onfray, a pseudo-philosopher who is a regular guest of the mainstream media and who used to be linked to the left (but is now associated with the far right), wrote: 'We are in a communitarian and racialist regime that has chosen the white heterosexual male as its enemy . . . in other words, a reverse apartheid'.

23   Sarah Mazouz, *La République et ses autres. Politiques de l'altérité dans la France des années 2000*, Lyon: ENS Éditions, 2017.

24   See Mathieu Rigouste, *La Domination policière*, Paris: La Fabrique, 2012. See also Fabien Jobard and René Lévy, *Profiling Minorities: A Study of Stop-and-Search Practices in Paris*, New York: Open Society Institute, 2009; Fabien Jobard, 'La couleur du jugement. Discriminations dans les décisions judiciaires en matière d'infractions à agents de la force publique (1965–2005)', *Revue française de sociologie*, 2007, vol. 48, no. 2, pp. 243–72.

25   See Olivier Le Cour Grandmaison, *La République impériale: politique et racisme d'État*, Paris: Fayard, 2009; Gérard Noiriel, *Immigration, antisémitisme et racisme en France (XIXe–XXe siècle). Discours publics, humiliations privées*, Paris: Fayard, 2007.

mid-1970s: as unemployment rose sharply, the right adopted positions hostile to immigration, followed, a few years later, by the Communists and then the Socialist Party. The weakening of the labour movement and the rise of the FN from the 1980s onwards accentuated this process. It was not until the 2000s, however, that the issue of race became truly omnipresent in the French public (media-political) sphere, largely as a result of the spread of Islamophobia. In this period, the 'common sense' that cast postcolonial immigrants and their children as the source of French society's ills (unemployment, crime, failure at school and so on) was combined with the constant demonisation of Islam and Muslims as a mortal danger to 'the Republic'.

It would be fair to say that the word 'race' is no longer used much in politics, including on the far right. In a move so extraordinarily revealing of the blindness to racism that dominates France, it has even been removed from the constitution, which had told us that the Republic 'ensures the equality before the law of all citizens without distinction of origin, race or religion'. Does this mean that racism has disappeared, seeing as the term 'race' has become obsolete? If we look only at its pseudo-biological variety, that is, an understanding of 'race' as a monolithic group defined by physical criteria said to decisively distinguish it from other groups (in turn allowing hierarchies to be established), then, clearly, most political leaders, and part of the population, have abandoned it in favour of the idea of the human species. But, if we see it as a political construct, whereby a group comes to be symbolically disqualified and materially devalued, considered inferior and/or dangerous, based in particular on the essentialisation of certain properties (real or supposed ethnic origins, skin colour, religion and so on),[26] it is obvious that we are not finished with 'race'. This is because the force that perpetuates 'race' as a social relationship of inequality and power – namely, racism[27] – continues apace. Today, racism can be expressed with all the less of a guilty conscience because it no longer need bother with the pseudo-biological category of 'race'. Conversely, it is all the more difficult to have racial discrimination recognised because it is no longer publicly defended in the language of an alleged 'hierarchy of races'. In neo-racist

---

26 As we said earlier, it matters little what criterion is used to establish this alleged otherness: 'culture' (whether assigned or rejected) can function, and very often has functioned, as a principle of exclusion in the 'racist mechanism'. On this point, see in particular Pierre Tevanian, *La Mécanique raciste*, Paris: La Découverte, 2017 [2008].

27 On this concept of races as statutory groups or 'social races', see in particular: Khiari, *La contre-révolution coloniale en France*, pp. 19–42.

ideology,[28] this has been replaced by the idea of the incompatibility of cultures. Still, the establishment of hierarchies is never far away, since certain cultures – and in particular religions – are often chastised as less able to live up to 'modern' and 'democratic' values.[29]

Éric Fassin's description of Roma-phobia[30] is a perfect illustration of this racism without races, in the sense that the 'races' produced by racism are generally no longer named as such and are no longer thought of in terms of pseudo-biological criteria. In this particular case, it is the combination of the systematic (and often illegal) dismantling of camps, the refusal to provide sanitary facilities, the unwillingness of local authorities to provide schooling for Roma children (again, completely illegally) and discrimination of all kinds, which has led to the marginalisation of Roma and to unhealthy living conditions. In turn, this situation enables the public authorities to legitimise this policy of exclusion by citing a 'cultural problem' said to irredeemably mark Roma people apart from the rest of society, through their own self-exclusion. 'Politics is hell-bent on producing the culture it is so ready to put the spotlight on, thus inverting cause and effect'.[31] This racism from above, based on marginalisation and otherising measures, is not simply a reaction to a popular racism, as if this latter were at the root of all government measures against the Roma (or refugees in general).[32] It is based on an active strategy designed to present minority groups and cultures as a fundamental problem for the nation, and in so doing to construct the nation and its greatness in opposition to these groups, or even on condition of their exclusion. Jews have long played this role for European nationalisms; Muslims and, more broadly, refugees from the Global South – and, to a lesser extent, Roma –have this function today.

---

28   On the genesis, logic and functioning of this neo-racism, see Étieene Balibar and Immanuel Wallerstein, *Race, Nation, Class: Ambiguous Identities*, London: Verso, 2011.

29   For example, one French interior minister, Claude Guéant, stated that 'not all civilisations, all practices, all cultures, are equal in terms of our republican principles'. See 'Claude Guéant persiste et réaffirme que 'toutes les cultures ne se valent pas'', *Le Monde.fr*, 5 February 2012.

30   Éric Fassin, Carine Fouteau, Serge Guichard and Aurélie Windels, *Roms et riverains. Une politique municipale de la race*, Paris: La Fabrique, 2014.

31   Ibid., p. 15.

32   See Jacques Rancière, 'Racism: A Passion from Above', diagonalthoughts.com. See also: Pierre Tevanian and Sylvie Tissot, *Dictionnaire de la lepénisation des esprits*, Paris: L'esprit frappeur, 2002 [1998]; Collectif Cette France-là, *Xénophobie d'en haut. Le choix d'une droite éhontée*, Paris: La Découverte, 2012.

The History of an Offensive, the Formation of a Consensus

So, it is not as if the FN introduced a xenophobia and a racism long absent from French politics and society before this party made its rise. Moreover, the Le Pen project would surely not have been so successful if the ground had not been prepared well in advance by the sharpening of anti-immigrant policies. First, the top state administration – which redefined immigration policy in the late 1960s[33] – then the political arena, across both the right[34] and the ranks of the Communist Party,[35] had indulged in a race to the bottom on xenophobia. Similarly, after the FN's initial electoral breakthrough, its ideological penetration would certainly have been slower had it not been for the fact that the right, and then part of the left, took up its obsessions. The FN's first successes in the early 1980s prompted the main right-wing party (then called the RPR), aware that the rise in the far-right vote was the result of disappointment and radicalisation among former right-wing voters,[36] to harden its anti-immigrant line. The RPR began a violently xenophobic and securitarian campaign in the 1986 parliamentary elections, against a backdrop of strong political polarisation following the left's return to the highest office in 1981. Conservative leader Jacques Chirac's statements in 1984 about the 'overdose of immigrants' and his oft-quoted speech about the 'noise and stink' of 'Muslims and blacks'[37] were, by no means, an accident or an unfortunate 'gaffe', but the product of a carefully thought-out strategy.

---

33   Sylvain Laurens, *Une politisation feutrée. Les hauts fonctionnaires et l'immigration en France*, Paris: Belin, 2009.

34   In the 1970s, three of Valérie Giscard d'Estaing's ministers – Jacques Chirac, Lionel Stoléru and Raymond Barre – argued that unemployment could be solved by doing without immigrants. In 1976, Chirac, the prime minister of the day, claimed that 'a country in which there are nearly a million unemployed but two million immigrants is not a country with an unsolvable unemployment problem'. Giscard went much further and was much more explicit in 1991, stating that 'the current problem we have to face is shifting from that of immigration to that of an *invasion*', and proposing the substitution of *jus sanguinis* for *jus soli* as the basis for acquiring French nationality. See in particular: Yvan Gastaut, 'Français et immigrés à l'épreuve de la crise (1973–1995)', *Vingtième siècle*, 2004, vol. 4, no. 84.

35   In January 1981, Communist Party leader Georges Marchais spoke of the need to 'stop official and illegal immigration', and Communist mayors in working-class towns took violent action against immigrant workers' hostels. For a detailed study of the relationship between Communist municipalities in the 'red suburbs' and postcolonial immigrants and their descendants, see Olivier Masclet, *La gauche et les cités. Enquête sur un rendez-vous manqué*, Paris: La Dispute, 2003.

36   See Chapter 5.

37   This speech is worth quoting at length in order to fully grasp its violent racism:

This far-right shift on the mainstream right was theorised and systematised by Nicolas Sarkozy between 2002 and 2012 – in what he called the 'unabashed right' – before it was taken further by most of the leaders of LR, from Laurent Wauquiez to Éric Ciotti. Caught between Macronism, which implements the policies dreamt up by the right, and Le Pen's party, which has beaten LR in every election since the mid-2010s, this conservative formation has worked to radicalise even further the neoliberal-identitarian synthesis proposed by its 2017 presidential candidate, François Fillon. This undeniably led the party down a blind alley: its candidate in the 2022 presidential election, Valérie Pécresse, obtained the lowest score ever achieved by the main party to emerge from Gaullism (4.8 percent). The increasing extremism of the right since 2002 prepared the ground for the political emergence of Éric Zemmour (7.3 percent in the 2022 presidential election), playing on a hypertrophied racist discourse, and then led Éric Ciotti – LR's own party president – to rally behind the RN in 2024.

The key player in this process of right-wing radicalisation, without which neither Zemmour nor Ciotti can be understood, was undeniably Nicolas Sarkozy. Far from sharing the Macronist illusion that the left–right divide could be overcome from the centre, he knew that the neoliberal right could not triumph in the long term without broadening its social base, well beyond the material beneficiaries of their policies alone. Hence, from his arrival at the Interior Ministry in 2002, he sought not only to subjugate and divide non-whites,[38] but also to systematically

> Our problem isn't foreigners, it's that there's an overdose. It may be true that there are no more foreigners than there were before the war, but they're not the same, and that makes a difference. Certainly, having Spaniards, Poles and Portuguese working here poses fewer problems than having Muslims and Blacks... How do you expect a French worker living in the Goutte d'or [a working-class district in the eighteenth *arrondissement* of Paris], who works with his wife and together earns around 15,000 francs, to see on the landing next to his council flat, crammed together, a family with a father, three or four wives, and around twenty kids, and who earns 50,000 francs in welfare benefits – without working, of course! If you add to that the noise and the stink, well, the French worker on the landing is going crazy. And you have to understand, if you were there, you'd react the same way. And that's not being racist. We no longer have the means to honour family reunification, and we must finally start the great debate that is needed in our country, which is a real moral debate, to find out whether it is natural for foreigners to benefit, in the same way as French people, from a national solidarity of which they are not part, seeing as they do not pay taxes [sic]!... Those who govern us need to realise that immigration is a problem, and that if we don't deal with it – and the Socialists being what they are, they will only deal with it under the pressure of public opinion – things will get worse, to the benefit of the most extremist.

38 Nicolas Sarkozy adroitly combined repression and domestication, rhetorical provocations and the co-opting of non-white women into his government (Fadela

target the white working classes through a hyperactive media strategy. The aim was to pit the white working classes against the *racailles* ('lowlifes') – the modern-day evil whom Sarkozy claimed he could rid impoverished urban neighbourhoods of by cleaning them out 'with a Karcher' high-pressure water jet (as he put it in 2005).[39] Sarkozy used the word *racailles* strategically to radicalise the right's traditional law and order stance. It was used to label young men from working-class and immigrant neighbourhoods as potential criminals, considered to be 'ever younger and ever more violent',[40] and even to cast them as terrorists in the making.

This rhetoric surely drew most of its strength from the fact that it was saturated with both class contempt (towards the most precarious elements of the working classes) and a racist imaginary (directed against the descendants of colonised people). The ethno-racial targeting was barely concealed, since Sarkozy constantly moved back and forth between the securitarian and xenophobic registers. He cast juvenile delinquency, for example, as a by-product of 'failed integration' (of the children of immigrants). He showed little hesitation in taking up the slogans of the far right – 'If there are those who are embarrassed to be in France, I say it with a smile but firmly, let them not be embarrassed to leave a country they don't like' – and to theorise this line in his speech in Grenoble in summer 2010. The far-right Identitarian movement, which likes to talk of 'Islamic *racailles*' or 'Islamicised *racailles*', and thus associates securitarian rhetoric with Islamophobia, merely made explicit what was already implicit in Sarkozy's rhetoric. In any case, by drawing on the rhetoric of the *racailles* said to dominate what are called 'neighbourhoods lost to the Republic' (itself a routine reference point in the racist 'common sense' that has spread throughout mainstream media and politics since the early 2000s), the aim was – and still is – to set this in opposition to the hard-working, disciplined 'good people' who do not complain or still less revolt.

While it is easy for the far right to claim that this vision is blind to differences of origin, religion or colour, based solely on effort and therefore on individual merit, it is clearly rooted in a set of stereotypes promoted

---

Amara, Rachida Dati and Rama Yade), the stigmatisation of Muslims in general and the integration of some Muslim elites into the state (through the creation of the French Council of Muslim Worship).

39   Paul Quinio, '"Nettoyage au Karcher": Sarkozy persiste', *Libération*, 23 June 2005.

40   On this point, see the critique by Laurent Mucchielli, *Violences et insécurité. Fantasmes et réalités dans le débat français*, Paris: La Découverte, 2001.

by the media-political sphere. These stereotypes support the idea that the 'France that gets up early to go to work' (to use an expression emblematic of Sarkozysm) is a white, European France. It can, at most, also add on those groups which have been constituted as 'model minorities' (immigrants and descendants of Portuguese – or, more recently, Asian – immigrants).[41] In reality, immigrants and the descendants of postcolonial immigrants occupy a large share of the lowest-paid, least-recognised, most precarious and most dangerous jobs (particularly in the case of undocumented workers), jobs which require them to get up early (to see this, you only have to take public transport at 6 am in any major French city). Yet these groups not only come to be excluded from this representation of the 'good people' but are blamed for 'social problems' and more generally for the difficulties encountered by the working class, and thus cast as enemies.

The whole of Sarkozy's criticism of 'welfare' thus served to fuel what the sociologist Olivier Schwartz called the 'triangular consciousness' of the popular classes: a perception of the social order organised not in a binary way (where those at the bottom are opposed to those at the top, the little people to the big people, the people to the elites, the working class to the bourgeoisie), but in a three-cornered one. Hence 'we' (who work hard and pay our taxes, without complaining or making demands) stand opposed to both 'the people on top' (untouchable and self-indulgent), and 'people below us' (those who are 'on handouts' or 'scroungers', the 'deadbeats', who have it easy because they receive benefits without having to work). In the first form of consciousness, privileges and parasitism tend to be seen as the preserve of the ruling class; in the second, they are associated with the most destitute sections of the population (refugees, immigrants more generally, Roma, racial minorities, poor neighbourhoods). The effects produced by this second form of consciousness are all the more powerful, and the boundaries it erects are all the more impenetrable, the more it is racialised. Just as, in the United States, the ideal-type person 'on benefits' is implicitly a Black woman living alone with several children (the 'welfare queen'), in France 'hand-out culture' is associated in racist ideology – and no doubt in the minds of a large share of the population – with large immigrant families from the Maghreb or sub-Saharan Africa.

What role has the left, and in particular the Socialist Party (its main force up until 2017), played in the racist offensive? Following the election of François Hollande in 2012, it was Manuel Valls who slipped effortlessly

---

41   See Ya-Han Chuang: *Une minorité modèle? Chinois de France et racisme anti-Asiatiques*, Paris: La Découverte, 2021.

into Sarkozy's shoes as first interior minister and then prime minister. He obsessively targeted Muslims, stepped up anti-migrant policy[42] and stigmatised Roma people, whom he considered 'impossible to integrate'.[43] But, here again, it would be wrong to see this as a clean break, ignoring the elements of continuity: for Valls's policy was the culmination of a long-term process. While the Communist Party abandoned the anti-immigration line it had taken in the second half of the 1970s and early 1980s, albeit without ever coming out in favour of freedom of movement and settlement, the Socialist Party has gradually moved towards an anti-immigration agenda.

In understanding this party's line, we should remember the turn that began already in the late 1980s. The then-president, François Mitterrand, said that the 'tolerance threshold [on immigration] had been reached in the 1970s', and Michel Rocard, prime minister, insisted that 'we cannot take in all the world's misery'. By introducing a purely imaginary scenario (did 'all the world's misery' really want to come to France?), this line sought to justify limiting entry, hunting down undocumented immigrants and dropping highly emblematic pledges (such as voting rights in local elections for foreigners). Having sought to project an image of 'firmness', Mitterrand and Rocard thus bear a heavy responsibility in this offensive: for, through their choices in government and public statements, the two foremost Socialist leaders aligned the left with the right, giving it a decisive point in the hegemonic battle. In so doing, they helped to create a new anti-immigrant consensus, which continues to shape the treatment of migration flows, the rights of foreigners, the situation of undocumented migrants, the right of asylum and so on. By accepting the premise that France had too many immigrants and – added to that – was suffering the consequences of 'uncontrolled' immigration, this part of the left, which was already on a sharp rightward course, headed into a losing terrain, in a manner that could only benefit the right and the far right. Mitterrand and Rocard were surely conscious of the damage caused by their statements: a few years later, as the right made hay out of these claims, these Socialist leaders each tried to have people believe that their comments had been taken out of context and that their intentions had been misunderstood.[44]

---

42   See 'Les expulsions se poursuit en 2013, Valls se défend de laxisme', *Le Monde .fr*, 13 June 2013.
43   See also Fassin, Fouteau, Guichard and Windels, *Roms & riverains*. See also the editorial in *Le Monde* on 25 September 2013: 'Roms: la faute lourde de Manuel Valls'.
44   Here is the full statement made by Michel Rocard, for example (not to mention other remarks in which he congratulated himself on having 'pushed back 66,000 people'):

What seemed like a clever short-term calculation turned out to be a disastrous choice. Firstly, for immigrants, but also for the (entire) left: by accepting the assumption that immigration, and thus immigrants and their children, represent only a 'problem',[45] it finds itself obliged to apologise at every turn for its supposed 'light-touch approach' on immigration. Above all, it has proven incapable of popularising a series of simple ideas about welcoming migrants – for example, the fact that given the number of vacant homes in France, recently estimated at more than three million,[46] a proactive policy would be able to solve the housing crisis while also finding homes for large numbers of people fleeing war and destitution. This same politically ruinous logic, which consists of deliberately playing on the enemy's ideological terrain, was also used by leading Socialist Laurent Fabius when, as prime minister, he declared in 1984 that 'the FN asks the right questions but provides the wrong answers'. Jean-Pierre Chevènement and his current in the Socialist Party – CERES, initially the Marxist left of the party – went the furthest down this road, moving in the 1990s towards an increasingly securitarian and nationalist orientation. While Chevènement never envisaged alliances with the FN, he devoted a great deal of energy to trying to unite the 'republicans of both shores', still calling in 2015 for an alliance ranging from Jean-Luc Mélenchon to national-conservative Nicolas Dupont-Aignan[47] (before rallying behind Emmanuel Macron in 2022).

Hence, the xenophobic and racist offensive cannot be identified with the far right alone. Firstly, because this offensive has material roots in

---

We must fight against all new immigration: with four million . . . a little more: four million two hundred thousand foreigners in France, we cannot take in all the world's misery: it's not possible . . . Refugees are not a statistical quantity, they are men and women living in Vénissieux, Les Minguettes, Villeurbanne, Chanteloup or Mantes-la-Jolie. And things happen when there are too many of them and there is a lack of understanding between communities. That's why I think we can't take in all the world's misery, and that France should remain what it is, a land of political asylum . . . but no more than that.

On the context, see Thomas Deltombe, '"Accueillir toute la misère du monde". Michel Rocard, martyr ou mystificateur ?', *Le Monde diplomatique*, 30 September 2009.

45   As Abdelmalek Sayad wrote, 'the only discourse about immigrants and immigration is an imposed discourse. And one of the forms of this imposition is to perceive the immigrant, to define him, to conceive him or, more simply, to talk about him always in reference to a social problem', in *L'immigration ou les paradoxes de l'altérité. 1. L'illusion du provisoire*, Paris: Raisons d'agir, 2006, p. 53.

46   See '1,2 million de logements vacants supplémentaires en France depuis 1990, surtout dans les zones en déprise démographique', *Insee Première*, January 2024, no. 1979, insee.fr.

47   See 'Chevènement veut un "mouvement d'idées" allant de Mélenchon à Dupont-Aignan', *Le Figaro*, 15 June 2015.

systemic discrimination and segregation (particularly in the labour force and in housing) that express an inequality of status between whites and non-whites. Secondly, because parties of both right and left have contributed to it, to varying degrees and in different forms. Macronism is no exception. In spring 2018, right at the start of Emmanuel Macron's first term in office, the Asylum-Immigration Act demonstrated the current government's desire to harden the anti-migration policies pursued by its predecessors, by toughening almost all existing provisions.[48] Despite this, the Macron government managed to present a 'balanced' package, seeing as the RN and LR insistently presented it as 'lax', proposing even more repressive and xenophobic amendments. But, with the erosion of its electoral base, and its lack of an absolute majority in the National Assembly from 2022 onwards, even this claim to moderation or balance has taken a back seat. In late 2023, Interior Minister Gérald Darmanin only managed to pass the Macron camp's second asylum-immigration law thanks to the votes of MPs from LR but also from the RN. Even for this agreement to be possible, many of the far right's programme points were incorporated into the law (including in the direction of the 'national preference' that the FN/RN has always called for), some of which were subsequently struck down by the Constitutional Council. Over and above these laws, the government's day-to-day policy towards migrants has, according to many observers, proven even more repressive than that of previous governments, right from the start of Emmanuel Macron's first term.[49]

The reversal on Islamophobia is just as spectacular. During his first presidential campaign, in 2017, Emmanuel Macron promised to stick to a liberal interpretation of secularism: in short, one faithful to the 1905 law which established the separation between church and state in order to better guarantee (particularly to religious minorities) freedom of conscience and worship, and equality before the state. However, it was this same Macron who pushed through a new law – 'strengthening respect for the principles of the Republic' – which calls into question certain rights of Muslims, particularly in terms of forming associations. This was so severe that it stirred the opposition of all religious denominations (representatives of the Muslim but also Catholic, Protestant,

---

48 On this point, see the set of articles in *Mouvements*: 'Les migrantes dans l'impasse des gouvernances', 2018, vol. 1, no. 93. See also the interview with immigration policy historian Patrick Weil: 'Immigration: "Aucun gouvernement depuis la Seconde Guerre mondiale n'avait osé aller jusque-là"', Europe 1, 27 December 2017, europe1.fr.

49 See, for example, Antoine Hasday, 'Sous Macron, une politique toujours plus répressive vis-à-vis des migrants', *Slate*, 24 November 2017, slate.fr.

Jewish, Buddhist and Orthodox faiths). They saw this new legislation as a challenge to religious freedom that could have collateral effects for all faiths and questioned its ability to genuinely combat 'separatism' and (terrorist) 'radicalisation'. In reality, the so-called 'separatism' law had no such objective. It was, rather, part of a political offensive aimed at 'triangulating' the far right by actively drawing on its rhetoric, while seeking to eliminate the left politically, in the name of its alleged indulgence of 'Islamism' (or at least what is referred to by this term, whose meaning is extraordinarily vague and ever-extended in France's media-political debate). This had, in fact, begun even earlier, since the Macron government had made a series of statements stigmatising certain Muslim practices, in particular the wearing of the hijab. Already in 2018, Macron himself said that the veil was 'not in keeping with the civility of our country', while his first interior minister termed the garment 'a deliberate marker of identity, a show of standing apart from French society'.[50] We should also recall the whole campaign waged jointly by the minister for national education, Jean-Michel Blanquer,[51] and the minister for higher education, Frédérique Vidal, against the danger of 'Islamo-leftism' infiltrating the republican school system.

Emmanuel Macron's first presidential campaign in 2017 was liberal in every sense of the word, seeking to realign the political field around an opposition between 'progressives' and 'populists'. On a number of issues that have shaped French politics over the last twenty years (migrants, the hijab, the Algerian War and so on), he took positions that seemed to run against both the right and the conservative and Islamophobic wing of the left. Many observers built up illusory expectations that he would break with the anti-immigrant and anti-Muslim consensus that had prevailed in France for several decades. And, yet, exactly the opposite happened: Macron quickly aligned himself, in deed and word, with some of the most reactionary positions in French politics. It seems as if Islamophobia and anti-migrant xenophobia were too central to the hegemonic construction built up by the French ruling class over the last thirty years for them to be abandoned in favour of a simple neoliberal pedagogy of trickle-down economics. When stripped to its bare essentials – a policy to destroy social rights and public services – this kind of

---

50   'Gérard Collomb trouve "choquant" qu'une porte-parole de l'UNEF soit voilée', BFMTV, 18 May 2018, bfmtv.com.

51   It has also filed a complaint against a trade union, Sud Éducation 93, for daring to talk about 'state racism' in France and organising training on this subject for school personnel.

pedagogy cannot alone withstand the pressures of the current moment, particularly in times of great economic turbulence (the crisis of capitalism, the pandemic, inflation and so on). The promises made by Macron to immigrants and minorities thus only lasted for the duration of the 2017 campaign and were then shelved in favour of the same strategy of 'triangulation' in which the Socialist Party had already become trapped under Hollande, consisting of occupying the terrain of the far right, thus pretending to pull the rug out from under it, and with the same result: the rise of the RN.

For thirty years, the Le Pen party has constantly benefited from this alignment of the main parties with its agenda and at least part of its language and programme. All it has had to do is play its usual part and wait for 'the voter to prefer the original to the copy', in the words of Jean-Marie Le Pen. Conversely, the presence of the FN/RN and its successes have enabled the so-called 'parties of government' to appear moderate – 'firm' but 'humane', as they say in the technocratic language used by the Socialist Party, LR and Macron's Renaissance. Meanwhile, these same parties step up the expulsion of illegal immigrants, curtail asylum rights, repress solidarity with migrants and whip up hostility towards Muslims.

Islamophobia in France: State-Sponsored Racism

It would be ethically unacceptable and politically wrong to ignore the variety of targets of racism in today's France – and even more so to set them in competition or somehow rank them in order of importance. But we should not overlook the fundamental role that Islamophobia has played in establishing a new nationalist and racist doxa since the 1980s, of civilisational and identitarian hues. Nor should we ignore the central role played by the state – and the parties that have governed France during this period – in establishing Islamophobia as a state ideology. This new 'common sense' has continued to develop and have new effects, in France and internationally, particularly since 11 September 2001. It was largely on the basis of hostility to Muslims that the *racial question* re-emerged, and that the 'shift to the right' of the French political arena, much discussed when Sarkozy won the 2007 presidential elections, took place. This must be understood both in terms of the radicalisation of the right (and its electorate) and the shift of part of the left to the right, as well-illustrated both by the poaching of 'left-wing' figures by the Sarkozy administration and then by the policies pursued by the Socialist Party in office between 2012 and 2017.

From this point of view, the rise of Islamophobia cannot be reduced to a somehow disguised recovery of a 'traditional' anti-Arab racism. Even if Islamophobia does in part follow on from this (but only in part, since it also targets a number of immigrants or descendants of sub-Saharan African immigrants, as well as people who have converted to Islam who do not hail from a postcolonial-immigration background),[52] it is not a simple costume in which to drape the 'real' racism (by which we mean pseudo-biological racism), as if, under the trappings of cultural differentialism, this latter remained unchanged. In other words, Islamophobia is not a mere *mask*, as if this could simply be removed, without damaging what lies beneath it. Rather, it is the main *ideological form* in which racism of colonial origin presents itself today. As such, this form has to be taken seriously. It makes it possible to assert the otherness and dangerousness of non-European immigrants and descendants of immigrants on the grounds of their – real or supposed – attachment to a 'Muslim community', which is seen as irredeemably alien if not hostile to the 'national community'. From this otherness and dangerousness derives the need to monitor them (and especially their religious practices), to control their every move, to constantly check their commitment to the 'values of the Republic' (flouted by the Republic itself, through its main institutions), and even to discriminate against them on the pretext of their alleged 'communalism'.[53]

Such an ideological and political endeavour in demonisation and discrimination could not prosper if it did not appear *respectable*.[54] It has thus relied on intense intellectual and political mobilisation, generally in the name of 'Judeo-Christian values' and/or 'republican principles', said to be jeopardised by the visible presence and activism of Muslims in France. From this point of view, secularism has undoubtedly been the

---

52   On this last point, see Solène Brun and Juliette Galonnier, 'Devenir(s) minoritaire(s). La conversion des Blanc-he-s à l'islam en France et aux États-Unis comme expérience de la minoration', *Tracés. Revue de science humaine*, 2016, no. 30.

53   On the rhetoric of 'communautarisme' and its ideological function, see Fabrice Dhume-Sonzogni, *Le communautarisme. Enquête sur une chimère du nationalisme français*, Paris: Demopolis, 2016.

54   For an exploration of this notion of 'respectable racism' as applied to Islamophobia, see Rachad Antonius, 'Un racisme "respectable"', in Jean Renaud, Linda Pietrantonio, and Guy Bourgeault (eds), *Les relations ethniques en question: ce qui a changé depuis l'11 septembre 2001*, Montreal: Les Presse Université de Montréal, 2002, pp. 253–71; Saïd Bouamama, *L'affaire du foulard islamique: la production d'un racisme respectable*, Roubaix: Geai Bleu, 2004; Tevanian, *La mécanique raciste*.

centrepiece of the Islamophobic machine.⁵⁵ Reshaped from the 1990s onwards, and especially in the 2000s, diverted from its original meaning and 'falsified',⁵⁶ it has continued to function as an *instrument of racialisation*.⁵⁷ It is increasingly regarded not as a fundamental legal principle guaranteeing freedom of conscience and worship and the equality of citizens before the state, but as an imperative of religious neutrality applying to everyone and on all occasions (and not just to state employees in the performance of their duties, as was previously the case). It is held up as a central element of French national identity or, even more audaciously, of 'Judeo-Christian civilisation'.⁵⁸ As a result, any practice considered 'contrary to secularism' – that is, contrary to the 'new secularism' that came into being with the law of 15 March 2004 on religious symbols in French schools⁵⁹ – can only be seen as demonstrating a failure or refusal to integrate. Worse, it may even represent a 'communalist' attempt to undermine the foundations of the Republic by imposing values contrary to France's own. It will thus justify, if we dare use the word, a *national-republican excommunication*. By increasingly stigmatising Muslims, we have helped to create a 'Muslim problem' under the cover of solving it.

This 'conservative revolution in secularism'⁶⁰ explains a lot. It alone can explain the media and political harassment to which Muslim women have been systematically subjected in recent years, for having the cheek to appear as Muslims in public, rather than stay in their socially assigned place (generally meaning the least valued jobs). Think, for example, of Ilham Moussaïd, who ran on an anti-capitalist list in the 2010 regional elections; the anti-racist activist Houria Bouteldja, who is constantly cast as antisemitic and homophobic; Maryam Pougetoux, president of students' union UNEF at the Sorbonne, accused by a member of Printemps républicain (an Islamophobic organisation initially set up

---

55 On this point, see in particular: Joan Wallach Scott, *The Politics of The Veil*, Princeton, NJ: Princeton University Press, 2010.

56 See Jean Baubérot, *La Laïcité falsifiée*, Paris: La Découverte, 2012.

57 On the concept of racialisation, see Didier Fassin, 'Ni race ni racisme. Ce que racialiser veut dire', in Didier Fassin (ed.), *Les Nouvelles frontières de la société française*, Paris: La Découverte, 2012 [2010].

58 'Judeo-Christian values' supposedly alone allow for the separation of religion and politics (even though the different European countries' situations in this regard remain highly diverse). In reality, the Catholic Church was historically hostile to secularism and fought it violently.

59 The expression 'new secularism' comes from a 2003 report by a right-wing leader, François Baroin. It explicitly emphasises the break between the secularism of 1905 and the secularism of the 2000s.

60 As Pierre Tevanian puts it. See *Dévoilements. Du hijab à la burqa: les dessous d'une obsession française*, Paris: Éditions Libertalia, 2012.

by Socialist Party activists) of fomenting nothing less than the 'infiltration' and 'subversion' of student unions by the Muslim Brotherhood,[61] and even the singer Mennel Ibtissem, who was forced by media and political pressure to quit the TV show *The Voice* following harassment because she wore a headscarf. We also remember that Latifa Ibn Ziaten, the mother of a soldier murdered by the jihadist Mohammed Merah, was jeered during a conference held in December 2015 at the French National Assembly, by participants criticising her for wearing the hijab: 'You're not French, madam. You say you have French nationality, but you can't talk about secularism when you're wearing a headscarf, you're a disgrace to France'.[62]

Similarly, journalist Rokhaya Diallo, community activist Marwan Muhammad, rapper Médine and comedian Yassine Belattar became the target of harassment and defamation campaigns simply because they publicly stood out as Muslims and criticised Islamophobia. In particular, these campaigns aimed to dismiss anything they had to say, prevent them from doing their jobs and even present them as feeding religious fundamentalism. Taken together, these examples show that behind the 'obvious issue' of religious symbols lies a 'latent issue': that of the acceptance of the presence of postcolonial immigrants and their descendants in France, the treatment they receive and the place they are assigned.[63] It is worth noting in passing that this Islamophobic harassment is not just the work of intellectuals, politicians and media on the right or far right. Certain 'left-wing' organisations such as Printemps républicain and the LICRA (International League Against Racism and Antisemitism), as well as certain magazines traditionally classified as 'left wing' such as *Marianne* and *Charlie Hebdo*, have greatly contributed to it in recent years. They have even sometimes been at the origin of polemics targeting prominent Muslims in the public arena, encouraging the spread of Islamophobic moral panics throughout much of the political and media field, and increasingly from the 'fashosphere' (Fdesouche, Valeurs actuelles, Causeur) to the dominant players in these fields. This shows how far intellectuals like Laurent Bouvet (one of the founders of the Printemps républicain movement) are not simply diagnosing 'cultural insecurity'

---

61   See Frantz Durupt, 'Voile, "islamisme"... de Mennel à Maryam Pougetoux, des polémiques et des méthodes qui se répètent', *Libération*, 14 May 2018.
62   'Huée à l'Assemblée nationale, Latifa Ibn Ziaten va porter plainte', BFMTV, 22 December 2015, bfmtv.com.
63   See Pierre Bourdieu, *Political Interventions: Social Science and Political Action*, London: Verso, 2008. Sources: Collège de France archives. Text dated November 1989.

but whipping it up by constantly feeding the obsession with threatened identity.

The Islamophobic use of *laïcité* is so forceful because no immigrant or descendant of non-European immigrants can oppose it without immediately being labelled 'anti-Republican', and therefore 'anti-French', or even 'Islamist'. If the criticism comes from someone who is not themselves suspected of being a Muslim (and we are, indeed, dealing here with a permanent logic of suspicion), they will invariably be accused of a 'soft-touch' approach on 'Islamism', of 'Islamo-leftism'. 'Islamo-leftists' are criticised for ignoring the danger of political Islam and the need to 'adapt' secularism (that is, to break with the spirit and letter of the 1905 law separating church and state). They are even taken for accomplices, unwitting or for opportunistic and electoral purposes, in a betrayal of France and 'Western values'. But the power of such a weaponised term is also connected to the fact that the underlying discriminatory logic is, by definition, *ever spreading*. The range of practices that can be prohibited by the 'new secularism' is potentially limitless. From the ban on so-called 'conspicuous' religious symbols for pupils in secondary schools (which – it is an open secret – was in fact targeted at Muslims, and, in particular, Muslim women), we have moved on to the dismissal of the deputy director of a private crèche because she was wearing a headscarf (on the grounds that, even though it was privately owned, it had a public-service mission). We have moreover seen the attempt to ban veiled mothers accompanying their children on school outings (the so-called Chatel circular); the ban on the full veil in the public space; and even the exclusion of young men and women from secondary school on the grounds that their beards and long dresses (which pundits call 'abayas', the better to make what are merely dresses seem alien to the majority of the population) are ostentatious religious symbols threatening the Republic. A 'guide to *laïcité* in schools' has institutionally enshrined what had until now amounted to controversial local practices,[64] before Gabriel Attal – then minister of national education – issued a circular banning 'abaya' and 'qamis' at the start of the 2023/24 academic year in the name of 'respect for the values of the Republic'.

The Labour Law, imposed in 2016 by Hollande, Valls and Macron, systematised this 'legal discrimination through micro-scale action'.[65]

---

64 Mattea Battaglia and Luc Cédelle, 'Signes religieux, dispenses de cours, enseignements contestés: l'école se dote d'un nouveau guide de laïcité', *Le Monde*, 29 May 2018.
65 See Abdellali Hajjat and Marwan Mohammed, *Islamophobie. Comment les élites*

Companies were authorised to 'insert a clause relating to the principle of neutrality into their internal rules, and to impose on employees a restriction on the expression of their beliefs, in particular political and religious beliefs, provided that it is justified by the exercise of other fundamental rights and freedoms or by the needs of the smooth running of the company'. Similarly, the Court of Justice of the European Union issued an opinion in 2017 to the effect that a private firm may ban the wearing of headscarves, subject to certain conditions that are so vague as to endorse and even strengthen discrimination against (especially female) Muslims.[66] Successive governments have thus left the door wide open for the 'new secularism' to be extended to the employees of private companies in general, thereby increasing the already especially widespread discrimination against Muslims.[67] Similarly, we have rising attacks on fundamental rights and arbitrary procedures targeting Muslims, in the name of the fight against 'radicalisation' and in an attempt to detect the 'minor signals' of this process (beards that are too long, prayers that are too frequent and so on). It should come as no surprise that, in response to all this discrimination, a growing number of Muslims in France are heading into exile, or considering doing so.[68]

In the name of the fight against the 'separatism' or 'communalism' for which Muslims are constantly blamed, but also against terrorism, the government has begun to roll out a policy that is itself separatist. The segregationist and racist logic which we described above in relation to the Roma is thus repeated: political leaders enact measures which objectively marginalise a group, or which endorse and amplify the practices of social exclusion which target it. They then justify these measures and practices in the name of the marginality and exclusion which this group is said to be wallowing in, citing its alleged 'cultural' inability to integrate socially and economically. It makes things so much simpler: to legitimise exclusion in terms of self-exclusion, segregation in terms of self-segregation.

---

françaises fabriquent le 'problème musulman', Paris: La Découverte, 2013, pp. 143–62.

66   See Jean-Baptiste Jacquin, 'Europe: les entreprises peuvent interdire le voile sous conditions', *Le Monde*, 14 March 2017.

67   One survey, for example, showed that Muslim men were four times less likely to be called for a job interview than their Catholic counterparts. See Marie-Anne Valfort, 'Discriminations religieuses à l'embauche: une réalité. Antisémitisme et islamophobie sur le marché du travail français', report for the Institut Montaigne, October 2015. More broadly, see the overview of Islamophobic discrimination in Hajjat and Mohammed: *Islamophobie*, pp. 25–70.

68   See the study by three sociologists: Olivier Esteves, Alice Picard and Julien Talpin, *La France, tu l'aimes mais tu la quittes. Enquête sur la diaspora française musulmane*, Paris: Seuil, 2024.

Once again, we see how far France presents a quite distinct picture, as compared to almost all Western countries. While Islamophobia is a rising ideology everywhere, sometimes driven by mass movements (PEGIDA in Germany, for example), in France it has been mainly pushed by governments, and has rapidly materialised through a series of state measures and provisions.

Islamophobia and French Nationalism

Islamophobia has another dimension that is less often mentioned, but which is crucial for what concerns us here. For its development is one of the main vehicles of a sharpening French nationalism.

First of all, we should be clear that nationalism is not inherently xenophobic, let alone racist (even though it certainly has an intrinsic 'oppressive potential'):[69] there are expansionist nationalisms and defensive ones, capitalist nationalisms and more or less socialist ones, imperialist nationalisms (in the most powerful nations) and emancipatory ones (in oppressed nations), exclusivist nationalisms and ones based on solidarity.[70] So, when it comes to discussions of nationalism, it is always important to evaluate its political profile, to assess its class content and to situate the nation with which it identifies within the international balance of forces.[71] From this last point of view, French nationalism is clearly associated with a nation that remains dominant in Europe, albeit economically outstripped by Germany, and which maintains an – albeit declining – hold on what is known as 'Françafrique' and the so-called overseas territories still under French domination.[72] In the name of its self-styled universalism or its claimed ideals of justice (which do not stop it selling arms to regimes like Saudi Arabia, Egypt or the State

---

69   See Balibar and Wallerstein, *Race, Nation, Class*, pp. 65–78.

70   We may point out, among many possible examples, that Cuban nationalism – formed in opposition to the predatory will of US hyper-imperialism – has fought in the frontlines of anti-racist and anti-colonialist battles, first among them its decisive contribution to Angola's victory over South Africa's apartheid regime. See Jorge Tamames, 'A War of Solidarity', *Jacobin*, 28 April 2018.

71   These questions were at the heart of the Marxist approach to the national question, in particular the distinction between oppressed and oppressor nations, and were the subject of crucial debates within the Second International and the Communist International (at least before it was Stalinised). On this point, see in particular: Georges Haupt, Michaël Löwy, and Claudie Weill, *Les marxistes et la question nationale, 1848–1914*, Paris: Maspero, 1974.

72   See in particular: François-Xavier Verschave, *Françafrique: le plus long scandale de la République*, Paris: Stock, 2003.

of Israel, who commit massacres against civilian populations), French power defends economic and geopolitical interests. It does not hesitate to resort to military interventions, as it deems necessary, including on repeated occasions in Africa over the last few decades.

French nationalism thus turns out, in practice, to be an imperialist and warlike nationalism. This is all the more true given that the military institution has had a decisive influence on the construction of the French state, including the formation of its current political regime (the Fifth Republic), but also its diplomatic choices and its methods of external intervention, as well as the industrial specialisation of its economy (crucial role of the arms industry); even the media have long been marked by the influence of the military-industrial complex.[73] But, if this nationalism is currently radicalising,[74] this owes not so much to long-term factors as certain features of the current period. This period is marked, in particular, by the decline of French imperialism – 'If we have fascistic, ultranationalist reaction, it's because we are great universalists-dominators *in decline*', said Pierre Bourdieu[75] – and the weakening of what René Gallissot called the 'national social state'.[76] It is against this backdrop that we should understand the revival of French nationalism and the growth of Islamophobia. This remains true even though Islamophobia, and racism in general, cannot be reduced to nationalism alone.[77] The 'Republic', with which the French nation is now unanimously identified – even though the nationalist right continued, up until the 1980s, to resist some fundamental republican principles, notably including secularism – is the institutional and ideological framework that allows for an imaginary unification of a social body increasingly fragmented by neoliberal counter-reforms. It is this context that allows the far right to occupy the political and symbolic vacuum created by the hollowing out of national-popular sovereignty. It is by now unsurprising that those like Nicolas Sarkozy who have done most to enthrone the 'supranationalism of capital',[78] in particular via the European Union, and thus to empty this sovereignty of all substance, are also the ones who have worked hardest to bring about a resurgence of aggressive, xenophobic

---

73   See Claude Serfati, *Le Militaire. Une histoire française*, Paris: Éditions Amsterdam, 2017.
74   See Claude Serfati, *L'État radicalisé*, Paris: La Fabrique, 2022.
75   In his lectures at the Collège de France on the state.
76   See in particular: René Gallissot, 'Lutte de classes et État national social', *L'Homme et la société*, 1995, nos. 117–18.
77   On this point, see the nuanced analysis by Étienne Balibar: 'Racism and Nationalism', in Balibar and Wallerstein, *Race, Nation, Class*.
78   The expression is by Cédric Durand. See in particular: *En finir avec l'Europe*.

and racist nationalism. As capitalism becomes deterritorialised and the bourgeoisie frees itself from its national roots – a process which is, moreover, very partial and far from complete[79] – nationalism develops, not only in reaction against this, but is also fuelled by the very people who promote this deterritorialisation and this peculiar market version of 'freedom'.

So, it is not enough to agree with Benedict Anderson that the nation is an 'imagined community' – in other words, a socio-historical construct in which intellectuals have played a central role.[80] For we still need to assess the effects of this construction process, which are anything but imaginary. We need to show the pivotal role played by political leaders, dominant parties and states in this process (by virtue of their 'monopoly of legitimate symbolic violence'), and to describe the political and symbolic struggles in which it is constantly being fought over (since nations are not fixed in place, except in the nationalist imagination itself). If nationalism makes the nation (and not the other way round, as postulated by nationalist thinking),[81] we must then ask how the nation can be reshaped by the transformations of nationalism, but also of capitalism and the state. What kind of French nation was created by the neo-nationalism promoted by Sarkozy and his followers, using rhetoric from the various parts of the far right – notably Patrick Buisson, the far-right journalist and activist turned Sarkozyist spin doctor – and going so far as to create a government Ministry of Immigration and National Identity?[82] Without an identified enemy, nationalism is scarcely able to develop and radicalise: hence, it also has to create other, enemy 'imagined communities', both vigorous and evil. In the case of oppressed nations, colonial or neo-imperial powers are a logical, obvious and legitimate target. In a dominant nation such as France, a constant political and cultural endeavour is needed to invent enemies, that is, to make certain ethnic-minority groups appear as traitors to the nation. Even though they suffer demonisation and discrimination, they find themselves cast as an omnipresent power and a threat to the white majority.

79   See Sébastien Chauvin and Bruno Cousin, 'Vers une hyper-bourgeoisie globalisée?', in Bertrand Badie and Dominique Vidal, *Un monde d'inégalités*, Paris: La Découverte, 2017.
80   See also the work of Anne-Marie Thiesse, in particular: *La Création des identités nationales. Europe, 18e–20e siècle*, Paris: Éditions du Seuil, 1999.
81   See Eric Hobsbawm, *Nations and Nationalism since 1780*, Cambridge: Cambridge University Press, 1992.
82   On this initiative of Sarkozy's, see Gérard Noiriel, À quoi sert 'l'identité nationale', Marseille: Agone, 2007. See also: Laurence De Cock (ed.), *Comment Nicolas Sarkozy écrit l'histoire de France*, Marseille: Agone, 2008.

From this point of view, the Islamophobic consensus undoubtedly serves to solidify the national imaginary, and hence the nation, by calling on the majority ethno-racial group – itself constructed through this operation – to stand united against the Muslim threat. The targeting of Islam, Muslims and their (real or imputed) cultural and religious practices, and the labelling of postcolonial immigrants and their descendants as potentially hostile and a threat to society itself, makes it possible to push an implicitly ethno-racial definition of France and 'French identity'. It also tends to harden the internal borders that run through French society,[83] while also providing ideological weapons that can be used against other minorities (in particular, the Roma and all groups defined as non-white, including also non-Muslim ones). These weapons can also be used against populations still colonised by France, as in Kanaky-New Caledonia or in the Caribbean, for example, particularly when they mobilise for their own rights and interests. So, we can easily understand why, at a September 2016 rally during the right-wing presidential primaries, Sarkozy claimed:

> If you want to become French, you speak French, you live like you are French. We will no longer be satisfied with an integration that no longer works; we demand assimilation. As soon as you become French, your ancestors are the Gauls.

Significantly, this profession of nationalist and neo-colonial faith was closely associated, in the same speech, with the fight against what Sarkozy called an 'extremist and political Islam' which seeks to 'provoke the Republic'. He promised to wage 'a merciless war', not only against terrorism of claimed Islamic inspiration, but also against the 'medieval practice which would have men bathing in swimming trunks while women are confined in burkinis'. Denouncing the alleged 'tyranny of minorities' (a theme imported from the American right), Sarkozy assured us that he would be 'the president of the national community, because in France, the only community that counts is the French community'.

Sarkozy's speech was striking because it revealed, more clearly than usual, how far Islamophobia is the main vector of the nationalist radicalisation in French politics. In its new fervour for assimilation,[84] the French ruling class is returning to an exclusivist nationalism. In this approach,

---

83 See Fassin (ed.), *Les Nouvelles frontières de la société française*.
84 See Abdellali Hajjat, *Les Frontières de l'identité nationale. L'injonction à l'assimilation en France métropolitaine et coloniale*, Paris: La Découverte, 2012.

membership of the 'national community' should not only *take precedence* over any other affiliation but should even *crush* any otherness (within the nation or the individual). The aim, then, is to break up the minorities deemed 'tyrannical' because they are accused of wanting to impose their idea of community on everyone else. In reality, minorities are generally content to demand equal treatment and rights – in other words, a consistent fight against the discrimination they suffer. Faced with all this, we can hardly stop at rebuffing the obviously absurd assertion that 'our ancestors' were the Gauls. In saying this, Sarkozy is not bothered with the historical reality – he knows full well that what he is saying is false, at least for his own family tree. Rather, his interest is in political intervention, and more precisely with pushing a nationalist policy. To make headway, such a politics needs to (re)construct a mythology that tends to function in two ways. First, as a call to order, imposed on postcolonial immigrants and descendants of immigrants. Second, as a nod and a wink to all those who see themselves and are perceived as 'truly French' because they are constituted as *white* (including descendants of European immigrants, who incidentally include key players in the rise of French state Islamophobia such as Nicolas Sarkozy or Manuel Valls), and – as such – as true members of the national community.

The paradoxical injunction to migrants and their descendants could be worded as follows: whatever your history and that of your ancestors, near or far, whatever the discrimination you have experienced in the French Republic and from its institutions, you are called on to accept that 'your ancestors are the Gauls'. In other words, you have to swallow without question – and even identify with – the grand narrative of the eternal French nation. This inevitably includes the claim that France is the 'homeland of human rights' even though, by definition, the presence in France of the children of postcolonial immigrants is linked to the fact that this great power colonised, massacred and pillaged. It requires that we forget how it repressively enlisted men to fight for France in wars that had little to do with them, and to toil in the most thankless jobs. Even the acceptance of the national narrative by the descendants of colonised people in no way guarantees that they will be considered fully fledged members of the 'French community'. Rather, everything suggests that they will continue to suffer labour market discrimination, racial profiling and even police brutality, as well as countless false accusations and abuses.

But the nationalist discourse also serves, and perhaps more importantly, as a nod and a wink to those who feel fully entitled to claim

France, French history, French heritage and French ancestors as their own 'property'. These are the people whom reactionary ideologues claim 'no longer feel at home', leading them to suffer from 'cultural insecurity'.[85] How could things be any different, given that they are recognised as the only people who genuinely belong to the French nation, and to whom the French nation genuinely belongs? The political leaders and pundits who have used Islamophobia to revive French nationalism promise these people that they will 'once again' feel at home, and that they will regain certain material and symbolic advantages (which have never disappeared). They will thus be able to keep their position above those others implicitly or explicitly deemed to have no rights over this country, who should either accept their place and give up on any idea of changing France, or else 'go home' (they should 'either love France or leave it', as Sarkozy put it already twenty years ago). The reason why it is so important to assert that the majority is no longer respected by minorities, and is even oppressed by them, is to encourage a politics of national-racial identification and the creation of the 'white bloc' referred to above.

Last but not least, the growth of Islamophobia has served to legitimise renewed Western military intervention, particularly in the Middle East and sub-Saharan Africa, in the context of the 'war on terror' prompted by the US war in Afghanistan and the invasion of Iraq. The rise of Islamophobia cannot be disconnected from these imperialist interventions, or more broadly from the rise in inter-imperialist tensions and the militarism associated with them.[86] Imperialism in the twenty-first century and Islamophobia go hand in hand. While this is expressed on an international scale in relations between dominant and oppressed nations (particularly in the Middle East), we can also see expressions of it within the dominant countries themselves. There, neocolonial racism takes on forms that vary according to national histories, the prevalent political and social power relations, the more or less mass and long-term presence of populations from the Global South and so on. More specifically, Islamophobia appears to be the main ideological form taken by

---

85 See Laurent Bouvet, *L'insécurité culturelle*, Paris: Fayard, 2015. For a critique, see in particular: Klaus-Gerd Giesen, 'L'insécurité culturelle: usages et ambivalences. Notes critiques à propos du livre de Laurent Bouvet', in De Cock and Meyran, *Paniques identitaires*. See also: Aude Lancelin, 'Laurent Bouvet, le nouveau radicalisé', *Le Media*, 17 February 2018, lemediapresse.fr.

86 On this new historical context, see Gilbert Achcar, *Clash of Barbarisms: September 11 and the Making of the New World Disorder*, New York: Monthly Review Press, 2002.

imperialism and militarism in the age of the 'war on terror'.[87] This makes it possible to justify military interventions abroad *as well as* hardening authoritarianism at home, targeting social movements but also and especially the 'colonised within', who are already suffering racist violence in all its forms. This means workplace discrimination, spatial and educational segregation, police harassment and state violence (including crimes that still go unpunished), and the constant suspicions levelled against them of terrorist 'radicalisation' or antisemitism.

We are now well-attuned to the systematic exploitation of Muslim women over the last twenty years. It was claimed that military intervention would liberate Afghan women from the Taliban, but it was also claimed that Muslim women wearing a hijab in France would be liberated from their fathers and older brothers through the ban on so-called 'conspicuous' religious symbols (although, because of these prohibitions, they are more discriminated against and marginalised than ever before). All this shows how imperialism and Islamophobia are intertwined, both in international relations of domination and in the domestic public life of Western-imperialist nations.

The Centrality of Racism in the Rassemblement National's Project

There are two kinds of temptation to avoid when trying to understand the place of racism in the RN's current project. The first is to refuse to make the slightest distinction between the dominant forces that make up and structure the French political field, in the name of the undeniable convergences that have developed between them on migration policies and Islam. On this view, to make such a distinction would be to absolve the mainstream parties of their responsibilities in the development of nationalism and racism in the political field. The second considers that xenophobia and racism have become marginal issues within the far-right party, citing the RN's political and programmatic reshuffles – in particular the ousting of Jean-Marie Le Pen and activists who were too outspoken in their antisemitism and Holocaust denial – and also the greater prominence today given to everyday economic issues in its discourse and programme.[88] This is said to have reshaped the choices of its

---

87   On this point, but focusing on the US and UK context, see in particular: Arun Kundnani, *The Muslims Are Coming: Islamophobia, Extremism, and the Domestic War on Terror*, London: Verso, 2014.

88   On this point, see Chapter 5.

leaders and members, and the aspirations of its electorate (or, indeed, the ideological foundations of its programme), with racism said to play only a secondary role in the party's rise.

Yet, it is important to remember two simple but politically critical facts. First, the FN/RN is the most brutally racist component of French nationalism. Second, racism has played – and still plays – a central role in its ideology and its development (which does not mean that this racism needs to be explicitly expressed at every turn in the party's propaganda). Contrary to what is often claimed, Marine Le Pen's party has not at all abandoned the political project which was that of the French far right when it embarked on building the FN in the early 1970s. That project is a so-called regeneration of the nation and its unity, based on the will to purification, through a policy aimed at breaking up the workers' movement, 'stopping immigration' and 'bringing to heel' all elements considered hostile or traitors to the nation, or perceived as potential sources of disorder and division. Nor does the party appear to be on the way to breaking from this project in the months or years to come. Its leaders maintain the movement's ideological base by regularly targeting Muslims, migrants and those considered to be their main accomplices (the left, the 'extreme left' or 'wokeism', which refers to an ill-defined group including politicians, cultural elites, trade union activists, feminists and so on). But they also target elites, whom they term 'globalists' – on both right and left – because they are said to be complicit in the 'migrant invasion', cast as a deliberate attempt to destroy the French nation and identity. Hence Marine Le Pen's twin targets in her campaign speeches: 'Islamist totalitarianism and globalist totalitarianism'.[89]

However, it has been argued that ultra-nationalism, xenophobia and racism no longer play the same role in the rise of this party as they once did, as its voters are no longer driven *primarily* by hostility to 'foreigners',[90] but also by social demands. It is also observed, and rightly so, that racism and xenophobia are present in other segments of the population

---

89 It is worth noting in passing that the rhetoric posing 'Islamist' or 'Islamic totalitarianism' as the main enemy was shared by both Fillon and Le Pen during the 2017 presidential election, the former having published a book entitled *Vaincre le totalitarisme islamique* ('Defeating Islamic totalitarianism') a few months previously.

90 In the racist ideology of the far right, the legal category 'foreigner' serves as an ethno-racial category, distinguishing between the 'true French' (also known as *de souche*, 'of French stock') and everyone else, that is, non-whites, whether of foreign or French nationality. In the latter case they are considered 'French on paper', according to an old far-right expression that continues to be used in the RN, and indeed by a former minister of Sarkozy's, Nadine Morano, with reference to Black writer Rokhaya Diallo.

who do not vote for this party. But one basic fact needs recognising: what makes the far-right electorate so special is both its exceptionally high level of hostility towards immigrants, Muslims, Jews and Roma, and the fact that it identifies the central political issues in immigration, security and the 'terrorist threat', as well as values and 'French identity'.[91] In 2017, economic and social issues did not rank first, second or third among voters' self-reported reasons for backing the FN: immigration (69 percent), terrorism (46 percent) and insecurity (42 percent) came far ahead, while social inequality and the cost of living were the main motivations for voting for left candidates Mélenchon (42 percent and 35 percent respectively) and Hamon (42 percent and 28 percent). The situation was slightly different in the 2022 presidential election, where the issue of the cost of living featured much more prominently for all the candidates, including Marine Le Pen's electorate. However, among her voters, this economic concern was itself associated with immigration, insecurity and identity, while among Jean-Luc Mélenchon's electorate, it was connected with the fight against social inequality, the defence of pensions, and the environment.

The RN thus continues to be perceived as the best defender not against rising inequalities or the undermining of social rights, but what its voters see as the danger of France's demographic dissolution ('it's not our country any more'), the cultural destruction of 'French identity' ('they want to impose their customs on us') and/or the socio-political marginalisation of the 'real French' ('everything's just for them now').[92] When this party does talk about the money in people's pockets, it is less about the vertical redistribution of wealth (between rich and poor) than the horizontal one (between French workers and foreign workers, seen as competitors). Hence, the RN has not simply succeeded in making 'analyses' and proposals that were once considered scandalous acceptable, and even respectable. As we have seen, it has benefited in this respect from the work of leaders on both right and left: they have all proposed to respond to the Le Pen camp's success by borrowing some of its proposals, and above all its language.

It is also clear that racism and xenophobia did not need to wait for the FN/RN to make their presence felt among the French population,

---

91 Among many studies on voters' motivations, see 'Comprendre le vote au 1ᵉʳ tour de l'élection présidentielle', *L'Express*, 23 April 2017.

92 This racial and racist dimension is central to the concerns of the RN electorate according to Félicien Faury's recent study: *Des électeurs ordinaires. Enquête sur la normalisation de l'extrême droite*, Paris: Seuil, 2024.

from the wealthier classes to the petty bourgeoisie and the working class (even when the latter was largely left wing, in particular, in the Communist Party), but also in France's institutions. This party's real coup is that it has managed to fix, at the heart of French politics, a divide pitting nationals against 'foreigners' and the nation against 'globalisation'. This divide remained marginal between 1945 and the early 1980s, despite the Algerian War. It is impossible to understand the rise of the party without focusing on racism and xenophobia, which have had a triple function for its electorate and activist base.[93] They have served to mobilise the emotions of a certain part of the population (*affect*), to bind together an imagined community (*culture*) and to rationalise a vision of the world (*ideology*). From this point of view, it is no coincidence that at Marine Le Pen's or Jordan Bardella's rallies, the audience seems most riled up when they are talking about immigration, particularly through the widely repeated slogan *On est chez nous!*: 'This is our country!'[94] Racism thus remains central to the construction and strengthening of the RN, providing the ideological cement of its activist base and a significant proportion of its electorate: in 2014, some 80 percent of *frontiste* supporters considered themselves 'racist' ('rather racist' or 'a bit racist').[95]

But are not immigration and national identity objectively taking up less space in this party's discourse, as a result of the 'de-demonisation' strategy and the 'turn to social issues'? No doubt this is, in part, true, given Marine Le Pen's three successive presidential campaigns (2012, 2017 and 2022). The RN no longer needs to constantly reiterate its positions on these issues; it benefits from a sort of rent from the xenophobic electorate. In order to broaden its appeal to sections of the population that have hitherto been distant from it, it has had to make inroads into areas – public services, environmental issues, women's rights, secularism and so on – that were not previously its own preferred terrain. However, this does not generally mean taking up 'left-wing' positions such as they are, but, rather, translating them into the political language of the far right: that of the nation threatened with decline, degeneration or even destruction as a result of immigration, the rise of Islam and 'globalism',

---

93 Here comes to mind Anne Tristan's excellent line about Front militants, at the end of her study of this party in Marseille: 'They love to hate together'. See Anne Tristan, *Au Front*, Paris: Gallimard, 1987.

94 You only have to watch a few of their rallies to see this. See, for example, the one given by Marine Le Pen at the Zenith in Paris on 17 April 2012: 'Meeting de Marine Le Pen au Zénith, 17/04/2012', Public Sénat, 18 April 2012, youtube.com.

95 See Nonna Mayer, 'Le mythe de la dédiabolisation du FN', *La Vie des idées*, 4 December 2015, laviedesidees.fr.

or that of the 'extreme left' (which, in the discourse of the current RN, includes most parts of the left). During her 2017 presidential campaign, Marine Le Pen built most of her rhetoric around the threat of France's 'disappearance', 'dissolution' or 'submission' under the impact of two 'globalisms' said to constitute two 'totalitarianisms': 'financial and business globalism' and 'jihadist globalism'; or 'globalisation from below with mass immigration, the lever for global social dumping, and globalisation from above with the financialisation of the economy'. The prophetic and catastrophist rhetoric of the 'destruction of France', which she so routinely deploys, has no other purpose than to serve a radical, exclusionary nationalism. Nationalism remains the guiding principle behind almost all the analyses and proposals on offer from the RN, and inevitably gives rise to xenophobia and racism.

One of the problems faced by the FN from its origins was how to give acceptable form to the obsession for purification that has always been at the heart of the fascist project. The universal condemnation of Nazism in the post-1945 context demanded that xenophobia and racism become more sophisticated. These now had to be expressed through euphemisms, innuendo, coded references or expressions with a double meaning, unless the heirs of Maurras, Barrès, Doriot and Brasillach were to be condemned to criminal convictions and electoral marginality. Historical and sociological research has revealed the work done within the party to train up cadres whose discourse would tone down the violent racism inherent in the far right. The historian Valérie Igounet, who had access to party training materials, quotes an internal FN memo circulated in the early 1990s, entitled 'The Image of the Front National'. It tells us that:

> To win people over, *you must first avoid frightening them and stirring a feeling of repulsion.* In our soft and fearful society, over-the-top language will worry a large part of the population and draw their mistrust or negative response. It is thus essential, when speaking in public, to avoid outrageous and vulgar language. The same thing can be said just as forcefully in a poised language that will be accepted by the general public. In an admittedly caricatural way, instead of saying 'rag-heads in the sea', let's say that we need to 'organise the return home of Third World immigrants'.[96]

---

96 Valérie Igounet, *Le Front national. De 1972 à nos jours, le parti, les hommes, les idées*, Paris: Seuil, 2014, p. 230.

The reworking of far-right ideology in an identitarian key – borrowing without saying so, and sometimes without knowing it, from the theoretical elaborations of the New Right (GRECE, Club de l'Horloge and so on)[97] – has made it possible to recycle the old racist stock-in-trade by embracing the recent 'culturalisation' of racism. Since the 1980s, this process has spread far beyond the far-right party, across the entire political spectrum. Young activists on both the far right and the more established right have now largely incorporated this reshaping. 'Through the discourse of cultural difference, the far right has in fact found an original mode of symbolic treatment of immigration, which legitimises a certain xenophobia while adapting to the political and legal condemnation of racism.'[98] It should also be noted that, even when the far right did wear its biological racism on its sleeves, cultural racism – that is, the othering of a group, it being relegated to an inferior place and discriminated against in the name of presumed cultural traits – was never far away, including in the case of Nazi antisemitism.[99] Perhaps the RN's proposals to ban ritual slaughter in France[100] would be viewed in a different light if we took seriously the fact that the Nazi Party repeatedly organised campaigns against Jewish ritual slaughter. The obvious aim was to publicly demonise Jews by presenting them both as radically alien to 'German traditions' and as guilty of barbarism.[101]

---

97 On GRECE, see in particular: Pierre-André Taguieff, *Sur la Nouvelle Droite. Jalons d'une analyse critique*, Paris: Éditions Descartes et Cie, 1994. On the influence of the New Right on the FN, see Jean-Yves Camus, "'Le Front national et la nouvelle droite'", in Sylvain Crépon, Alexandre Dézé and Nonna Mayer (eds), *Les faux-semblants du Front national*, Paris: Presses de la FNSP, 2015.

98 See Sylvain Crépon, *La Nouvelle extrême droite. Enquête sur les jeunes militants du Front national*, Paris: L'Harmattan, 2006.

99 On this point, see Roger Eatwell, 'Fascism and Racism', in John Breuilly (ed.), *The History of Nationalism*, Oxford: Oxford University Press, 2013.

100 See, for example, 'Le Pen veut interdire l'abattage des animaux sans étourdissement préalable', *Le Point*, 25 April 2017.

101 See in particular: William S. Allen, *The Nazi Seizure of Power: The Experience of a Single German Town 1930–1935*, London: Eyre & Spottiswoode, 1966, p. 57:

> the Nazis next decided to arouse the populace against Orthodox Jewish methods of cattle slaughtering. Consequently they sponsored a speech on this subject, with color slides, by the chairman of a Hanoverian society for the prevention of cruelty to animals. At the speech, Northeim's Nazi leaders put themselves on record as being opposed to such practices.

The Front/Rassemblement National: From Antisemitism to Islamophobia?

So, has this party broken with the antisemitism that has been a staple of the nationalist right since the final quarter of the nineteenth century? On this point, it is important to distinguish between the voters and the current leadership of this far-right party. Antisemitism among FN/RN supporters, as measured by opinion polls,[102] is much higher than among other parts of the electorate. This should be enough to disprove the media-political commonplace, loudly relayed by some ideologues and political leaders, according to which the radical left and 'Arab-Muslims' now have a monopoly on antisemitism (renamed the 'new Judeophobia'), because of their anti-Zionism or, simply, their critical attitude towards the State of Israel. Incidentally – as shown by Nonna Mayer some fifteen years ago and confirmed by numerous studies since – negative prejudices and mistrust of Jews, or indeed antisemitic stereotypes, are least prevalent among left-wing voters, whether in the early 2000s or in the 2023 report by the National Consultative Commission on Human Rights (CNCDH).[103] Conversely, it is among voters on the right and far right that these prejudices, stereotypes and mistrust are strongest, as are stereotypes and hostility towards Muslims, Roma, immigrants, foreigners and so on. The fact that racist attitudes are easily transferable from one minority to another, from Muslims to Jews or vice versa, should hardly be surprising. Logically, according to the same CNCDH report, it is among left-wing voters that we find the part of the electorate most convinced of the need for a vigorous fight against racism (68 percent compared to 40 percent for right-wing voters), antisemitism (62 percent compared to 43 percent) and Islamophobia (64 percent compared to 36 percent).

While antisemitism remains a powerful force among the far-right electorate, this party's leadership surely has sought to curtail antisemitic outbursts from its activist base, and particularly from its election candidates, and to put an end to the denial or downplaying of the genocide

---

102 See in particular: Mayer, 'Le mythe de la dédiabolisation du FN'.
103 See 'Nouvelle judéophobie ou vieil antisémitisme?', *Raisons politiques*, 2004, 4, no. 16. For more recent data, see the study published in December 2017 by Ipsos for the Fondation du judaïsme français, which shows once again that antisemitic prejudice is by far the most widespread among this party's supporters: 'L'évolution de la relation à l'autre au sein de la société française – vague 3', Fondation du Judaïsme français and Ipsos, December 2017, ipsos.com. For the CNCDH survey, see 'Lutte contre le racisme, l'antisémitisme et la xénophobie', Commission nationale consultative des droits de l'homme, 2024, cncdh.fr.

of the European Jews. In December 2013, Louis Aliot, at the time the FN's vice-president, pointed out the vote-catching dimension of this about-turn:

> When I was handing out leaflets in the street, the only glass ceiling I saw was not immigration or Islam ... Others are worse than us on these issues [sic]. It's antisemitism that stops people from voting for us. That's the only thing. The moment you break through that ideological barrier, you free up the rest ... As long as I've known her, Marine Le Pen has agreed with that. She couldn't understand why and how her father and the others couldn't see that this was the blockage ... This is the thing that needs to be blown apart.[104]

The FN thus abandoned antisemitism in a purely opportunistic manner: the demonisation of Jews or the Holocaust-denier sympathies that its leaders, from Le Pen to Gollnisch, routinely expressed are now seen by the party leadership more as a millstone around their necks than as a means of winning over new parts of the electorate. It should also be remembered that many of the current leaders of the RN were already members, and often leading members, of the FN when its top leader made numerous antisemitic interventions, and that, until 2009, they worked alongside the leading antisemitic ideologue of the last four decades in France, Alain Soral.

To demonstrate that it has changed, the FN/RN has taken up the rhetoric of the 'new Judeophobia'. In this vein, it has sought in recent years to pit Jews against those who are called their real enemies, namely Muslims and non-European immigrants (but also the left, constantly denounced as an accomplice of the latter). In this effort to racialise antisemitism, the far-right party has been supported by the Jewish Defence League (LDJ), a fascist group considered a terrorist organisation in many countries (including the United States and Israel) but which Marine Le Pen defended in summer 2014, when this tiny group attempted to attack demonstrations in solidarity with Gaza. The LDJ returned the favour by providing Le Pen with security on several occasions during demonstrations against antisemitism.[105] In 2018, after insulting and threatening

---

104 See Valérie Igounet, 'Jean-Marie Le Pen est-il trop antisémite pour le "nouveau" FN?', Derrière le Front blog, 6 May 2015, blog.francetvinfo.fr.

105 On Friday, 1 August 2014, she told broadcaster RTL: 'There is a Jewish Defence League because there are a large number of Jews who feel insecure. They have the feeling that a new antisemitism is rising in France and that it is the result of communalist clashes.'

elected members of La France insoumise and forcing them to leave the 'White March' in honour of Mireille Knoll (an eighty-five-year-old Jewish woman, Holocaust survivor and victim of an antisemitic murder), LDJ activists provided an escort for the leaders of the RN. During the 2002 presidential elections, Roger Cukierman, then president of the Representative Council of Jewish Institutions in France (CRIF), went so far as to term Jean-Marie Le Pen's strong first-round result 'a message to Muslims to keep quiet'.[106] In 2015, the same Roger Cukierman, still president of the CRIF, claimed that Marine Le Pen was 'beyond reproach' on antisemitism. More generally, this rhetoric of the 'new Judeophobia', said to be the work of Muslims and the radical left, was put into circulation in France in the 2000s by intellectuals like Pierre-André Taguieff or Alain Finkielkraut. It has spread much more widely over the last ten years as support for Palestinian resistance has been criminalised,[107] to the point where it has become a spontaneous media ideology to delegitimise, by way of principle, any demonstration of solidarity with the Palestinians, including during the genocidal Israeli war in Gaza after the 7 October attacks.[108] This equation of unconditional support for Israel with defence of the Jews, and criticism of Zionism with an apology for terrorism, provides the RN with an almost insuperable argument for ridding itself of a cumbersome stigma, even though its electorate is still steeped in antisemitism.

But, if antisemitism has been muted by the party leadership, without any real critical reckoning with the previous period (Jordan Bardella even recently claimed that he does not 'believe that Jean-Marie Le Pen was antisemitic'), it is only to replace it with racism specifically targeting Muslims. It's a fact that Islamophobia is not only less likely than antisemitism to be politically condemned but is also constantly encouraged by key players in the political and media spheres. Islamophobia increased considerably among the population as a whole between 2009 and 2014, even though the FN electorate continues to stand out from supporters of other parties on this point:

---

106 See Karl Laske, 'Le président du Crif dérape sur le vote FN', *Libération*, 23 April 2002.

107 An opinion piece in 2018, issued by editorial writer Philippe Val, attracted 300 signatures from artists, intellectuals and politicians. See 'Manifeste "contre le nouvel antisémitisme"', *Le Parisien*, 21 April 2018. See the critical comments on this text by Dominique Vidal: 'Contre l'antisémitisme, avec détermination et sang-froid', Le Club de Mediapart, 23 April 2018, blogs.mediapart.fr.

108 On this point, see Didier Fassin, *Une étrange défaite*, Paris: La Découverte, 2024.

FN supporters' refusal to see Muslims as citizens like any others exceeds that among supporters of other parties by 48 points (compared with 23 points in the case of French Jews). Their negative judgment of the Muslim religion is 42 points higher (compared with 20 for the Jewish religion). Their feeling that Muslims form a 'group apart' is 35 points higher (compared with 14 when it comes to Jews) and their refusal of legal sanction for offensive remarks is 28 points higher (compared with 21 [with regard to Jews]).

In this context, Mayer concludes: 'a characteristic feature of FN supporters is a heightened anti-Islamic polarisation, far more marked than their antisemitism'.[109] As we have seen, Islamophobia can be found – in crude or euphemised, explicit or roundabout forms – almost across the political field. The fact remains that the RN is its most overt and violent political expression. In other words, it is the party most likely to implement, if not Éric Zemmour's sinister dream of deporting millions of Muslims, then at least a policy of bringing them to heel and systematically discriminating against them. This would mean not only banning Muslims from existing publicly as Muslims, but also establishing a complete inequality of rights, to which governments have already contributed over the last twenty years.

The heart of the conflict between Jean-Marie Le Pen and his daughter is, then, not so much about a change in the 'nature' of the party, or even of its overall strategy, but a difference in political tactics. The real change brought about by Marine Le Pen is to have foregrounded 'France's Islam problem'.[110] In so doing, she has used Islamophobia to radicalise the party's xenophobic rhetoric, even as she recodes its discourse in a 'republican' key. If this has conveyed the illusion of a deep transformation of her party, that is in part because Islamophobia is, in any case, mainstreamed, tending to make it acceptable to publicly express hostility towards Muslims.[111] But it is also because of a wider shift in public discourse since the 1970s, which has cast immigration

---

109   See Mayer, 'Le mythe de la dédiabolisation du FN'.

110   Bruno Mégret and the Mouvement national républicain (MNR) – the party he founded after being expelled from the FN – had already built up a violently Islamophobic discourse in the early 2000s, some ten years before the Le Pen party. On the tortuous history of far-right Islamophobia, see Nicolas Lebourg, 'Marine Le Pen, l'extrême-droite et l'islamophobie', *Le Nouvel Observateur*, 2 May 2012.

111   Tellingly, a recent poll used across mainstream media to show that antisemitism is rife in French society, actually showed that Islamophobia is far stronger. For instance, 22 percent of people would react badly if their daughter married a Jewish man, and 55 percent a Muslim one (the figures among RN voters were 18 and 71 percent). See 'Antisémitisme en France: où en est-on en 2024?', Ipsos, 21 November 2024, ipsos.com.

and immigrants as a 'problem' to be solved. This combined rise in Islamophobia and xenophobia – coupled with the assertion of a 'new *laïcité*' that allows the demonisation of Muslims in the name of defending the 'Republic' – tends to legitimise in advance all the RN's most openly racist statements, at least when they target Muslims and (non-European or Roma) migrants. It is also worth noting that the clash between father and daughter, which is only falsely presented as a dispute between a 'hard' and a 'moderate' line, was not triggered by past racist statements by Jean-Marie Le Pen. Take the example from May 2014 when, speaking of the alleged 'risk of France being swamped' by immigration, Le Pen *père* remarked that 'Monseigneur Ebola can sort it out in three months', here alluding to the epidemic then raging in Africa. At the time, this statement did not prompt any condemnation from the FN leadership or its daughter, at the time party president; rather, she supported him.[112]

Marine Le Pen herself never hesitates to use the rhetoric of the 'invasion', 'occupation' or 'colonisation' of France by foreign populations, and more specifically non-European and Muslim ones. Here she finds not just Renaud Camus,[113] but the Edouard Drumont of *La France juive* of 1886 and the pre-fascist writer Maurice Barrès.[114] In September 2015, for example, she said of the influx of refugees: 'The migrant invasion to which we are subject will be on a par with that of the fourth century and may have the same consequences.'[115] She also stood in the 2015 regional elections on a platform that included 'denouncing and eradicating all bacterial immigration'.[116] A few weeks later, she resorted to the rhetoric of civil war:

---

112   See 'Marine Le Pen affirme que les propos de son père sur Ebola ont été 'dénaturés'', *Libération*, 22 May 2014.

113   Camus notes in passing that

now the FN would love to recuperate the content [of 'great replacement' theory]. It is thus saying, rather ridiculously, that there is indeed replacement, yes, but that it is not so 'great' [in the sense of big]; that the word 'great' adds a suspicious, unscientific quality to the phrase . . . If this isn't such a great replacement, what [evidence] would they need]? A full-scale genocide?

See Renaud Camus: '"Si le remplacement n'est pas grand, qu'il leur faut?"', *Boulevard Voltaire*, 9 July 2017, bvoltaire.fr.

114   On the older origins of the rhetoric around 'great replacement', see Grégoire Kauffmann, *Le Nouveau FN. Les vieux habits du populisme*, Paris: Seuil, 2016, pp. 88–91. On Maurice Barrès, see Zeev Sternhell, *Maurice Barrès et le nationalisme français*, Paris: Fayard, 2016 [1972].

115   See 'Pour Marine Le Pen, l'afflux de migrants pourrait ressembler aux invasions barbares "du IVe siècle"', *Le Parisien*, 14 September 2015.

116   See 'Régionales: "éradiquer l'immigration bactérienne", l'improbable proposition de Marine Le Pen', *Libération*, 10 November 2015.

We have no choice but to win this war. If we fail, Islamist totalitarianism will take power in our country, as it did in Libya with the help of Nicolas Sarkozy, and as it is trying to take power in Syria, Egypt, Tunisia, etc. . . . Sharia law will replace our Constitution, radical Islam will replace our laws, our buildings will be destroyed, music will be banned, religious purges will bring their trail of horrors, etc.[117]

Shortly before, she tweeted an invitation to re-read *Le Camp des saints*, a dystopian book that has become a classic of the far right. It is based on the premise that 'races are incompatible when they share the same environment'. In this book, far-right author Jean Raspail portrays the colonisation of France by a million migrants, and the armed resistance of a few natives 'of French stock', who resist the 'invaders' guns in hand only to be betrayed by a 'multiracial' government.[118] While Marine Le Pen said she hoped for a different ending, she defended the book on the grounds of its 'incredible modern relevance' and 'sharpness'. She also praised Michel Houellebecq's *Submission*, saying that the prophecy on which the book was based – an Islamist candidate winning the presidency in 2022 after François Hollande's two terms in office, and appointing a certain François Bayrou as Prime Minister – 'could one day become the reality'. She also congratulated the author for pointing to the 'complicity' of the Socialist and Gaullist parties in driving the rise of 'Islamic fundamentalism'.[119] François Bayrou has indeed since been appointed prime minister, but by Emmanuel Macron and as part of a government that is stepping up xenophobic and Islamophobic attacks, supported de facto by the RN. By using this rhetoric of the 'colonisation' of France by non-natives, Marine Le Pen follows fully in line with an old *frontiste* strategy. François Duprat, one of the main strategists of the neofascist far right in the post–World War II period (and, for a time, the number two figure in the FN)[120] made it clear back in 1976: 'Anyone who believes that our nation is being colonised will sooner or later accept our methods of action to liberate it.'[121] When Jordan Bardella took over as

---

117   See 'Marine Le Pen: "Si nous échouons, la charia remplacera notre Constitution"', *Le Point*, 3 December 2015.
118   See Dominique Albertini, 'L'un des livres favoris de Marine Le Pen décrit une apocalypse migratoire', *Libération*, 16 September 2015.
119   See 'Pour Marine Le Pen, le dernier livre de Houellebecq "pourrait devenir une réalité"', *Le Lab politique/Europe 1*, 5 January 2015, lelab.europe1.fr.
120   See Nicolas Lebourg and Joseph Beauregard, *François Duprat. L'homme qui réinventa l'extrême droite*, Paris: Nouveau Monde, 2012.
121   Ibid., p. 205.

party president, he said: 'The French people's vital prognosis is at stake ... A change of population is taking place through influxes of legal and illegal immigration, in unprecedented proportions and at unprecedented speed.'[122]

In this way, the far-right party's leaders offer a xenophobic and Islamophobic prophecy of the conquest of France by 'Islam'[123] even more than they defend an identitarian prophecy of French national rebirth. But, even in so doing, they claim that they are targeting immigration as a socio-political phenomenon, not immigrants as individuals. In this narrative, migrants today suffer not from anti-migration policies, but rather from the destruction of nations by 'globalism' (in the form of the uprooting of populations and the loss of their cultural bearings). In this account, opposing immigration is the only real defence of immigrants. But this rhetorical ruse does not generally hold up for long. Marine Le Pen has made a series of statements in which she presents non-European immigrants and/or Muslims (many of whom are not immigrants but the descendants of immigrants, not to mention converts) as a threat, a fifth column or even an occupying force. In 2010, she developed this discourse of 'occupation' – obviously playing on the subtext of the occupation of France by Nazi Germany – to refer to the prayers performed by Muslims in the street, taking great care to exaggerate their scale and conceal their cause (the very low number of mosques in France in relation to the number of practising Muslims).[124]

But the leaders of this far-right party do not stop at the idea of occupation or colonisation. Non-European immigrants and their children are systematically equated with delinquency and even the most revolting crimes. This inevitably appears as an implicit call not only to expel them, but to punish them in the most brutal fashion. At her rally at the Zénith

---

122   See Julien Lemaignan, 'La candidature de Louis Aliot contre Jordan Bardella permet au RN de poser en parti 'mature' et démocratique', *Le Monde*, 3 August 2022.

123   As early as 1987, the FN put up posters featuring an alleged quote from a Hezbollah official: 'In twenty years' time we can be sure that France will be an Islamic republic.'

124   Her words left little room for ambiguity:

Today there are ten or fifteen places where a certain number of people regularly come to take over the territory. I'm sorry, but for those of you who like to talk about World War II, if we're talking about occupation, we could talk about it in this case, because that's an occupation of territory. It's an occupation of swathes of territory, of neighbourhoods where religious law applies, it's an occupation. Of course, there are no tanks or soldiers, but it's an occupation all the same and it's weighing on the local residents.

See Valérie Igounet, 'Une histoire d'un hold-up idéologique sur le FN loin d'être terminée', Derrière le Front blog, 4 December 2017, blog.francetvinfo.fr.

indoor arena in Paris in April 2012, Le Pen replied to the thousands of people shouting '*On est chez nous*':

> And because you are in your own country, you have the right to no longer want these Franco-Algerians like Mohammed Merah [a jihadist who killed seven people, including three Jewish children, in March 2012], these Franco-Angolans like the Bouguenais murderer, these Franco-Malians like the Paris madman! We want French people who love their flag and are proud of their country!

In another speech in Nantes on 25 March 2012, she said: 'How many Mohamed Merahs are on the boats and planes that arrive in France every day full of immigrants? ... How many Mohamed Merahs are there among the children of these unassimilated immigrants?' These words leave little room for ambiguity: according to Marine Le Pen, non-European immigrants, but also their children (Mohamed Merah was not himself an immigrant, since he was born in Toulouse), must be considered not just as potential troublemakers, but as potential murderers and terrorists, and treated accordingly. In the summer of 2023, during the uprisings that followed the death of Nahel Merzouk (a seventeen-year-old killed by a police officer at point-blank range, on the pretext that he had refused to obey a traffic stop), Marine Le Pen claimed that 'almost all street crime is committed by foreigners or people of foreign origin', arguing for the abolition of birthright citizenship (in force in France since 1889).[125]

The RN's rise has owed much to the normalisation of its claims by parties and intellectuals on both left and right; it could not have taken root without a pre-existing impregnation of French society by xenophobia and racism, as we have highlighted here. Yet it would be wrong and dangerous to claim that the arrival of a Le Pen government would simply mean continuity in the policies already being pursued. A party whose success is so heavily based on xenophobia and racism, and which is so widely understood as the best defender of a distinct white majority, could not rise to power and stay there without constantly showing seriousness of intent to its own electorate. It would have to give free rein to the repressive state apparatus, a large proportion of whose personnel are already committed to its positions. It would thus go much further in subjugating immigrants and descendants of postcolonial immigrants,

---

125 See Clément Guillou, 'A Beauvais, Marine Le Pen tente de se tenir distance des émeutes', *Le Monde*, 13 July 2023.

Muslims, Roma and surely also Jews (whatever the party leaders are currently saying).

Marxist approaches to fascism have sometimes underestimated its cultural dimension and the importance of the ideological crisis in its emergence and further development. They have often used fascists' (well-demonstrated) programmatic opportunism[126] as a pretext for concluding that they lacked ideology or that ideology played only a marginal role in their rise. This habitually means reducing fascism to a myth of action or a simple militia in the service of capital. However, nothing could be further from the truth, both if we look at fascism as a movement, that is, the way in which fascism takes root and progresses until it is finally in a position to conquer political power, and if we study fascism as a regime, that is, the way in which fascism rules, establishes and consolidates its dictatorship. Fascist ideology – if expressed in different ways according to historical situations and national contexts – surely did play a driving and central role in the victories achieved by fascist movements.[127]

Having duly noted the risks of this underestimation and the need to remedy it, it is nevertheless worth also highlighting one of the strong points of the Marxist approach. It consists in refusing to understand capitalist democracy and fascist dictatorship as two radically distinct phenomena, essentially alien to each other.[128] When, instead, we connect them, this allows us to understand the fascist dynamic on the basis of the economic, social, political, ideological and cultural conditions created by capitalism, liberal democracies and the associated hegemonic apparatuses (parties, media, churches and so on). We should, therefore, understand fascism as the most catastrophic expression of the *political and ideological* contradictions of capitalism at a certain stage of its development. For our purposes here, this means showing what fascists do, in particular the kind of discourse they develop in order to gain the ear of different classes and thus a mass audience, but also the way in which non-fascist political leaders encourage the fascists' advance, through direct or indirect collusion.

---

126   On this point, see Chapters 1 and 5, particularly concerning the positions of the contemporary far right on economic and social issues.
127   See the introduction to this book, but above all the fundamental studies by historians Zeev Sternhell, Roger Griffin, Roger Eatwell and Stanley Payne.
128   This does not mean that they should be flatly identified as one and the same thing, as the Communist International did in the era of 'Third Period' Stalinism.

This is why we have focused not only on the FN/RN action in terms of ideas or 'values' – and we will come back to this in the next chapter – but, above all, on the revival of a nationalist policy consciously pursued by the main French political leaders of both right and left since the 1980s. How are we to understand this revival, as expressed in the building of a xenophobic and Islamophobic, anti-migration and anti-Muslim consensus? It is no coincidence or paradox that this occurred at the very moment when the ruling class, by imposing neoliberal policies, was undermining the foundations of the 'national social state' that had been built up throughout the twentieth century, and indeed the foundations of a relatively independent national economic policy. It should come as no surprise, therefore, that Emmanuel Macron is pursuing the most offensive neoliberal policy and the most brutal anti-migration policy *in combination*. We have no intention here of harking back nostalgically to the 'good old days' of Gaullist economic nationalism or the postwar social compromise. Rather, our concern is to point out that the internationalisation of capital in no way renders nationalism obsolete. Rather, precisely because it pits workers from all over the world against each other, and because the European institutional architecture built by the dominant parties makes economic nationalism unthinkable, the ruling classes are tempted to radicalise nationalism in a racist and xenophobic direction. It is also striking that the European authorities (ECB and European Commission) react swiftly and brutally whenever there is some threat to the euro or economic orthodoxy[129] – deploying or at least threatening to use the monetary weapon and sanctions – but confine themselves to mere pious words whenever European governments are targeting the rights of migrants and minorities. Neither xenophobia nor racism are really their concern, unlike troublesome deficits or the prospect of a member-state leaving the euro. The far right is only criticised for its Euroscepticism or Putinophilia, not for its reactionary policies.

While the sharpening of nationalism is generally acknowledged, it is sometimes argued that it this fundamentally different from the type of nationalism that characterised historical fascism, which was an expansionist nationalism. The contemporary far right is said to have no desire for annexation and is thus hardly in a position to project its designs onto the international stage. Yet some qualification is in order. First of all, it is not true that expansionism is absent from some of the varieties of

---

129 On this point, see in particular: Cedric Durand, 'The Workers Have No Europe', *Catalyst Journal*, winter 2018, Vol. 1, no. 4.

fascism or regimes currently in power that are in the process of fascisation (whether in Israel, Russia, Turkey or India). It is also important to remember that fascism, in the process of gaining power, did not always clearly display its expansionist aims, at least not as openly as we tend to imagine today. Even several years after rising to power, Hitler still took great care, in his international and diplomatic speeches, to present himself as simply defending a just peace, as opposed to the iniquitous one imposed by the Treaty of Versailles. The same applies to Fascist Italy, which, even in the case of the invasion of Ethiopia – whose unprecedented brutality we often forget[130] – tried to present its action in such a way that it did not appear to be an invasion at all, especially as Ethiopia was an independent member of the League of Nations. Here, again, we should always be wary of giving too much credence to what the leaders of the contemporary far right have to say, even with hand on heart. Doublespeak is part of what this political current is.

One final remark is necessary on this point. What is ideologically pivotal to classical fascism is not expansionism per se (which we also do not find in fascist movements of the dominant nations which benefited most from colonial expansion, such as France and Britain) as two other dimensions. These are, firstly, the organicist, monolithic and ultimately totalitarian conception of the nation, and, secondly, the claim to resolve the contradictions of present-day society, not by breaking with capitalism or at least reducing inequalities, but at the expense of enemies – particularly internal ones (the Jews, the left) – alleged to be plotting against the nation. We might assume that present conditions would preclude any expansionist aims in Europe, seeing as nation-states and the system of states are now more stable and firmly established than they were in the interwar period. In that case, however, the neofascist attempt to overcome present contradictions would inevitably be to the detriment, not of other nations, but of a section of the population considered to be non-native, non-assimilated or unassimilable, and even traitors to the nation. It would target – all the more brutally because it has no other, external outlet – the millions of individuals who are already *regarded as foreigners and enemies within*, even if they were born in France and of French nationality, and even as the offspring of parents born in France and of French nationality.

To put it another way, if, in the conditions created by World War I and the Treaty of Versailles, expansionism and war in Europe were part

---

130 See in particular Marie-Anne Matard-Bonucci, *Totalitarisme fasciste*, Paris: CNRS Éditions, 2018.

of fascism's horizon of expectations (especially for countries like Italy and Germany where nationalist currents thought they lacked sufficient *Lebensraum*), racism (including with genocidal tendencies) and civil war are no less fundamentally part of the matrix of neofascism. Unable at this stage to direct its exclusivist and bellicose nationalism outward against rival peoples and states, as classical fascism once did, neofascism would turn this nationalist aggression inwards. In other words, it would turn it against ethnic minorities who are already stigmatised and discriminated against. In both cases, we cannot underestimate the 'cumulative radicalisation'[131] in which fascism almost necessarily finds itself caught. This is, indeed, what happens as the vacuousness of its claims to tame capitalism or punish elites, the consequences of its ultranationalist project (for war) and the totalitarian truth of its 'national revolution', become apparent to a growing share of its social base.

---

131   Hans Mommsen, 'The National Socialist Seizure of Power and German Society', in Neil Gregor (ed.), *Nazism*, Oxford: Oxford University Press, 2000.

5
A Fascist Party on the Road to Power

Fascism clearly has a symbolic dimension, as well as cultural and ideological conditions that prepare its rise.[1] Yet it cannot be reduced to a simple mood ('the spirit of the 1930s'), or a zeitgeist, that is, a set of representations, symbols and myths said to be the distinctive traits of an entire era. Nor, as we have seen, can fascism be boiled down to a psychological type connected to what the Frankfurt School in their day called the 'authoritarian personality'[2] – even if such a mentality clearly is embodied in fascist subjectivities – and nor can it be reduced to an endogenous process inherent to capitalist states. Barring exceptional conditions,[3] fascism will tend to crystallise in the form of structured parties, which strive to conquer political power and exercise it by pursuing objectives that distinguish them in part from the (liberal and/or conservative)

---

1   We need to take seriously the force of fascist culture and its ability to unite an imagined community behind the fascist leader and party. On this point, see the classic works of the historian George L. Mosse, in particular: *Nazi Culture: Intellectual, Cultural and Social Life in the Third Reich*, Madison, WI: Wisconsin Press, 1966; *The Nationalization of the Masses: Political Symbolism and Mass Movements in Germany from the Napoleonic Wars through the Third Reich*, New York: Howard Fertig, 1975.

2   Theodor Adorno, Else Frenkel-Brunswik, Daniel Levinson and Nevitt Sanford, *The Authoritarian Personality*, New York: Harper and Row, 1950.

3   Here, I am thinking of the German military occupation of France between 1940 and 1944, which allowed for a regime to be imposed with some fundamental features reminiscent of fascism, but which was not itself the product of a conquest of political power by a mass fascist movement (even though mass organisations did play a role in establishing, and above all maintaining, the Vichy regime). On this point, see Robert O. Paxton, *Vichy France*, New York: Columbia University Press, 1972. The Spanish and Portuguese cases could also be mentioned in this regard. On Salazarism, see in particular: Fernando Rosas, *Salazar e o poder. A arte de saber durar*, Lisbon: Tinta da China, 2012.

right – even if the fascists then always ally with these latter in power. So, we need to analyse how fascism takes embodied form in organisations whose programmes, modes of action and strategies vary greatly across national and historical contexts. In France, this means focusing on the major party that has succeeded since the mid-1980s in remoulding and thus updating the fascist legacy: the Front National (FN), which became the Rassemblement National (RN) in 2018. This political and strategic revamp, which is clearly visible in the party's public communications, is obviously never presented as such. After all, the current leaders of the RN are perfectly aware that any explicit reference to historical fascism, and, more generally, to the far-right movements and intellectuals of the interwar decades, has, since 1945, been a sure route to the political margins. Nevertheless, the fundamentals of the party's project have hardly changed: and, if, in the 1980s, this was considered neofascist in content, it is hard to see what would justify the consideration that its project no longer has anything to do with fascism. This seems especially true when we realise that the FN/RN's strategy, since its creation in 1972, has *always* consisted of winning power through the existing institutions.

The mass audience achieved by the FN in the 1980s cannot be explained solely in terms of the FN's own decisions. While Jean-Marie Le Pen's rhetorical talents obviously played a certain role, as did certain organisational and strategic choices made by old hands of French fascism (Victor Barthélémy and François Duprat), it is equally clear that none of this would alone have been enough to lift it to its current position. Proof of this is the fact that, ten years after its foundation in 1972, the FN was still a tiny group with just a few hundred members and no electoral hearing.[4] So, to understand the rise of the FN/RN, we need to turn our attention to other players in the French political arena, starting with the direct support this party received from François Mitterrand and the Socialist Party in the 1980s, with the express aim of dividing the right. In June 1984, Pierre Bérégovoy, who was then minister for social affairs and national solidarity (and later became prime minister), was quoted as saying: 'We have every interest in pushing the FN. It makes the Right unelectable. The stronger it is, the more unbeatable we'll be. This is the Socialists' historic opportunity.'[5] It is also worth remembering that it was under pressure from Mitterrand that Jean-Marie Le Pen was invited

---

4   In fact, it failed to gather the 500 signatures of elected representatives needed to stand in the 1981 presidential elections.

5   See Valérie Igounet, *Le Front national. De 1972 à nos jours, le parti, les hommes, les idées*, Paris: Seuil, 2014, p. 127.

for the first time to appear on prime-time political TV shows (at a time when the FN leader's poll ratings were merely derisory).[6] While this complicity on the part of the centre-left would obviously not alone suffice to explain the rise of the FN/RN, it did have a real impact. Following his first appearance in 1984 on the most popular TV politics show of the day, *L'heure de vérité*, the FN's poll scores doubled. The party's coffers were replenished by a large number of donations and, the very next morning, hundreds of people were reported to be queuing up outside the FN's Paris offices to join the party: 'Whereas the party used to receive an average of fifteen membership applications a day, within a few days these had risen to a thousand.'[7]

Given how far the main political forces have – directly or more often indirectly – encouraged the rise of the FN/RN, it can hardly be seen as the inevitable consequence of the natural appeal of xenophobia and racism in times of crisis. It is true that far-right parties have grown almost everywhere over the last four decades, and particularly over the last fifteen years. And, yet, the pace of their growth and the levels they have reached vary greatly from one country to another. The rise of the far right cannot therefore be understood as the product of an irresistible 'right-wing turn' in French society, or still less of populations on a European or even global scale, as a simple collateral effect of economic crisis. If we look at France alone, recent research tends to contradict this idea of a 'right-wing turn' which tends to be confined to the political and media spheres, marked by a steady shift of forces from the centre and the right towards the positions of the far right.[8] The best way to understand this party's rise is not through a general, mechanical and abstract model (the economic crisis is said to encourage xenophobia, which then feeds the success of the far right). Rather, we need an analysis that takes seriously a conjunction of political, economic, social and ideological dynamics (so a variety of actors – most of whom do not come from the historical far right).[9] While each has a relative autonomy, their effects combine to shape and to feed the *protracted crisis of hegemony* described in the second chapter of this book, on which the rise of neofascism feeds.

The electoral advance of the FN/RN, which has allowed it to bear weight across the entire political field these last forty years, is one of the

---

6   Ibid., p. 132.
7   Ibid., p. 149.
8   See Vincent Tiberj, *La droitisation française, mythe et réalités*, Paris: PUF, 2024.
9   See the previous three chapters.

main expressions of this crisis – one which essentially began in the late 1970s and has continued to deepen ever since. Its rise reflects the inability of the ruling classes, through the various political parties serving their fundamental interests, to prepare and implement a political project able to unite a majority social bloc in an enduring way. But it also signals a certain political impotence of the working classes and oppressed groups – that is, their inability to achieve a unified political representation of their own, able to defend their fundamental interests both in the field of social mobilisation and in the electoral arena. In keeping with the entire fascist tradition,[10] the FN/RN seeks to reorder the political spectrum to its own advantage by constructing an ideological synthesis that claims to transcend the opposition between right and left, and indeed that between employers and workers. It does this in the name of an ideal of national rebirth and the unity of 'nationals' (against what is said to be an ever-present, multi-form 'foreign' or 'globalist' threat) – and, ultimately, in the aim of coming to power by legal means. Yet, in this respect, it would be wrong to contrast it with historical fascism in Italy and Germany. Although Hitler did attempt an insurrection in 1923 (the 'Beer Hall Putsch' in Munich), imagining that this was how Mussolini had come to power (although the March on Rome was in fact largely a combination of political theatre and military failure), these movements essentially sought a constitutional route to power. In fact, they only succeeded in reaching power because they were lifted to the head of government by a large section of the traditional elites, the bourgeoisie, the large landowners, the conservative right and the highest representatives of the state (King Victor Emmanuel III in Italy and President Paul von Hindenburg in Germany).[11]

The Stages of the Far Right's Rise

It is not as if the FN/RN's rise has always been straightforward. It has been punctuated by many internal crises and strategic reorientations, expulsions and acts of score-settling. This has, through its history, led

---

10 See Zeev Sternhell, *Ni droite ni gauche. L'idéologie fasciste en France*, Paris: Gallimard, 2012 [1983] (*Neither Right nor Left: Fascist Ideology in France*, Berkeley, CA: University of California Press, 1986).

11 Among an enormous bibliography on the rise to power and the conquest of power by fascist movements, see in particular: Robert O. Paxton, *The Anatomy of Fascism*, New York: Knopf, 2004.

to the departure of certain currents from its ranks and the arrival of others. Examining this far-right party's path to the gates of power, we can distinguish among several stages of development, allowing us better to understand certain tactical and strategic choices that it has made in different moments.

The first stage, from the FN's creation in 1972 up until the start of the 1980s, were wilderness years, both electorally and in terms of building much of an activist presence. Throughout this period, which ended with the party's first breakthroughs in the Dreux local elections in 1983 and the European elections in 1984, the FN was a mere groupuscule. Initially, it sought to unite different far-right factions, in this mainly recruiting activists who had their political initiation in four different arenas: the Vichy regime between 1940 and 1944 (that is, former collaborationists, ex-Waffen SS and Milice members, and so on); the Poujadist movement in the 1950s (allowing Jean-Marie Le Pen's first election as an MP, in 1956, aged twenty-eight); the colonial wars (in Indochina and then Algeria) in which many young neofascists had taken up arms; and, finally the neofascist movements of the 1950s and 1960s (Jeune Nation, Fédération des étudiants nationalistes, Europe Action, Occident and so on),[12] notable for raising up a new generation of activists. The FN's initial difficulties immediately belied its founders' grandiose ambitions, in particular those of the neofascists of Ordre nouveau, who had initiated this party-building project and soon questioned the advisability of continuing along this path. Following a series of electoral setbacks, only two years after its founding the FN descended into internal warfare, despite having only a few hundred supporters. Many believed that this crisis would seal Jean-Marie Le Pen's fate and put a premature end to the nationalist movement of which he was the figurehead. This crisis, in fact, gave rise to a separate party, the Parti des forces nouvelles (PFN). For a time, the PFN was a marginal group just like the FN, but, as Jean-Marie Le Pen's party gained ground in the 1980s, this rival lost all political influence, and hence many of its members, including its leaders, gradually joined his grouping.

The second stage was the period during which the FN conquered, expanded and then consolidated its initial social and electoral base (1983–2002). What were the key factors behind the far right's electoral successes in this period? First of all, the established right-wing parties'

---

12 On these different movements, see Jean-Paul Gautier, *Les extrêmes droites en France, de 1945 à nos jours*, Paris: Syllepse, 2017.

adoption of the neoliberal agenda in the 1970s left part of the traditional petty bourgeoisie – small shopkeepers, craftsmen, farmers and small business owners – without political representation, as they faced increasingly heavy competition from mass retailers (booming in this era), large-scale industry and agri-business. Added to this were more conservative layers of the working class, including blue-collar workers, who had largely voted for Gaullist forces in the previous period. Added to this were the 1981 elections, with both setbacks for the right – pitching its two main parties (the RPR and UDF) into crisis – and electrifying the right-wing base in opposition to the Socialist–Communist coalition (it was said that Russian tanks would soon be rolling down the Champs-Élysées . . .). It was into this breach that the FN first jumped, claiming to be the sole embodiment of a 'social, national and popular right', particularly attentive to the 'little people' (that is, the petty bourgeoisie in the traditional sense). Its first national successes thus relied on the traditional right-wing electorate: some 54 percent of FN voters in the 1984 European elections (its first major breakthrough) had voted for the right (Chirac or Giscard d'Estaing) in the first round of the 1981 presidential election.[13] Secondly, the Socialist Party's conversion to neoliberalism, barely a year after coming to power,[14] allowed the FN to win over certain segments of the white working classes.[15] It is also worth noting that it was among former Mitterrand voters – who may have felt disoriented, betrayed or even despairing after the 'austerity turn' of 1983 – and not among the electorate of the French Communist Party, as is so often claimed – that the FN recruited almost all of its first voters from the left.[16] Indeed, some 24 percent of FN voters in 1984 had backed Mitterrand in the first round of the 1981 presidential election and just 1 percent backed Georges Marchais (the Communist Party candidate). Finally, the working-class electorate in which the FN began to make inroads from

---

13   See the data compiled from polls at the time by Alain Bihr: *Le Spectre de l'extrême droite. Les Français dans le miroir du Front national*, Paris: Éditions de l'atelier, 1998, p. 24.

14   See Chapter 2. See also: Ludivine Bantigny, *La France à l'heure du monde. De 1981 à nos jours*, Paris: Seuil, 2013.

15   Over the period as a whole, the vast majority of immigrants and descendants of non-European immigrants remained opposed to voting for the far right (and largely hostile to the right). This contradicts a sort of journalistic cliché that the FN has gradually spread its influence across the whole French population, with mass appeal even among the children of postcolonial immigrants. See for example Sylvain Brouard and Vincent Tiberj, *Français comme les autres? Enquête sur les citoyens d'origine maghrébine, africaine et turque*, Paris: Presses de Sciences Po, 2012.

16   Ibid., p. 24.

the late 1980s[17] was also made up of new voters (that is, young voters). With no established political roots, they came of age – and thus had their electoral-political socialisation – in a moment when the communist movement was in marked decline and the FN remained at a persistently high level, routinely being presented as a major opposition force.

The third stage was a kind of growth crisis. In 2002, the FN reached the second round of the presidential election for the first time, but it was unable to use this as a springboard to continued development in the years that followed. In fact, the far right's electoral scores declined sharply during the 2000s. If, in the 2002 first round, the FN scored 16.9 percent support (to which we should add the 2.3 percent for Bruno Mégret, Jean-Marie Le Pen's former lieutenant), in 2007, this sank to 10.4 percent (to which we could add the 2.2 percent for Philippe de Villiers). In the parliamentary elections that followed in June 2007, the FN sank to 4.3 percent support. Le Pen's success in reaching the second round in 2002 owed less to a surge of support than to the extreme fragmentation on the left: the 'plural left' coalition that had governed between 1997 and 2002 fielded five different candidates in the first round (in addition to the three candidates from the revolutionary left). The entire left-wing vote added up to much more than the far right's (around 43 percent, compared with 19 percent) and remained at that level throughout the 2000s. The Sarkozyan offensive was another crucial feature of this period. First as interior minister between 2002 and 2007, then as president from 2007 to 2012, Nicolas Sarkozy set himself the goal of rebuilding a 'right-wing base' on a staunchly neoliberal basis. More exactly, as we have seen, he combined a meritocratic ideology ('work more to earn more'), a securitarian agenda (the promise to use the high-pressure hose to clean up working-class neighbourhoods) and xenophobia (the demonisation of young people from immigrant backgrounds). This last dimension was to become increasingly pronounced as Sarkozy's poll ratings declined, as demonstrated by the Grenoble speech in 2010, which asserted – much in the manner of Le Pen – the link between immigration and crime. Sarkozy's aim was to tap into the language and programmes of the far right in order, he promised, to 'bring FN voters back into the fold of the Republic'. In so doing, he set in motion a radicalisation on the right that would gradually reconfigure what the Macron administration has since called the 'republican arc' – progressively excluding all or part of

---

17   The FN and Jean-Marie Le Pen made their first real breakthrough among blue-collar workers in the 1988 presidential election, but at levels still well below those achieved in the 2017, 2022 and 2024 elections.

the left while increasingly explicitly including the far right. The Sarkozyan dynamic would initially destabilise the FN, which the activist and electoral mobilisation of 2002 had put on the back foot and helped to delegitimise. Yet the radicalisation of the conservative camp would ultimately benefit the far right, once Sarkozy was voted out in 2012.

Thus began a new period for the FN/RN in 2011–12, the result of the arrival of Marine Le Pen as its leader, the ebbing of the Sarkozyan wave and the erosion of the left's electoral base. This was the second stage in the development of the far-right party's audience: the shattering of what had been thought to be its 'glass ceiling' at under 20 percent support. Indeed, the FN gradually started achieving much higher scores: 24.9 percent in the 2014 European elections (obtaining twenty-three MEPs), 27.7 percent in the first round of the 2015 regional elections (winning 118 regional councillors), and a huge 34 percent in the runoff of the 2017 presidential election – almost double the score that Jean-Marie Le Pen achieved against Jacques Chirac back in 2002. Since then, the party's electoral successes are no longer just in presidential elections. While the FN used to be closely associated with Jean-Marie Le Pen and seemed utterly dependent on his personal aura and his talents as an agitator and speaker,[18] in the 2010s, its vote reached previously unknown levels at all elections. It then became irreducible to his brand alone, and indeed increasingly less volatile, to the point where it now has the strongest electoral bedrock of any party (particularly in terms of the carry-over of its voters from one election to the next). At this stage of its development, Marine Le Pen's strategy has essentially consisted of three elements. Firstly, she had to reassure the movement's activists and its traditional electoral base, by showing that she remained faithful to the legacy of her father (whom she appointed the FN's honorary president in 2011) and to the party's core ideology. 'I embrace my party's entire history,' she told delegates at the Tours Congress in 2011. She thus waged her 2012 presidential campaign by riding the party's fundamental battle horses, in particular anti-immigrant xenophobia. She linked this loyalty to two elements that were hardly new, but which she gradually put more emphasis upon in order to change the profile of the FN/RN through small steps.

These two strategic focuses – often summed up in the expressions dedemonisation and 'the social turn' – were closely associated with Florian

---

18   While the party did manage to make inroads at town-hall level in the 1980s–90s (first in Dreux in 1983, but especially in the 1995 local elections, when major towns such as Toulon, Orange and Marignane fell to the FN), it generally secured lower scores than in the presidential elections.

Philippot, who became her lieutenant after 2012. The de-demonisation process essentially involved a change of attitude on the issues of antisemitism and the Holocaust. In particular, the expulsion of Jean-Marie Le Pen from the party was seen to corroborate the idea of a break with the past and was greeted by most of the mainstream media. The strategy of seeking establishment respectability also benefited from the adoption of increasingly xenophobic rhetoric on the right, as well as among some Socialists (notably Manuel Valls, François Hollande's interior minister at the time). Indeed, this had the automatic effect of *normalising* the FN/RN, making it appear no longer as an extremist force but as the most consistent party in the face of what was now widely presented as an 'immigration problem' or 'problem of law and order'. Moreover, politicians across the board have increasingly taken up the Le Pen camp's longstanding association of these themes – notwithstanding judicial and police statistics to the effect that crime levels have declined in recent decades, particularly when it comes to the most serious incidents. As far as the 'social turn' is concerned, the change in tone had already come in the 1990s with the criticism of 'Euro-liberalism', itself a break with the pro-European but also Reaganite line which the FN had pursued in the 1980s. Nevertheless, after the financial crisis of 2007–8 and the sharply neoliberal course taken by the Hollande government, Marine Le Pen realised that it could pay off politically to step up her criticism of 'financial globalism' and advocating various measures (which have since been abandoned) that backed up her 'anti-system' message. These included re-establishing retirement at age sixty, increasing low wages and pensions, renationalising certain companies and so on. It was on the basis of this program, and through the skilful use of social demagogy, that the far-right party succeeded in winning over a new electorate in regions hard hit by deindustrialisation (particularly in the north and east of France). Still, here, we should push back against a certain received wisdom. For it was not so much former left-wing voters who switched to the far right as individuals who had already voted for right-wing parties previously: while 59 percent of Marine Le Pen's voters in 2017 had already supported her in 2012, 15 percent had voted for Sarkozy, 7 percent for Hollande and just 1.5 percent for Mélenchon, to which we must add former abstainers and new voters (those who had been too young to vote in the previous contest).

A final stage in the development of the FN/RN began in 2017. This can be described as a march towards power, although we should also be clear that its victory is not assured, as was also signalled by its unexpected setback in the runoffs of snap parliamentary elections on 7 July 2024. Many commentators had presented Le Pen's defeat in the second round of the 2017 presidential contest as irrefutable proof that her party would never come to power (in particular, by going on endlessly about her incompetent performance in the debate with Macron in between the two rounds). Added to this failure were the party's low scores in the parliamentary elections that immediately followed, as well as the departure of two of its leading figures (Marion Maréchal and Florian Philippot). And, yet, the whole period since 2017 has mercilessly refuted these doom-laden forecasts for the party's future, as the FN/RN has made further great strides, crossing a new threshold in its electoral reach. It held its own in the European elections in 2019 (with 23.3 percent support) before achieving an exceptional score at the same contest in 2024, with some 31.4 percent of the vote, taking advantage of the decomposition of Macronism as well as the divisions on the left. In the 2020 local elections, the RN held on to almost all the towns it had won in 2014 and even secured a few new ones, in particular winning – for the first time in many years – a town with more than 100,000 inhabitants, namely Perpignan. Moreover, Marine Le Pen's score in the runoff of the presidential election in 2022 was some 41.5 percent (up from 34 percent in 2017). Perhaps most important, in parliamentary elections, in which the party was historically weak – but which are also crucial in terms of public visibility and the state funding of parties – it has made major progress, winning 89 MPs in 2022 (to general surprise) and then 126 in 2024.

Beyond its electoral scores, a number of factors back up this idea of a new stage starting in 2017, qualitatively different from the previous one. These elements each point to a new relationship between the ruling classes and the far right (in general, and especially the FN/RN). Le Pen's party has become a possible option for a section of the propertied classes. This is true for part of the bourgeois electorate (in the broadest sense) previously attached to the historic party of the French right (the RPR, which became the UMP and then LR): unfortunately, we have no data on how employers as such vote, but we do know that the far right as a whole rose from a 13–14 percent score among senior executives and professionals in 2012 to 26 percent in 2022. Les Républicains' candidate Valérie Pécresse slumped to a feeble score in the first round of the 2022 presidential election (4.8 percent), and not only because Éric Zemmour succeeded in tapping into the most right-wing parts of this traditional conservative electorate, taking advantage of the radicalisation effects associated with the Sarkozyan offensive of the 2000s–10s (extended and amplified by the mass homophobic movement that was the Manif pour tous protests against same-sex marriage). It was also because, for a section of this electorate, Marine Le Pen appeared to be the 'pragmatic' choice to block the left (most notably Mélenchon and La France insoumise, with their 20 percent–plus support) and Macronism, which, despite its authoritarian and racist drift, this electorate blames for not having gone far enough. Among the 2017 voters for LR candidate François Fillon, in the 2022 first round some 16 percent of them opted for Zemmour and 17 percent for Le Pen. The other striking new development in this respect was the alliance sealed ahead of the 2024 parliamentary elections between the RN and the man who was then still LR's party president, Éric Ciotti. Even though Ciotti was disowned by the vast majority of the party's senior figures after this decision, and eventually had to leave to found a new party – destined to become a mere affiliate of the RN – this was a historic coup for the far right, which had previously only managed to attract rather more minor figures from the right-wing camp.

But the new relationship between the ruling classes and the far right is also, and perhaps above all, reflected in the support it now receives from a handful of billionaire backers, particularly Vincent Bolloré and, more recently, Pierre-Edouard Stérin. For political rather than economic reasons, Bolloré has built up a real media empire that includes not only the written press (the newspaper *JDD*), but also TV and radio stations (CNews, C8, Canal+, Europe 1), publishing and distribution (via the huge Hachette group) and cinema (via Canal+, one of the main funders of French cinema). Most importantly, he has put this empire at the service of the far right and fostered the emergence of a swarm of new figures – pseudo-journalists, presenters-interviewers, pundits – previously condemned to second-rate media with low ratings and attracting little public interest (TV Libertés, Boulevard Voltaire and so on). Following an ultra-conservative and libertarian line, Stérin's project is to fund, to the tune of €150 million (over ten years), training structures designed to bring up a new generation of far-right political personnel at the crossroads of the RN, Reconquête and LR. They will thus be both better versed in effective PR strategies and more capable of holding positions within the state in the event of victory. This plan also includes building up think-tanks that will constantly supply the media with fake experts who are also quite real far-right ideologues. Another notable aspect of this situation is the new attention paid to the RN by business circles. Informed by the Italian experience of a coalition of the right dominated by the party that is heir to postwar neofascism (Fratelli d'Italia), growing sections of French business circles, dissatisfied with the social and political instability that Macron has not managed to resolve during his two terms in office, are clearly attracted by an even more brutal solution than the current president's authoritarian neoliberalism. They doubtless see an opportunity in the social base that the RN has built up among the population, which might enable it to impose the counter-reforms it deems necessary, with fewer bumps along the way.

Finally, and perhaps most importantly, over the last few decades, the RN has succeeded in popularising its ideas, or rather its obsessions, at the heart of the French political and media spheres. These notably include the four 'big I's' of RN discourse: immigration, insecurity, Islam and (national) identity. It has been so successful in this regard that, over the last fifteen years or so, much of the political and media debate has been centred around these same themes. This process of eating away at the mainstream has gone so far that the Socialist Party, when it was in power, proposed measures like stripping perpetrators of terrorist attacks of their French nationality (before President Hollande backed down in the face of the uproar). This was a demand that no party other than the FN/RN was making a decade previously, and that has no precedent in French history apart from the Vichy regime. As we saw in the previous chapter, the far-right party could never have expanded its reach so deeply or so quickly without the convergence of a significant proportion of political and media personnel with the proposals, language and even worldview of the far right. A perverse mechanism is in operation here: the more the RN gains ground, the more the ruling parties tend to adopt its themes, language and proposals. The more this transfer intensifies, with the obvious effect of legitimising the RN's 'ideas', the more the far-right party progresses ideologically and electorally – in turn redoubling the incentive to adopt elements of Le Pen's ideology.

An Enduring Strategic and Political Project

A number of politicians and journalists, and more rarely intellectuals, have sown dangerous confusion by claiming that the political and strategic project of the RN has undergone a qualitative transformation, to the point where some claim that there is no longer any reason to associate it with the far right, and still less with fascism. The party is said to have moved from its original fascist matrix to a 'populist' or 'national-populist' one, and indeed now cast as just another right-wing party.

According to the philosopher Marcel Gauchet, commenting in 2022, 'Marine Le Pen embodies something very different from what the far right has been in the past'. That same year, Michel Onfray claimed that Marine Le Pen is 'obviously not far right' seeing as this term means 'the violence of the streets, the rejection of democracy, the rejection of the Republic, the rejection of the National Assembly'. In 2023, even Nicolas Sarkozy took offence at the 'charge of [this party] being far-right', asking 'how can anyone say that the RN is not republican?' There confusion is such that often nowadays the RN is no longer criticised for its racist and ultra-authoritarian line, the antisemitic or Islamophobic statements of its candidates and suchlike, but because its economic agenda is allegedly too 'left-wing'. Hence, in spring 2015, we saw François Hollande claiming (as president of the Republic, no less) that Marine Le Pen 'talks like a Communist Party leaflet from the 1970s', in particular because of her party's alleged 'statism'. More recently, when Bruno Le Maire was Macron's minister for the economy and finance, he said that the RN's economic programme was 'Marxist'.

While such preposterous statements are unlikely to convince the public that the RN is not 'serious' about economic issues, or to limit the far-right party's growing appeal in business circles, they do foster a confusion that objectively serves Marine Le Pen's purposes. Indeed, after a first period in which she had just taken over the leadership and her main concern was to reassure her party's base that she remained loyal to her father's legacy, she instead turned to constantly repeating that the new FN was no longer Jean-Marie Le Pen's party, and, in particular, that it had overcome the past left–right divide. The quarrel between Marine le Pen and her father and his eventual expulsion are often perceived – or rather, presented – as proof of a fundamental break with the FN's past. This so-called turning point was also symbolised by the arrival in the party's ranks of figures such as Florian Philippot (who claimed to have come through Chevènement's patriotic-social-democratic tendency), Robert Ménard (former head of Reporters Without Borders), lawyer Gilbert Collard (once close to the Parti des travailleurs, a Trotskyist group),[19] and trade unionist Fabien Engelmann (also formerly a far-left activist).

---

19 In response to those who see the arrival of these figures in the FN as clear evidence of its thoroughgoing transformation, it would be useful to re-read historian Philippe Burrin's excellent book on prominent defectors (notably Jacques Doriot and Marcel Déat). He shows that these movements are common historically, and that they lead defectors to adapt to the far right, or even to become even more radical nationalists, racists and anti-communists, and not the other way round: *La dérive fasciste. Doriot, Déat, Bergery: 1933–1945*, Paris: Seuil, 2003 [1986].

It should also be noted that the media, by routinely giving noisy publicity to these new arrivals (who are nevertheless very marginal figures within their political currents of origin and far less numerous than defectors from the traditional right), have insidiously contributed to the FN's de-demonisation strategy.[20] In the case of Philippot, his chosen presentation of his contested political origin has been constantly and indulgently relayed by journalists, generally without recalling that his support for Chevènement was only episodic, during the 2002 presidential election, and that he was never a member – let alone a leading member – of Chevènement's party, the MRC. Besides, after leaving the FN, Philippot founded a new far-right party – Les Patriotes – on a quite radical ideological foundation based on conspiracy theories (especially in the context of the pandemic).

From its foundation until the early 2000s, there was a general tendency – at least on the left – to see the FN as an update of the fascist project, or at least as an heir to the far right of the interwar period (including fascist movements). From the 1980s onwards, the increasing use of the category of 'populism' – the shortcomings of which have already been highlighted[21] – gradually marginalised the characterisation of the FN as 'fascist'.[22] However, while the term 'populism' is used in

---

20   For a broader analysis of the contribution of the 'mainstream' media to the construction of the idea of a 'new FN' after Marine Le Pen became its leader, see A. Dézé, 'La construction médiatique de la "nouveauté" FN', in Sylvain Crépon, Alexandre Dézé and Nonna Mayer (eds), *Les faux-semblants du Front national*, Paris: Presses de la FNSP, 2015. See also: E. Darras, 'Ordre politique et désordre médiatique. Que sait-on de la médiatisation du Front national', in Lorenzo Barrault-Stella, Brigitte Gaïti and Patrick Lehingue (eds), *La politique désenchantée?*, Rennes: PUR, 2019.
21   See Chapter 1.
22   Many specialists have sought to draw an unbridgeable separation between a 'national populism' said to be specific to the French far right since the Boulangism of the late nineteenth century, and fascism, instead deemed little more than an import, unable to take root in France. This is the dominant interpretation in French historiography, whether among historians of the French far right from the end of the nineteenth century to the Vichy regime (René Rémond, Michel Winock, Serge Bernstein and so on), or among specialists in the far right after World War II. See the position taken by many of the latter: 'FN, un national-populisme', *Le Monde*, 7 October 2013. Again, on this point, it is worth referring to the volume edited by Michel Dobry, which emphasises, in particular, the porous divides between the different currents of the French far right during the interwar period, and the many elements that this far right drew from Italian or German fascism. It further stresses both the difficulty of classifying in definitive terms a mass movement such as the Croix-de-feu (which became the Parti Social Français in 1936), and the significance of organisations of clear fascist profile and memberships in the hundreds of thousands (in particular, Jacques Doriot's Parti Populaire Français). See Michel Dobry (ed.), *Le Mythe de l'allergie française au fascisme*, Paris: Albin Michel, 2003.

public debate with the clear intention of denying this party credibility, it also obviously bears far less stigma than the label 'fascism' (which has long hung over the FN, to the extent that its leaders have on several occasions taken legal action against those who have described them using this term).[23] In addition, the far-right party has been able to exploit this to vaunt its closeness to the working classes:[24] as a 'populist' party, the FN is imagined to have 'naturally' become the party of ordinary people. It is said to have replaced the Communist Party in this role, with this latter party's voters supposedly turning en masse to the FN – an untruth that is time and again empirically refuted yet nonetheless constantly repeated.[25] What is more, this overlooks the fact that only a minority of the working classes vote for the FN, that this party's activist presence in working-class areas remains very weak and that its leadership bodies remain – as we shall see later – largely dominated by members of the ruling classes, notably company bosses and the professions (especially lawyers), and the middle classes (small shopkeepers and artisans, estate agents and so on).

So, the question of the political characterisation of the FN and its project – fascist or not – clearly needs revisiting. This issue is too often reduced to the problem of the presence in its ranks of individuals considered to be 'authentically' fascist, because they explicitly claim a line of descent from Mussolini or even Hitler, or because they adopt a visibly fascist style (explicitly racist slogans, marches in close military-style ranks, outstretched arms, neo-Nazi symbols, styles of dress associated with fascist movements and so on). However, given the anathema that comes with such a self-identification or with such external markings (which remains relative, since the most violent far-right movements are regularly seen marching with Celtic crosses or other symbols associated with the fascist and neofascist traditions), very few RN activists and even fewer leaders express such direct links between their project and historical fascism. This often leads to the hasty assumption that the RN is, if not actually free of such ills, at least a non-fascist organisation to which fascist elements have attached themselves through so-called 'entryist' strategies. It is admitted that the FN may well have been fascist

---

23 Marine Le Pen took Jean-Luc Mélenchon to court over his use of the term 'fascist' but lost the case: 'Marine Le Pen définitivement déboutée contre Jean-Luc Mélenchon', *Libération*, 28 February 2017. More recently, Louis Aliot – former number two in the party and current mayor of Perpignan – took a local CGT trade union activist to court on the same grounds, and also lost.
24 Annie Collovald, *Le 'Populisme' du FN, un dangereux contresens*, Bellecombe-en-Bauges: Le Croquant, 2004.
25 See below.

when it was founded back in 1972, due to the strong and undeniable presence of individuals and currents from the old networks of the Nazi-collaborationist far right and explicitly neofascist groups or leaders (in particular, Ordre nouveau). And, yet, it is said to have definitively distanced itself from this original flaw in the decades since – for some, as early as the 1980s, and for others more recently thanks to Marine Le Pen's efforts in particular. By this argument, the key factor is a kind of demographic turnover which – through the gradual death of the collaborationists of the Vichy regime, the terrorists of the OAS and the militants of Ordre nouveau – has eliminated from the RN most of the individuals with the most notorious links to historical fascism and the violent currents of postwar neofascism.

It is important to remember that two of the early key figures who developed the FN's organisation in the 1970s (in effect, modelling the FN on the Communist Party's structure) and built its ideological and strategic profile – making up for Jean-Marie Le Pen's shortcomings in these two areas – were men closely bound to historical fascism. The first, Victor Barthélémy, general secretary of the FN from 1975 to 1978,[26] was Doriot's right-hand man during World War II and the working-class linchpin of the Parti populaire français (PPF), making him a prominent collaborationist and, as such, one of the organisers of the Vel d'Hiv' roundup of Jews. The second, François Duprat, who was in charge of the FN's press and its electoral committee from 1974 until his violent death in 1978 (having been expelled in February 1973 and reinstated a few months later), was one of the main theorists, historians and strategists of the so-called 'revolutionary-nationalist' (NR) neofascist far right in the 1960s and 1970s.[27] Do their deaths and the political marginalisation of currents such as Ordre nouveau and the NR mean that we can conclude that there was a break between the FN of the past and that of the 1980s and 1990s? Firstly, it should be noted that other currents with links to historical fascism joined the FN from the late 1970s onward: for example, the Union solidariste headed by Jean-Pierre Stirbois – who joined the

---

26 As Franck Timmermans – one of the founding members of the FN and its future deputy general secretary – wrote much later: 'Victor was . . . undoubtedly the one who helped build the structure with loyalty and patience, without ostentation, and by building up a constant, almost paternalistic contact with the local-level cadres. *We owe the first web of organisation to him*': Nicolas Lebourg and Joseph Beauregard, *Dans l'ombre des Le Pen. Une histoire des numéros 2 du FN,* Paris: Nouveau Monde, 2012, p. 60 (emphasis added).

27 See Nicolas Lebourg and Joseph Beauregard, *François Duprat. L'homme qui réinventa l'extrême droite*, Paris: Denoël, 2012.

FN in 1977 and quickly became the party's number two leader – and the Nouvelle Droite, some of whose leaders joined the organisation in the 1980s (Jean-Yves Le Gallou, Pierre Vial, Yvan Blot and also Bruno Mégret). Secondly, it seems unlikely that nothing was handed down politically from this generation of old-timers on the fascist(-adjacent) far right – some of whom may have left the FN at various points in its history – to those who are at the head of the movement today, many of whom joined the FN in the 1980s and 1990s at a fairly young age. These latter include Marine Le Pen, of course (she joined aged eighteen in 1986), but also Louis Aliot, Gilles Pennelle, Laure Lavalette, Bruno Gollnisch, Marie-Christine Arnautu and Philippe Olivier.

Furthermore, it is vastly simplistic to frame the question of the RN's fascist character solely in terms of the presence therein of activists who explicitly claim to be part of the fascist tradition or who show the most visible signs of belonging to it. The political trajectories of the men and women who currently head the organisation are surely an important consideration, and one which deserves more than a simple examination of how they choose to present their own record. We cannot read into their souls and their inner thoughts. But we can ask questions about such issues as their ideological hinterland, their intellectual influences (sometimes cited implicitly or indirectly) and the imaginaries that they draw upon in their discourse. Doubtless even more important, in pinning down the forms of continuity or discontinuity with fascism, is an analysis of the operation of this party, its ideological orientations, its strategic project, its tactics (for laying down roots, for developing support and so on) or, indeed, its social base.[28] When we base our analysis on these elements, then questioning the fascist or non-fascist nature of the RN no longer consists only of checking whether it resembles in every aspect the fascisms of the interwar period (which are themselves very diverse), or whether it is an exact replica of them. For that would be easy to answer: clearly, the RN and the contemporary far right have significant differences from classic fascism. How could it be otherwise, almost a century later?

Most importantly, we should ask whether – given the current state of the political field, of French society and, more broadly, of capitalism – the RN fulfils a function similar to that performed by the historical fascisms. In other words: does it constitute what historian Robert Paxton

---

28 Peter Fysh and Jim Wolfreys took just such a line of research in what remains one of the best books analysing the FN. See *The Politics of Racism in France*, London: Palgrave MacMillan, 2002 [1997].

would call a 'functional equivalent' of fascism? This is a much more intellectually demanding task than the 'analyses' offered by media scribes who generally take at face value the reassuring speeches of Marine Le Pen or Jordan Bardella, marvelling at the fact that they do not advocate the overthrow of the Republic or explicitly call for violence against the groups whom they verbally target. In particular, this presupposes an in-depth analysis of the social and political situation in France, in order to assess whether the conditions are conducive to the development – or even the victory – of a force that could be characterised as a 'functional equivalent' of fascism, that is, one whose rise to power would have effects that are similar, all due differences considered, to those produced by the classical fascisms.

A more specific question concerns the changes in the RN: are they real or illusory, superficial or profound? The programmatic changes have more to do with communication strategies – with cosmetic changes like speaking of 'national priority' instead of the former policy of 'national preference' – than with a genuine *aggiornamento*. At a deeper level, the fundamental and structuring elements of the FN's original political, strategic and organisational project persist within the current RN, and these are in continuity – at least in part – with the fascist project. The first of these is, undoubtedly, the desire to give a new respectability to the far right, delegitimised in the first place by its collaboration with the German occupier and its involvement alongside the Nazis in the project of a fascist Europe. In the minds of the FN's founders, from the early 1970s onwards, this meant adopting a new language and, above all, making more considered and systematic use of the electoral arena. This meant putting on the back burner the violent militancy that had been the hallmark of the far right of the 1960s (particularly Occident, which became Ordre nouveau after this first group was banned, and then the Groupe Union Défense). This shows how far the de-demonisation strategy attributed to Marine Le Pen has merely deepened an approach that has been present in the party since its foundation, and which Bruno Mégret – Jean-Marie Le Pen's former right-hand man – took up in the 1990s.

The second element was the need to unite the 'national camp': the founders of the FN set out to overcome the sectarian divisions and fragmentation of the far right,[29] which had already clearly emerged in the

---

29   See probably the most comprehensive book on the French far right, in all its diversity, after World War II: Jean-Paul Gautier, *Les extrêmes droites en France*, Paris: Syllepse, 2017. See also: Arianne Chebel d'Appollonia, *L'extrême droite en France. De Maurras à Le Pen*, Brussels: Éditions Complexe, 1988.

interwar years.[30] For the FN's founders hailing from Ordre nouveau, this party was meant to be a broad structure within which 'nationalists' – in their minds, neofascists – could attract, manoeuvre and give leadership to a 'national' milieu – in other words, nationalists considered more moderate because they came from the traditional right or, like Jean-Marie Le Pen, from Poujadism. Marine Le Pen has got rid of a number of figures or currents who caused problems because of their overly visible proximity to historical fascism and in particular to Holocaust denial (her own father, l'Œuvre française, some fundamentalist Catholics and so on). Still, this has not stopped her from handing important roles to unrepentant ex-leaders of the GUD (Groupe Union Défense), one of the main neofascist groupings in France since the 1970s, namely Axel Loustau and Frédéric Chatillon; integrating militants from the Identitarian movement (the best known being Philippe Vardon, one of the founders of the Bloc identitaire, later deputy campaign director and head of communications for the FN/RN in the 2019 European elections, then a candidate for the party in local elections in Nice); and also attracting leaders from the most radicalised fringes of the conservative right (notably Nicolas Dupont-Aignan's party Debout la France), in the spirit of what Maurras called a 'nationalist compromise'.

A third pillar of the FN since its foundation has been its insistence on maintaining its political independence from the parties of the traditional right. This differed from the PFN, its direct competitor on the far right in the 1970s, which had split from it early on in its history. The PFN, though made up of former radicals from Ordre nouveau, instead sought to forge relations with Valérie Giscard d'Estaing's UDF and then with Jacques Chirac's newly created RPR. Jean-Marie Le Pen, at various times, and more recently Marine Le Pen, have always staunchly opposed the idea of binding themselves to the established right-wing parties through national-level agreements that would place the FN in a subordinate position. This stance long prevented the party from having a number of elected representatives commensurate with the size of its electoral base. Still, this choice has paid off in the long term, as they have never had to take responsibility for a disappointing government record. As a result, the RN can continue to be seen as an 'anti-system' party, one that 'has never been tried out' as its voters often say, precisely because it has never governed at national level. Still, since its first electoral breakthroughs

---

30   We need only think of the differences, tensions or sometimes total absence of relations between organisations such as Action Française, the Croix-de-feu which became the PSF, the PPF, the Jeunesses Patriotes and Dorgères's Chemises vertes.

in 1983, it has sometimes built alliances with the right at the local or regional level, and has taken over a number of town halls (in the 1990s and again since the mid-2010s).

Anti-communism, and more broadly a radical hostility towards the labour movement (particularly the trade unions) and the left as a whole, constitutes a fourth fundamental element that has always been at the heart of the FN/RN project. This obviously expresses a certain continuity with the fascist matrix, in which the left in general, and the communist movement in particular, are seen as the 'party of foreigners'. First there was the 'Socialist-Communist' threat, raised in the 1970s at the time of the Union of the Left and these parties' 'Programme commun' (which promised a break with capitalism). This allowed the FN to attract sections of the traditional right-wing electorate when the right lost the presidential and parliamentary elections in 1981 and the left returned to power after twenty-three years of right-wing rule. A whole section of the right's electoral base clearly aspired to an anti-working class and anti-immigrant policy, and was not satisfied with what Jacques Chirac's RPR and Valéry Giscard d'Estaing's UDF had to offer at the time. Since 'communism' left the scene in 1989 (even if the right-wing press still often clutch their pearls about its alleged resurfacing, during major social mobilisations), and insofar as the Socialist Party has long since converted to neoliberalism, what was once seen as a threat to the capitalist status quo no longer frightens the right-wing base. Today, the spectres of 'Islamo-leftism' and 'wokeism' are variously mobilised by the ideologues and leaders of the right and far right, thus presenting themselves as defenders of 'freedom of expression'.

A final element, the most important ideologically – the one which we explored in the previous chapter – refers to ethno-nationalism. This is the principle around which the whole of the FN/RN's distinctive worldview is organised, and which necessarily carries with it anti-immigrant xenophobia and racism in all its varieties. It was François Duprat, in particular – a figure who, as we have noted, had a decisive influence on the development of the organisation – who long insisted (at the time when Jean-Marie Le Pen was essentially preoccupied with anti-communism) that the FN should adopt the anti-immigrant line as the fundamental thread of its agitation and propaganda.[31] It was also Duprat who devised the campaign that made the FN's name, even before its first electoral

---

31 On this point, see Igounet, *Le Front national*, pp. 91–7; Lebourg and Beauregard, *Dans l'ombre des Le Pen*, pp. 97–102.

successes, notably through a poster that was regularly reprinted and updated as unemployment rose: '1 million unemployed means 1 million too many immigrants. France and the French first.'

On this persistent political and strategic basis, how should we interpret the ideological mutations of the FN/RN, spearheaded in particular by Marine Le Pen since she took over the leadership at the Tours Congress in 2011? Far from constituting a symptom of normalisation and marking a clean break with historical fascism, the changes in the party's political discourse are bringing it *closer to it,* particularly through three shifts: the so-called 'social turn', the adoption of a 'neither right nor left' posture and the role that the FN/RN claims to be playing for the state. The 'social turn' refers to the borrowing from the left of rhetoric about the living conditions of workers or the safeguarding of public services, and of a few manifesto pledges which – as we shall see later on – are of very limited real substance. In this respect, Marine Le Pen has merely amplified a tactical shift that began in the 1990s in response to the demise of the Eastern Bloc and the upsurge in social struggles. The FN leadership theorised that the decline of the Communist Party and the labour movement offered it a huge opportunity to win over the working classes, and shifted from the ardently neoliberal line of the previous period to include a critique of the policies of competition (particularly those associated with the European Union).[32] By claiming to integrate both the values of order promoted by the right, and the left's values of social justice, the FN then began to rediscover the 'neither right nor left' that was the original inspiration for fascism.[33] This, in fact, contradicted Jean-Marie Le Pen's approach in the 1970s and 1980s, which consisted of claiming that the FN was the (only) embodiment of a 'national, social and popular' right, or more simply of a 'true right'. Lastly, Marine Le Pen's talk of the 'strategic state' goes back to the fundamentals of historical fascism, in which the state intervened heavily in the economy: not to redistribute wealth, but to serve the big capitalist interests, 'a strong state for a free market'.[34]

---

32   See below.
33   On the specifically ideological aspects of fascism, see Sternhell, *Ni droite ni gauche.*
34   See Grégoire Chamayou, *La société ingouvernable*, Paris, La Fabrique, 2018 (*The Ungovernable Society: A Genealogy of Authoritarian Liberalism*, Cambridge: Polity Press, 2021). The corporatist ideal of a compact between workers and employers within the framework of new organisations (the corporations) – an ideology of the third way between socialism and communism, which fascism promoted throughout Europe – was never more than window-dressing aimed at appealing to the small self-employed in particular (farmers, artisans, shopkeepers) and promising workers an improvement in their lot through negotiation rather than social struggle. The reality of the economic

When Florian Philippot was still one of the main leaders of the FN, he made every effort – citing the changes we have just mentioned – to present the party in the respectable trappings of Gaullism.[35] In its day, Gaullism, too, had drawn on the rhetoric of overcoming the left–right divide (and even what De Gaulle called the 'regime of the parties'). Yet, Gaullism as a practice of power was possible in the specific context of the rapid development of French capitalism and the high level of organisation of the working class. The ruling classes were thus forced to make social and political compromises that had previously been deemed unacceptable. In France and elsewhere, the state was tasked with a central role in reviving the accumulation of capital and in forging agreements between business figures – who had in part been delegitimised by the economic collaboration with Vichy and Nazi Germany – and a powerful workers' movement. This historical situation is nothing like today's. If fascism is to rotting capitalism what Bonapartism (in the Marxist sense of the term) is to developing capitalism, the RN could well be to today's crisis capitalism what Gaullism was to the flourishing capitalism of the much-misnamed 'Trente Glorieuses' or 'Golden Age'.[36]

So, the RN's strategic and political project has not fundamentally changed. Racism and xenophobia continue to occupy a central place therein, even if Marine Le Pen's party no longer needs to return to them constantly, particularly in its media interventions. Even the emergence in the political and media arena of a figure – Éric Zemmour – who is constantly trying to outmatch the RN on the terrain of racism, has not

---

regime under the fascist dictatorships was one of total domination by capital over the workers, since the latter were forbidden to organise collectively (within the framework of independent trade unions) and to defend their interests through their own specific means of action (strikes).

35 This is yet another of the FN's old 'de-demonisation' tactics. As early as 1988, the FN was able to declare, with regard to Yvan Blot (RPR MP and prominent member of the Club de l'Horloge), that he was joining the FN 'as a Gaullist because the RPR is not faithful to the major orientations of Gaullism'. Quoted in Lebourg and Beauregard, *Dans l'ombre des Le Pen*, p. 165.

36 There is much to be said about the degeneration of Gaullism, starting by remembering its profoundly authoritarian and xenophobic dimensions. The former aspect is now repressed from the collective memory, but it was apparent in the existence of an armed militia (the 'Service d'action civique', in which Charles Pasqua played a prominent role) and, above all, in the Constitution of the Fifth Republic (the product of a coup d'état). As for xenophobia, we should not forget de Gaulle's ethnic vision of immigration policy. In a letter to the minister of justice in June 1945, for example, he proposed 'limiting the influx of Mediterranean and Oriental immigrants, who have profoundly changed the composition of the French population over the last half-century', and instead giving 'priority' to 'Nordic naturalisations (Belgians, Luxembourgers, Swiss, Dutch, Danes, English, Germans, etc.)'. See Gérard Noiriel, *Le creuset français: histoire de l'immigration, XIXe–XXe siècle*, Paris: Seuil, 1988.

managed to dislodge it from its central position. When people want to express their rejection of immigrants and their hostility to minorities, they spontaneously and overwhelmingly vote RN. Not only have Zemmour and his Reconquête party not succeeded in peeling away Le Pen's electorate, but they have contributed – by way of contrast with their violent rhetoric – to 'softening' the political image of the RN. This radical rival has itself made Le Pen's party more respectable, even though their programmes on immigration and Islam are, in reality, virtually identical ('zero immigration', discrimination against foreigners and dual nationals enshrined in law, mass closures of mosques, bans on the hijab in all public spaces and so on). What is more, the issues that provide the most fertile ground for the far right – immigration, insecurity, terrorism, Islam – as well as the framings specific to this political family, are at the heart of the dominant ideology as co-produced by the political and media elites and have become increasingly so over recent decades. Indeed, today, the RN no longer needs to devote as much effort as it once did to forcing the ethno-racial divide into the centre of the political debate, or indeed in pushing a framing centred on the opposition between 'real French people' ('ours') and foreigners ('the others'). For this divide is already invariably raised in public debate even when it comes to issues such as household incomes and inflation, the public debt, employment, school failure and so on.

How Deep are the FN/RN's Popular Roots?

But we still need to analyse the RN's social base, in order to understand what roots it has among the general population. What are its specific areas of strength? Can we identify classes or fractions of classes, or indeed sections of the population as defined by other variables (gender, age, geographical location, origin, religion), or even types of territory, in which electoral support for the RN is particularly high? And where does the RN electorate come from politically? Is it actually true that, in the most recent period, the far-right party has managed to win over voters on the left (the oft-mentioned *fâchés pas fachos*: 'angry but not fascists')? Finally, what are the dynamics of the vote for the RN? Has it grown at the same rate in all groups? Have its areas of strength become more pronounced, or has it caught up in the groups where it was historically weak?

The question of the relationship between the RN and the working classes is generally obscured by two kinds of propaganda: firstly, by the media, which often unquestioningly gives Marine le Pen's party the title of 'France's leading workers' party'; and secondly, by the RN itself, which presents itself as the embodiment of 'the people' in the political arena. As we know, this category of 'people' is polysemous and disputed by the nationalist right and the internationalist left. The RN has an ethno-racial conception of 'the people' (hence it means the French people in a restrictive and exclusivist sense, in which 'French' always ultimately refers to the 'true French' or those of 'French stock', now generally extended to 'native Europeans' to include the descendants of European immigrants). The left remains attached to a class meaning: 'the people' is the popular or working classes, over and above any national, ethno-racial, religious and other divides. In the lexicon of the far right, the people thus refers to Maurras's 'real country', in other words the whole of the 'Nation' once the enemies (those who are foreign to the nation, not just in a formal and legal sense) and traitors (both the 'globalist' elites and the 'immigrationist' left) have been taken away. But Marine Le Pen has shown herself to be particularly adept over the last ten years at alternating between one register and the other: the RN presents itself as the representative of the 'people' in an ethno-racial sense (which involves using dog whistles sufficiently implicit to comply with the de-demonisation strategy) but also in a class sense (the party of the 'little people', 'people without station' and so on), a line that the FN took up from the 1990s.[37] From this point of view, we would more accurately discuss this party in terms of 'social nativism' than those of 'populism', 'national populism' or 'right-wing populism'. For these categories underestimate the centrality of the ethno-racial opposition between a community of 'natives' (openly asserting their homogeneity in terms of culture or identity, but often also at a pseudo-biological level) and minority groups considered fundamentally alien to the national body because they are immigrants or immigrants' descendants (particularly from outside Europe), whether or not they are French nationals.

Turning to election results, it is true that the FN/RN has seen a significant increase in its scores among blue-collar workers (its results are also high, if not quite as strong, among white-collar workers) over the last few decades:

---

37 It is worth remembering Jean-Marie Le Pen's speech on the night of the first round of the 2002 presidential election:

> Don't be afraid, dear compatriots. Return to hope . . . Don't be afraid to dream, you small people, the downtrodden, the excluded. Don't let yourselves be trapped in the old divisions of left and right . . . You, the miners, the steelworkers, the workers in all those industries ruined by Maastricht's Euro-globalisation. You, the farmers with the meagre pensions, driven to ruin and extinction.

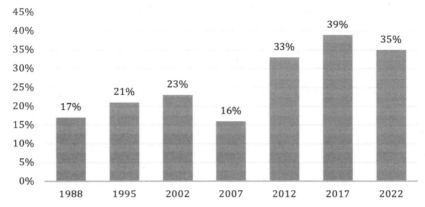

Data: CEVIPOF/IFOP.

Here, we see two phases: the first, during which the FN conquered a blue-collar electorate and ranged between 15 and 25 percent support in this category; and a second phase, after Marine Le Pen became party leader in 2011, during which the FN has consistently achieved 30 percent–plus of this vote. It should also be pointed out that, in order to accurately measure the far right's overall electoral reach, we need to add the scores of Debout la France and, for 2022, the vote for Reconquête: the far right would then stand at 35 percent among blue-collar voters in 2012, 42 percent in 2017 and 44 percent in 2022. To complete this picture, we should also note the high scores obtained by the far right among low-ranking public employees (category C), with 37 percent support compared with 27 percent for the left. Indeed, the left surpasses the far right only among those public employees (a group that is one of its historical bases) in the middle (B) and upper (A) categories, respectively outmatching the far right by 39 to 29 percent and by 43 to 20 percent. Inside the public sector, the far right is doing extremely well among police and soldiers: 47 percent in the first round of the 2022 presidential election and 53 percent in the first round of the snap parliamentary elections in 2024 (compared with 16 percent and 8 percent for the left in these same votes).[38]

It is possible that a third phase has begun, with the FN/RN making further gains among the blue-collar electorate between 2022 and 2024.

---

38   These data on the civil servant vote are taken from two research notes by Luc Rouban: 'Le vote des fonctionnaires à l'élection présidentielles de 2022', Vagues 13 et 13bis, Sciences Po Paris, 2022; and 'Le vote des fonctionnaires aux élections de 2024 ou la fin de la gauche d' État', Sciences Po - CEVIPOF; CNRS - INSH, 2024.

In the European elections in June 2024, Le Pen's party won 49 percent of the blue-collar vote (and a further 6 percent went to Reconquête), which puts the far right at a total 55 percent among those blue-collar voters who cast a ballot. The FN/RN had in fact already won 46 percent support among this electorate in the 2014 European elections, and 47 percent in 2019. The most striking point is the score for Marine Le Pen's party among blue-collar workers in the snap elections in July 2024: 51 percent (compared with 36 in the 2022 parliamentary elections, in which Reconquête garnered a further 5 percent). This amounts to an increase of ten points for the far right between the parliamentary elections of 2022 and those of 2024, even though abstention fell sharply (from 63 to 45 percent among blue-collar workers).

So, it would be absurd to deny that there is a strong and growing blue-collar – and more broadly working-class – vote for the far right in France. Nevertheless, it is important to add at least four further considerations. Firstly, the real electoral strength of the FN/RN among the working classes is systematically overestimated by failing to take into account the crucial influence of differential abstention. While, up until the early 1980s, there were no significant differences in the propensity to abstain between social classes in France – or in most European countries in general[39] – the working classes now refrain from voting significantly more than their better-off counterparts (and are also more likely not to be registered to vote).[40] In the 2022 elections, only 31.1 percent of unskilled workers and 35.4 percent of skilled workers over the age of twenty-five voted in all rounds (first and second rounds of the presidential and parliamentary elections), compared with 49.9 percent of managers and

---

39 This highlights the fact that, contrary to a miserabilistic account that essentialises (and eternalises) the distance between the working classes and the political arena, what is at issue is less the intrinsic 'political incompetence' of these classes than the absence of any suitable political expression – or more precisely, the decline of the Left (especially the Communists but also the Socialists) among the working classes. On these issues, see the important study by Guy Michelat and Michel Simon: *Les ouvriers et la politique. Permanence, ruptures, réalignements*, Paris: Presses de Sciences Po, 2004. See also Florent Gougou, 'La droitisation du vote des ouvriers en France. Désalignement, réalignement et renouvellement des générations', in Jean-Michel De Waele and Mathieu Vieira (eds), *Une droitisation de la classe ouvrière en Europe?* Paris: Economica, 2011. More generally, on issues of electoral participation, see Peter Mair, 'Ruling the Void', *New Left Review*, 2006, no. 42.

40 To take the level of qualification as an indicator: in 2018, according to INSEE, 23.5 percent of people with no qualifications were not registered to vote, compared with 7.6 percent of people with higher education qualifications. To this should be added what is known as 'misregistration', that is, not being registered in the municipality of one's main residence, which particularly affects young people (37.8 percent of 18–25 year olds compared with 5.5 percent of 70–74 year olds).

Abstention and far-right voting among blue-collar and white-collar workers in the European elections (2014 and 2019), in the first round of presidential elections (2017 and 2022) and in the first round of the snap elections to the National Assembly in 2024 (as percentage of registered voters)

		2014 EU election	2017 presidential election	2019 EU election	2022 presidential election	2024 EU election	2024 National Assembly election
Blue-collar	Abstention	62	24	56	29	53	45
	Far-right	17.5	32	20.5	31	26	28
White-collar	Abstention	67	24	58	25	53	38
	Far-right	13	26.5	16	30	20.5	27

Data: IFOP surveys / exit polls.

upper-ranking intellectual professionals. If we want an accurate picture of the FN/RN's reach among the working classes, we therefore need to think not only about the votes actually cast, but about all potential voters (although, unfortunately, we cannot here cover the question of unregistered or mis-registered voters, for lack of adequate data). We can see that in all so-called intermediate contests (at the regional, European, municipal and *département* levels), withdrawal from the electoral process – in the form of one-off or long-term abstention, or even non-registration – is the main party of the working classes. In presidential elections, the preference to abstain is never all that far from the propensity to vote for the far right.[41]

This counting of the vast mass of abstentionists, which represent a particularly large share of the working classes, should not be used for the purposes of self-consolation. We clearly should not ignore the decline of the left (as a whole) among the working classes since the 1980s, and the difficulties that it has encountered in rebuilding in any lasting way. We have to take seriously the fact that a large and growing proportion of the blue- and white-collar voters who do turn out at election time are voting for the FN/RN, and that the far right does not lose out when abstention is relatively lower, notably in presidential elections. It may even benefit from a rebound in turnout, as was the case in the snap parliamentary elections in summer 2024.

---

41 On this point, see Patrick Lehingue, 'L'électorat du Front national', in Gérard Mauger and Willy Pelletier (eds), *Les classes populaires et le FN*, Bellecombe-en-Bauges: Le Croquant, 2016. This proportion would in fact be slightly lower if we also included foreign workers in the blue-collar group. Indeed, there are far more non-French citizens in this socio-occupational category than in the managerial category, and they do not have the right to vote in national elections (and do not have the right to vote in any elections if they are not some kind of EU citizens).

What's more, not only did the FN/RN vote increase significantly among blue-collar workers (and white-collar workers) over the 2010s, but it accentuated even the FN/RN's relative strength among blue-collar workers compared with more privileged socio-occupational categories (particularly managers). In short, the increase in the FN/RN vote among blue-collar workers is not simply following the curve of its increase in the population as a whole but has far exceeded it: the FN's extra strength among blue-collar workers (compared with the population as a whole) rose from 3 points in 1988 to 12.6 points in 2012, and some 17.5 points in 2017. This is a major development, part of the 'electoral realignment' beginning in the 1984–6 period, when the right, and even more so the far right, made powerful gains among working-class voters.[42] Nevertheless, even if there is nothing to indicate that abstainers are immune to the far-right vote – or still less so the 'ideas' for which it stands – recent studies have shown that the left united in the Nouveau Front Populaire had 'a non-negligible electoral potential' among abstainers, including 'as compared to the RN'.[43] There is a quite simple reason for this: the tendency to abstain is higher among parts of the population that tend to favour the left, namely young people and the poorest parts of the working classes.

This brings us to a second point. It is important to enrich the class analysis of the vote for the far right using the indicator of income (rather than that of occupational category). This allows us to take greater account of underemployment but also of the differentiations within the working classes themselves (between skilled workers, who have a stable contract and have been able to progress in their careers, and unskilled workers, who are insecure and at the bottom of the scale, particularly in terms of wages). It is thus striking that, while the far right (adding up the scores for the RN, Reconquête and Debout la France) was far ahead of the left among blue-collar workers in the 2022 presidential election (by 44 to 33 percent), the left enjoyed a strong lead among those on the lowest incomes (under €900 a month): 48 percent compared with 32 percent for the far right.[44] The same was true of the parliamentary elections that

---

42 On this process, see Michelat and Simon, *Les ouvriers et la politique*. See also: Florent Gougou, 'Les ouvriers et le Front national. Les logiques d'un réalignement électoral', in Crépon, Dézé and Mayer (eds), *Les faux-semblants du Front national*. The figures quoted above are taken from this article (except for 2017, which I added using IFOP data).

43 See Tristan Haute, 'Élargir les bases socio-électorales de la gauche: nécessités, difficultés et incertitudes', *Contretemps*, 9 October 2024, contretemps.eu.

44 It should be noted that the forces further left than the Socialists and the Greens

followed in June 2022: for this same income bracket, the left outstripped the far right (35 percent of votes against 31 percent), but it was also ahead among the €900–€1,300/month and €1,300–€1,900/month income brackets. Jean-Luc Mélenchon's particularly high score among the lowest income groups in the 2022 presidential race and the 13-percentage-point drop for the left-wing vote between the presidential and parliamentary contests no doubt provide arguments for the idea that there are reserves of votes for the left among the most precarious sectors of the population, in which young people, women and people from ethno-racial minorities are over-represented.

Furthermore, the RN's electoral base cannot be considered as a bloc, and still less so as a popular bloc united by a charismatic leader. It is much more a 'conglomerate'[45] of different electorates than one homogeneous force mobilised around a unifying programme. The RN scores well not only among blue-collar and white-collar workers, but also among managers (see above) and, above all, among the petty bourgeoisie (the self-employed and small business owners). In the 2022 presidential election, 36 percent of tradespeople and shopkeepers voted for the far right (in addition to 9 percent for Valérie Pécresse, the conservative LR candidate who ran a particularly right-wing campaign). In 2024, during the European elections, 46 percent of artisans and tradespeople voted for the RN or Reconquête: hence, more than the far-right vote among white-collar employees. Added to this is the fact that these groups have systematically higher turnout than blue-collar workers: as a percentage of registered voters, the RN's vote among artisans and tradespeople is thus close to its absolute number of blue-collar votes. What limited the far-right vote in the snap parliamentary elections in summer 2024 was the fact that these groups – perhaps more worried about the instability that could have resulted from the FN/RN coming to power – turned more to the right-wing parties (Renaissance and LR), which they had largely rejected in the European elections a few weeks earlier, when they had favoured the RN. The profile of this electorate is therefore clearly right wing, with an increasingly marked tendency towards the far right.[46]

---

received some 39 percent of the votes of people on under €900 a month (with 34 percent for Jean-Luc Mélenchon alone).

45 See Daniel Gaxie, 'Front national: les contradictions d'une résistible ascension', in Mauger and Pelletier (eds), *Les classes populaires et le FN*.

46 These social roots go back a long way and preceded the FN's breakthrough among the working classes. The FN's first breakthrough, between 1984 and 1988, corresponded to a crisis on the right and a political radicalisation of the traditional middle classes (particularly the less wealthy parts of the self-employed) as well as the

From a gender perspective, there is an undeniable trend towards the feminisation of the RN electorate, with the end of the previous gender differential (although a significant gender gap has appeared in Zemmour's wing of the far right).[47] As can be seen in the following graph, this differential remained stable between 1988 and 2002 in the FN/RN's first phase of development – with the male vote for this party around 6 or 7 points higher – before gradually disappearing in the 2010s. Recent studies also show an interaction between gender and class, as well as between gender and age, with the FN/RN particularly gaining ground in the 2010s among working-class women (commercial and blue-collar women workers), as well as young women.[48] The fact that the list led by Jordan Bardella for the European elections in June 2024 also did slightly better among women than men also shows that this trend cannot be reduced to the individual role of Marine Le Pen – although it is also notable that in the following month's snap parliamentary elections, a significant gender gap of 4 points re-emerged (35 percent for the RN among men compared with 31 percent among women). This perhaps suggests that women were more sensitive to a campaign that highlighted the mortal danger posed by the far right, particularly to women's rights.

In terms of age, there has been a lot of media chatter in recent years about the rise of the RN, and the far right in general, among young people. It is true that eighteen- to twenty-four-year-olds now vote more for the FN/RN than they did in the past: 26 percent in the first round of the snap parliamentary elections in 2024, compared with 16 percent in the first round of the presidential election back in 2012. However, this increase needs to be qualified in light of several other important facts.

---

more conservative parts of the bourgeoisie. In the context of the left's return to power, these class fractions were sometimes attracted by the anti-communism and Reaganism vaunted by Jean-Marie Le Pen. In the 1988 presidential election, 27 percent of industrial and commercial bosses voted for Le Pen (as compared with 19 percent of blue-collar workers and 14.4 percent of the overall vote). The FN's rhetoric did all it could to appeal to these groups, including its claim to be the only full-throated right-wing party, and its visceral criticism of May 1968 and its alleged consequences (moral and educational 'laxity', and so on). See in particular: Alain Bihr, *Le Spectre de l'extrême droite. Les Français dans le miroir du Front national*, Paris: Editions de l'Atelier, 1988, pp. 57–64; Nonna Mayer, 'De Passy à Barbes: deux visages du vote Le Pen à Paris', *Revue française de sociologie*, 1987, vol. 37, no. 6.

47 For a detailed analysis, see Abdelkarim Amengay, Anja Durovic and Nonna Mayer, 'L'impact du genre sur le vote Marine Le Pen', *Revue française de science politique*, 2017, vol. 67, no. 6.

48 Anja Durovic and Nonna Mayer 'Un vent de renouveau? La recomposition des gender gaps électoraux à l'élection présidentielle française de 2022', *Revue française de science politique*, 2022, vol. 72, no. 4.

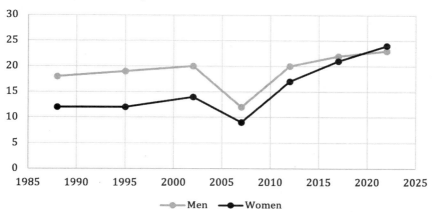

Data: CEVIPOF (1988–2007) then IFOP (2012–22).

First of all, the youngest categories of voters are also – by far – the ones who abstain the most: 41 percent of eighteen- to twenty-four-year-olds abstained in the first round of the 2022 presidential election, whereas abstention was between 22 and 27 percent in all other age brackets. There was a mighty 34-point turnout gap between the eighteen to twenty-four age group and those aged sixty-five and over at the June 2024 European elections. Secondly, young people have been voting for the far right for a long time, contrary to the popular belief that young people used to be allergic to Jean-Marie Le Pen's FN, and that their electoral support for the far right exploded in the 2010s. In fact, as early as 1988, the far right scored 14 percent of the vote among eighteen- to twenty-four-year-olds, and, by 1995, it had risen to 18 percent, stabilising at 17 percent in 2002.[49] The far right's vote share in this age group increased between 2012 and 2017 (from 16 percent to 27 percent), but has stagnated since then.

In addition, the most striking fact since 2017 is not the far right's growing reach among young people, but the gap between the eighteen to twenty-four age bracket and older ones (with the exception of those aged sixty-five and over, who continue to vote more for the right than for the far right). Twenty-five- to thirty-four-year-olds, who voted for the far right less than eighteen- to twenty-four-year-olds did in 2017, stand out in 2024 with a 7 percent higher RN vote. If, in 2017, the FN/RN score among thirty-five- to forty-nine-year-olds was 4 percent

---

49 See Nonna Mayer, 'Les hauts et les bas du vote Le Pen 2002', *Revue française de science politique*, 2002, vol. 52, no. 5.

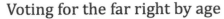

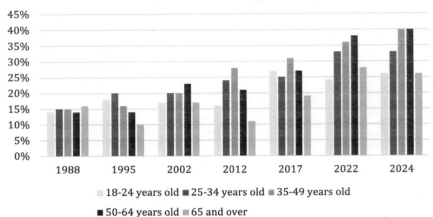

Data: CEVIPOF surveys (for 1988, 1995 and 2002) then IFOP exit polls. For 2002, 2017 and 2022, these numbers refer to the first round of the presidential election only, and for 2024 to the first round of the snap parliamentary election. The far right includes votes for Marine Le Pen, Nicolas Dupont-Aignan and (in 2022 and 2024) for Éric Zemmour and his Reconquête party.

higher than among eighteen- to twenty-four-year-olds, by 2024 this figure was 14 percent. Meanwhile fifty- to sixty-four-year-olds – who voted for the FN/RN at a similar level to eighteen- to twenty-four-year-olds in 2017 – in 2024, expressed fourteen points higher support for this party than did these youngest of voters. Finally, it is worth noting that the growth of the radical left is much more marked among eighteen- to twenty-four-year-olds and twenty-five- to thirty-four-year-olds than rising scores for the far right: the vote for parties to the left of the Socialist Party and the Greens rose from 19 percent in 2012 (12 percent among twenty-five- to thirty-four-year-olds) to 31 percent in 2017 (26 percent among twenty-five- to thirty-four-year-olds) and 39 percent in 2022 (33 percent among twenty-five- to thirty-four-year-olds). In the first round of the 2024 snap parliamentary contest, the left came out clearly ahead in these two age categories: 43 percent among eighteen- to twenty-four-year-olds and 42 percent among twenty-five- to thirty-four-year-olds (compared with 26 percent and 33 percent respectively for the far right).

It is also important to look at the FN/RN's electoral base in terms of its territorial presence, which can be captured statistically in two ways: either in terms of differentiation according to the type of locality (from rural villages to the Paris conurbation, via various small and medium-sized towns); or according to *département* or region (insofar as there are generally significant continuities over time).

Taking this first line of approach, there has been a clear increase in the far-right vote in rural areas over the last thirty years: 34 percent in 2022 compared with 25 percent in 2012, 23 percent in 2002, 14 percent in 1995 and 12 percent in 1988. This is the opposite disparity compared to an earlier FN/RN electorate, which was more urban (scoring 20 percent in municipalities with more than 200,000 inhabitants in 1988, compared with 12 percent in rural ones). Today, the more people live in big cities (particularly the Paris metropolitan area), the less they vote for the far right. In the first round of snap parliamentary elections in 2024, the FN/RN scored 18 percent in the Paris conurbation (and much less in inner Paris, particularly in the less bourgeois *arrondissements* of the north and east of the city, where it was below 10 percent), compared with 35 percent in provincial urban municipalities and 41 percent in rural ones. It should be added that, in 2022, in the first round of the presidential election, the score of the far right as a whole was particularly high in small towns (between 2,000 and 20,000 inhabitants): some 39 percent, higher than its score in rural villages (34 percent).

In terms of its electoral geography, the far right has gained a massive following in a considerable number of *départements*, particularly those around the Mediterranean (from the Alpes-Maritimes to the Pyrénées-Orientales), but also in the north and east of France (particularly the Aisne, Pas-de-Calais, Moselle, Ardennes and Haute-Marne). It is true that it was in these same areas that the FN achieved its best results in 2002 (between 20 and 30 percent). But the party made an especially strong breakthrough there between 2012 and 2024, competing with the right and then supplanting it, and recently achieving results of between 45 and 55 percent in the European elections of June 2024 in these *départements*. In addition, the far right was able to increase its audience in geographical areas where the FN had historically been weak, particularly in the *départements* from Bretagne to the south-west of France – rising between 2002 and 2024 from 12.8 to 32.5 percent in Côtes-d'Armor, from 11.6 to 35.8 percent in Landes and from 14.2 to 40 percent in Dordogne – but also in départements in the centre of the country, with some particularly impressive increases: from 15.9 to 42 percent in Allier, and from 18 to 43.7 percent in Cher.[50]

---

50 To find out more about the FN's territorial roots, see in particular: Joël Gombin, 'Le changement dans la continuité. Géographies électorales du Front national depuis 1992', in Crépon, Dézé and Mayer (eds), *Les faux-semblants du Front national*. For an analysis of the joint effects of social and territorial dynamics, see in particular: Antoine Jardin, 'Le vote intermittent. Comment les ségrégations urbaines influencent-elles les comportements électoraux en Ile-de-France', *L'Espace politique*, 2014, vol. 2, no. 23.

To conclude this overview of the far-right electorate, it is important to say a few words about its ethno-racial and religious dimensions. The blindness to race that is so characteristic of French republican ideology means that this factor is studied very little in political science research in France. Even such an important dynamic as the electoral behaviour of the descendants of immigrants is very rarely considered as such (and never by pollsters). It is rarely pointed out, or only mentioned in passing, that FN/RN voters – and even right-wing voters – are overwhelmingly white (or recognised as white, to use a more sociologically precise formulation). It is likewise little mentioned that people identified as non-white vote very little for the right, or still less the far right. The few studies on this issue have shown that the descendants of people born in France's overseas territories[51] and of non-European immigrants, who make up a large proportion of racialised minorities, place themselves much less to the right of the political spectrum than the rest of the population.[52] Indeed, less than 10 percent – and just 2 percent of the descendants of immigrants from the Sahel – identify as right wing, compared with 30 to 48 percent as left wing (depending on their precise origin), and 30 to 40 percent 'neither right nor left-wing'.[53] A quantitative survey conducted during the 2017 presidential election in two urban working-class areas in the Paris suburbs and the north of France also showed that ethno-racial characteristics are one of the main factors in the differentiation of votes within the working classes (if not the main one), particularly in the

---

51 We are talking here about people from overseas France living in mainland France. The situation is much more complex to interpret in several overseas territories where Jean-Luc Mélenchon came out well ahead in the first round (56 percent in Guadeloupe, 53 percent in Martinique, 51 percent in French Guiana) but where Marine Le Pen scored very well in the second round against Emmanuel Macron (70 percent in Guadeloupe, 61 percent in Martinique and 61 percent in French Guiana). On the interpretation of the far-right vote in the French West Indies during the 2022 presidential election, see Silyane Larcher, 'La tentation du fascisme en postcolonie? Sur la victoire de Le Pen aux Antilles', *AOC*, 27 May 2022, aoc.media.

52 See Patrick Simon and Vincent Tiberj, 'La fabrique du citoyen. Origine et rapport au politique en France', INED, Working Papers, 2012, no. 175. These results confirm an earlier study by Sylvain Brouard and Vincent Tiberj: *Français comme les autres? Enquête sur les citoyens d'origine maghrébine, africaine et turque*, Paris: Presses de SciencesPo, 2005.

53 Conversely, the descendants of immigrants from Asia and southern Europe appear to have similar left/right positions to the majority population, which no doubt reflects the specific representations surrounding these groups and in particular the way in which some political forces (including the far right), the media and the cultural industries have tended to construct them as 'model minorities'. On the case of immigrants and descendants of immigrants of Asian origin in France, see Ya-Han. Chuang, *Une minorité modèle? Chinois de France et racisme anti-Asiatiques*, Paris: La Découverte, 2021.

division of votes between the anti-neoliberal left (Jean-Luc Mélenchon) and the far right (Marine Le Pen). If we add up the results in the two municipalities, descendants of North African immigrants and people of sub-Saharan African origin voted 54 percent and 35 percent respectively for Mélenchon, compared with 2 percent each for Marine Le Pen. Conversely, 29 percent of people with no migrant background voted for Mélenchon, compared with 16 percent for Le Pen.[54] Here, the descendants of immigrants from Asia and southern Europe (Spain and Portugal) were at an intermediate level, voting as much for the anti-neoliberal left as the children of sub-Saharan immigrants, but more than them in favour of the various right-wing parties. From the point of view of religion, the most recent period has seen the far right breaking through among practising Catholics. Historically, until 2017, this part of the electorate voted overwhelmingly in favour of the traditional right, with the result that the far right scored lower among practising Catholics than among people who identified as Catholics but who were non-practising. In 2022, if we add together the results of Marine Le Pen, Eric Zemmour and Nicolas Dupont-Aignan, it appears that 40 percent of Catholics who said they regularly practised their religion voted for the far right, compared with just 14 percent in 2017, with Le Pen alone rising from 12 percent to 21 percent among this electorate, and from 18 to 26 percent among occasional churchgoers. Conversely, the far right's vote declined among Protestants (from 27 to 22 percent) and stabilised at a very low level among Muslims (9 percent in 2022 compared with 8 percent), while the anti-neoliberal left made strong gains (71 percent among Muslims in 2022 compared with 39 percent in 2017). Finally, it should be noted that among people declaring no religious belief (a growing population), the far right is in slight decline (25 percent in 2022 compared with 27 percent in 2017), while the anti-neoliberal left is on the rise (from 30 to 36 percent over this same period).

Class Vote or Racist Vote?

How did the FN/RN develop its social roots and, in particular, what role do identity and socio-economic issues play in its electoral success? Does the far-right vote mainly express racism and xenophobia, a feeling of abandonment, or a form of social grievances? This also raises the

---

54 See also Collectif Focale, *Votes populaires*, Bellecombe: Le Croquant, 2022, p. 135. It should be noted that, in their book, the authors note the strong under-reporting of the FN vote in their sample, interviewed face-to-face at the exit polls.

following question: how has a party whose leadership is almost exclusively made up of members of the privileged classes (as we will come back to later), and whose main figure – Marine Le Pen – is herself an heiress from the bourgeoisie of western Paris, been able to gain significant and lasting support well beyond these classes, particularly among the working classes?

Let us start by saying that voting for the FN/RN and the far right more broadly is neither a vote by default or out of pique – as Thomas Piketty and Julia Cagé erroneously assert – nor a simple protest vote or reactive choice of the moment as it has long been portrayed. If this electorate used to be especially volatile, since 2012 this has become much less the case,[55] to the point that the RN now certainly has the most robust electorate of any party. Today, it is voters for other parties who appear less firmly attached to the organisations or personalities they vote for. Not only is a majority of the RN electorate no longer voting for the party only sporadically, but doing so repeatedly and consistently (and, in some cases, systematically), or else essentially choosing between this party and abstention. Moreover, these are also the voters who make up their minds the earliest in the campaigns. Their behaviour has thus gradually turned from a kind of sceptical interest in FN/RN discourse, of the type of which Richard Hoggart spoke when discussing the relationship of the working classes to the dominant ideology and mass culture,[56] to a more open assent and even a strong attachment – to the RN and its main leaders, but also to some of its slogans (in particular 'the French first'). The fact that most of the party's voters are unfamiliar with its manifesto commitments, or even know nothing about them, makes little difference. On the contrary, we might even argue that this underlines the trust they place in this party – at least enough to vote for it, sometimes consistently – without needing to examine its policies. We should not confuse the party ideology – to which people may adhere (however weakly or ardently) without necessarily being able to outline what it is – with the electoral manifesto, which is generally known only to a small minority of voters.

In their book on electoral behaviour in France over more than two centuries, Julia Cagé and Thomas Piketty put forward the thesis that the RN vote today is essentially a class vote, unlike in the 1980s and 1990s

---

55 See Patrick Lehingue, 'L'objectivation statistique des électorats: Que savons-nous des électeurs du Front national?', in Jacques Lagroye (ed.), *La Politisation*, Paris: Belin, 2003.

56 See Richard Hoggart, *The Uses of Literacy: Aspects of Working-Class Life*, London: Chatto and Windus, 1957.

when the FN vote was primarily an identitarian-racist vote. This vote is said to express a feeling of abandonment among the rural working classes, and their anger at worsening public services in the areas furthest from the major urban centres. In fact, these authors' interpretation goes far beyond what their empirical material justifies: the data they have is about the socio-demographic composition of voters' municipalities of residence, but offers no information on the 'causes' or 'motivations' behind their electoral behaviour, let alone their ideological positions. As a result, Cagé and Piketty must deduce the meaning of the far-right vote – and what it means for the voters themselves – from the socio-demographic composition of the areas in which they live (indeed, without even knowing precisely which segments of the electorate in each of these municipalities are voting most for the far right).

They add two further arguments in support of their assertion, though neither is convincing. First of all, they tell us that, unlike in the 1980s and 1990s, today's RN voters no longer live in areas with a high proportion of immigrants. This assertion is essentially correct, but to say that this belies the idea of an anti-immigrant vote suggests that xenophobia can only be generated by spatial proximity to immigrants (or even that xenophobia arises almost naturally from living with immigrants in the same neighbourhood or town). This idea is, moreover, refuted by the Zemmour vote in wealthy areas, particularly in the well-heeled districts of western Paris, where immigrants are largely absent as residents. Another argument put forward by Cagé and Piketty runs as follows: if this vote for the RN were specifically or mainly racist, then surely these voters would have swung over to Zemmour, whose campaign in 2022 had an even more explicitly identitarian – and particularly Islamophobic – profile than did Le Pen's?

On this last point, it should be remembered that the RN and Reconquête programmes on immigration and Islam were virtually identical in 2022 (see above). But, above all, surveys of people's ideological positions (or 'values') show that those who say they are close to the RN are, in fact, quite ready to describe themselves as 'racist' and, from this point of view, are very close to Zemmour's voters (and much closer to his following in this respect than the electorates of other parties are). In a survey carried out by the National Consultative Council for Human Rights (CNCDH) in 2023, some 54 percent of RN voters said they were 'a little' or 'very racist').[57] This was far higher than the levels for sympathisers of other

---

57   While this percentage is down on the 2014 survey (when it stood at 82 percent), it is difficult to say whether this is due to survey bias and, in particular, whether in a society where explicit racism is increasingly frowned upon, the cost of calling oneself

parties, including LR (26 percent of whom said the same). The specific nature of the RN electorate can also be gauged from the fact that 'only' 23 percent of blue-collar workers in general declared themselves to be 'a little' or 'very racist'.

Furthermore, when voters themselves are asked why they voted for a particular candidate (what pollsters call the 'determinants' of voter behaviour), the issues of immigration, insecurity and terrorism counted most among RN voters.[58] True, in 2022, these numbers were even higher among Éric Zemmour's electorate. And yet, contrary to what Cagé and Piketty assert, these are, in fact, quite similar electorates in this regard, each distant from the Macronist electorate (at least in terms of these self-reported motives for voting), and even more so from the electorate of Jean-Luc Mélenchon and the left more broadly.

So, we should avoid a form of patronising paternalism towards FN/RN voters that leads to the assumption that they know neither what they are doing when they vote for this party nor what they are saying when they say they vote for it because of their concerns about immigration. It simply must be acknowledged that these reasons, and more generally xenophobia and racism (judging by the CNCDH survey in particular) remain central to far-right voting.

A slightly more subtle way of minimising these dimensions is to recognise that they are indeed present, but that they coexist with other determinants, which these researchers often consider more significant: issues of income and the cost of living, insecurity, or abandonment by the authorities. However, what the qualitative surveys of FN/RN voters[59]

---

racist has increased (in other words, if this data expresses a tendency towards self-censorship). For example, in 2014, only 39 percent of people said they were 'not racist at all', compared with 59 percent in 2023. Does this reflect an increase in anti-racism or an increase in the cost associated with publicly declaring oneself a racist? Another illustration of the potential power of these biases: in a survey conducted by Luc Rouban in 2023, a few months after the CNCDH survey, but this time online, 62 percent of respondents said that Muslims were a 'group apart in society', compared with 31.5 percent of respondents to the CNCDH survey, which was carried out face-to-face. See Luc Rouban, *Les ressorts cachés du vote RN*, Paris: Presses de Sciences Po, 2024, p. 31.

58 In all likelihood, the issue 'the fight against terrorism' captures a large proportion of hostile attitudes towards Islam and Muslims. After all, media and political Islamophobia systematically associates terrorism with Islam, while underplaying the far-right terrorism which has made such great strides internationally over the last fifteen years.

59 Read Félicien Faury's recent book, the result of an immersive study of an area of southern France with a strong far-right vote. It includes repeated interviews with FN/RN voters. *Des électeurs ordinaires. Enquête sur la normalisation de l'extrême droite*, Paris: Seuil, 2024. See also, for a series of contributions from recent surveys: Safia Dahani, Estelle Delaine, Félicien Faury and Guillaume Letourneur (eds), *Sociologie politique du Rassemblement national. Enquêtes de terrain*, Lille: Presses du Septentrion, 2023.

Determinants of voter behaviour in the first rounds of the 2017 and 2022 presidential elections and in the 2024 European elections

	Presidential elections 2017			Presidential elections 2022			2024 EU election		
	Mélenchon	Macron	Le Pen	Mélenchon	Macron	Le Pen	France insoumise	Renaissance	RN
The fight against unemployment	**71%**	**69%**	69%	57%	49%	51%	55%	34%	**47%**
The fight against terrorism	43%	54%	**93%**	35%	**56%**	76%	43%	**66%**	80%
Health	69%	**59%**	62%	**75%**	**71%**	71%	**73%**	**63%**	69%
Education	63%	**62%**	57%	67%	**56%**	55%	**72%**	51%	56%
Raising wages and purchasing power	**76%**	51%	66%	**81%**	55%	**80%**	**75%**	39%	**70%**
The fight against crime	35%	40%	**85%**	41%	52%	**83%**	43%	58%	**88%**
The fight against precarity	**70%**	46%	55%	**73%**	42%	56%	/	/	/
Controlling tax levels	47%	48%	55%	51%	53%	59%	45%	34%	56%
Fighting illegal immigration	25%	26%	**92%**	21%	31%	**79%**	26%	42%	**89%**
The climate around political and judicial affairs	53%	53%	36%	/	/	/	/	/	/
Safeguarding public services	64%	40%	45%	60%	37%	48%	59%	42%	51%
European integration	/	/	/	/	/	/	38%	**69%**	33%
Environmental protection	63%	33%	29%	64%	42%	34%	62%	49%	32%
Reducing public debt	29%	45%	46%	29%	32%	40%	37%	36%	51%
The war in Ukraine	/	/	/	28%	55%	29%	32%	58%	27%
The fight against racism and discrimination	/	/	/	/	/	/	69%	41%	34%
The Israeli-Palestinian conflict	/	/	/	/	/	/	56%	26%	19%

Data: IFOP. The top three concerns of each electorate are shown in bold. Where data is missing, it is because the issue concerned was not mentioned in the survey following a particular election.

clearly show is that these 'determinants' do not exist side by side, as if merely piled one on top of the other. Rather, they are interwoven, with racism and xenophobia generally binding them together. And, even if this is not always entirely coherent – most ordinary voters are not ideologues who vote according to a systematic doctrine, and may draw on different and competing ways of reading social reality – most issues tend to be seen through a nativist prism. For example, it is striking to note how far the perceived level of insecurity – and therefore of concern about crime, which favours the FN/RN vote – is statistically linked with attitudes towards immigration: the more a voter is 'concerned' about immigration, the more they tend to feel insecure (and this statistical correlation is particularly strong in France): 57 percent of individuals 'concerned' about immigration feel insecure, compared with 25 percent of those who are not concerned about immigration.[60] The same applies to the cost of living: if we follow the sociologist Félicien Faury, we can see that demands in terms of income, the cost of living and spending power are not generally associated, in the discourse of FN/RN voters, with a criticism of social inequalities or, for example, with a call to increase taxes on the rich and corporate profits. Rather, they are associated with the demand to pay less tax and a criticism of public spending considered to unfairly favour immigrants (State Medical Aid, benefits for refugees and so on).

It is therefore strange that the racist dimension of the FN/RN's project and this part of its appeal often tends to be denied or played down. It has sometimes been claimed that using racism and xenophobia to interpret the FN/RN vote would serve no other purpose than to point an accusing finger at the working classes, thereby masking the 'social' causes of the FN/RN vote (which also means assuming, incidentally, that racism is not itself a *social* phenomenon). The denunciation of the FN/RN's racism and that of (most of) its voters is thus said to function in the public arena as a denunciation of the working classes, expressing a form of class contempt that is all the more pernicious because it is disguised as a false or at least superficial solidarity with immigrants and minorities.[61]

---

60 See the graph presented by Luc Rouban in his *Les ressorts cachés du vote RN*, Paris: Presses de Sciences Po, 2024, p. 79. In this book he devotes a great deal of energy to trying to refute the idea that xenophobia and racism are at the heart of the far-right vote, often in contradiction with his own data.

61 This is the argument put forward by Gérard Mauger and Willy Pelletier, based on an earlier article by Claude Grignon (whose main target was the work of Pierre-André Taguieff), when they write:

Yet there is nothing contradictory about pointing out the class contempt that permeates much of the discourse on the FN/RN electorate, while, at the same time, acknowledging the influence of xenophobia and racism on the electoral behaviour of those who do repeatedly vote for this party. As we said earlier, numerous studies – both old and recent, quantitative and ethnographic[62] – show that xenophobia and racism are at the heart of the perception of the social world and politics that distinguishes FN/RN voters. These are indeed central reasons for voting for the far right, whether it is by members of the working classes or individuals from other backgrounds, and whether these motives are captured through surveys or interviews. Moreover, to claim that the FN/RN vote can be explained solely and without mediation in terms of living conditions (the famous 'social causes' of its support)[63] would inevitably justify the (false) assertion that it is exclusively or almost only the most impoverished and precarious voters who support the FN/RN. In that case, we could never understand the logic that leads *some* members of the working classes to give their vote to the far right when *many others* – indeed, the majority – are not drawn in by its sirens. We would likewise be at a loss to pin down the growing vote for the FN/RN among better-off categories; unless, that is, we assert that racism explains the far-right vote only in the case of voters belonging to the affluent classes (which the surveys deny), for example Éric Zemmour's supporters, whereas the rest of its electorate is driven by so-called 'social' reasons (cost of living, feelings of abandonment and so on).

So, it is quite legitimate to highlight the causes of the growth of the far right – in particular, the rise in competition on the labour market,

---

All these studies show the dead ends which 'anti-FN' activists run into . . . [they are] ever-ready to denounce discrimination and racism at any opportunity and sometimes out of place . . . and associate, in complete ignorance of the facts, their hatred of 'narrow-minded, racist proles' with the unconditional defence of 'immigrants', systematically identified, if not with the vanguard of the international proletariat, at least with exemplary victims. Thus, they work, more surely than to combat racism, to assert its distinctive distance from common sense and the common morality.

See Mauger and Pelletier (eds), *Les classes populaires et le FN*, p. 281.

62   Indeed, the ethnographic studies compiled by Mauger and Pelletier contain a wealth of observations and testimonies in support of the idea that it is essentially xenophobia and racism that distinguish those – a minority within the working classes, as the authors rightly say – who consistently stand on the far right. See, for example, the studies by Emmanuel Pierru and Sébastien Vignon, Violaine Girard, Romain Pudal, Lorenzo Barrault-Stella and Clémentine Berjaud, and Ivan Bruneau.

63   Frédéric Lordon is right to warn against a certain pseudo-Marxist vulgate that denies the power of 'ideas', which is sometimes greater than that of material conditions themselves. See his *Les Affects politiques*, Paris: Seuil, 2017, pp. 47–51.

widespread precarity and the uncertainty associated with it, the increase in urban segregation and its series of knock-on effects, the weakening of collective solidarity in the places where people work, live or study and so on. Or, likewise, to offer a useful reminder that the working classes have no monopoly on racism (which is obviously very present, coupled with classism, at the top of the social hierarchy).[64] Yet it is quite another thing to deny the hold of xenophobia and racism over a significant part of the population, including the working classes, and the effects that this has on electoral behaviour.

Political scientists Guy Michelat and Michel Simon show that it is impossible to understand the FN/RN vote without taking seriously the ideological cleavages that structure the population in general, and the working classes in particular.[65] Thus, among individuals with two 'working-class attributes'[66] (categorised as 'very working-class'),

> electoral behaviour varied in 2002 according to both fear of unemployment and attitudes towards immigrants. When these 'very working class' people had no fear of unemployment and were not violently hostile to immigrants (in other words, when they did not completely agree with the statement 'There are too many immigrants in France'), the FN vote was zero (0 percent). When people feared unemployment but were not violently hostile to immigrants, the FN vote remained marginal (only 2 percent). On the other hand, when they did not fear unemployment but were violently hostile to immigrants, the FN vote jumped to 17 percent.

---

64   On this point, see in particular Samuel Bouron and Maïa Drouard (eds), 'Les beaux quartiers de l'extrême droite', *Agone*, June 2014, no. 54. In an earlier article, Nonna Mayer analysed the high scores for the FN in the middle-class neighbourhoods of western Paris. She interpreted this 'mobilisation of the upper-class neighbourhoods in favour of [the FN] in 1984' as the product of a

> radicalisation among the right-wing electorate, exasperated by the arrival of the Socialists in power, and not identifying with the moderate list presented by Simone Veil, [and who] seized on the opportunity of this election, which had no national stakes, to express their discontent.

See Mayer, 'De Passy à Barbès'.

65   Guy Michelat and Michel Simon, 'Appartenances de classe, dynamiques idéologiques et vote Front national', *La Pensée*, October–December 2013, vol. 4, no. 376.

66   The indicator of an individual's social position – and more specifically their relationship to the blue-collar condition, as constructed by Michelat and Simon – consists of taking the individual's socio-occupational category and that of their father, resulting in three possible positions: 0 working-class attributes (neither the individual nor their father is a worker), 1 working-class attribute (either the individual or their father is a worker) or 2 working-class attributes (both the individual and their father are workers).

Finally, when people were both very anxious about unemployment and violently hostile to immigrants, the FN vote reached its maximum level (25 percent).

In other words,

> it is not enough to be very working class and anxious about unemployment to vote FN. You also have to attribute this risk to the presence of immigrants who should not have been allowed to 'invade' us and who should have been sent 'home' to give French workers access to the rare commodity that employment has become.[67]

These are, admittedly, relatively old data points. But the most recent surveys remind us of the centrality of this dimension in the FN/RN vote,[68] without denying the wide variety of circumstances that can lead some voters to take the plunge.

Sociologist Olivier Schwartz takes us further in his exploration of the forms of popular consciousness. As we mentioned above, he shows that, in many cases, this consciousness is not 'bipolar' – that is, structured according to a binary divide between us and them, opposing 'those at the top' and 'those at the bottom' – but rather 'triangular'.[69] In seeking out those responsible for the difficulties that they face, the working classes look not only to the top of the social hierarchy (the bosses, the elites, those in charge, the rich and so on) according to a logic that would fall under what Pierre Bourdieu called a 'class sense' and which, in certain circumstances of strong polarisation and class politicisation, can lead to a real 'class consciousness'. They also – and sometimes mainly – look downwards, to those who are singled out by media-political elites' neoliberal rhetoric and presented as 'welfare junkies' or 'fraudsters'. However, when racist principles for reading and dividing up the social world are legitimised and promoted by these same elites – as has been true in France since the 1980s – this line-up of 'scroungers' and 'scammers' generally become saturated with racist representations. They are spontaneously associated with the eminently expandable category of 'foreigners', including the most recent newcomers, non-European immigrants in general, and their descendants: in other words, all racialised minorities.

---

67 Michelat and Simon, 'Appartenances de classe', p. 13.
68 See Chapter 4.
69 See Olivier Schwartz, 'Vivons-nous encore dans une société de classes? Trois remarques sur la société française contemporaine', *La Vie des idées*, 22 September 2009, laviedesidees.fr.

It is this triangular dimension of popular consciousness that can lead to what Antonio Gramsci called a 'contradictory consciousness'.[70] In this form of consciousness, the (vertical) class polarisation – which pits the 'us' against those above – does not disappear, but is articulated and subordinated to the (horizontal) ethno-racial polarisation, which pits the 'us' against those from elsewhere (or at least perceived as such, since many of them were in fact born in France). Those at the top can continue to be criticised, but not in the sense that they exploit or dominate, but insofar as they refuse to protect the 'French' (against immigration, crime or terrorism), or have even put themselves at the service of foreigners (or those perceived as such), living unduly off the solidarity among fellow nationals. Fundamentally, it is the crumbling of class solidarity built up over two centuries of social resistance – gradually broken down, suffocated or incorporated by the stratagems of bosses and the state – that has weakened the feeling of belonging to the common fate of the 'exploited' or 'those at the bottom', and the entire perception of the social world built around this feeling. Consciousness abhors a vacuum, and racism – both as ideology and as affect – is precisely what can fill that void. For those whose 'resources' include being identified as being of French (or at least European) origin, because they are perceived or recognised as *white*, the claim to be *from here* or *at home* is very often what enables them to maintain a 'last difference'.[71] It is this difference that restores the dignity of the individual by assuring them that those who are perceived as outside or even antagonistic to the legitimate social body are not only (socially and morally) *beneath* them but are the source of most of the 'problems' that they encounter.[72] In a way, what the far right is

---

70   Antonio Gramsci, *Selections from the Prison Notebooks*, London: Lawrence & Wishart, 1971, pp. 323–43.

71   See Pierre Bourdieu (ed.), *La Misère du monde*, Paris: Le Seuil, 1993.

72   This explains why the FN/RN vote remains so low among the descendants of non-European immigrants, despite the fact that a large proportion of them belong to the working classes, which, as we have seen, vote for this party in higher-than-average numbers. See Céline Braconnier and Jean-Yves Dormagen, 'Le vote des cités est-il structuré par un clivage ethnique?', *Revue française de science politique*, 2010, vol. 60, no. 4; Brouard and Tiberj, *Français comme les autres?*; Jérôme Fourquet, 'Le vote Front national dans les électorats musulman et juif', in Crépon, Dézé and Mayer (eds), *Les faux-semblants du Front national*. It is not just that they may (quite rightly) see themselves as targets of this party's rhetoric, particularly in its Islamophobic vein. It is also that the FN/RN cannot offer them a vector of 'positive' identification, that is, the fact of being recognised as 'really from here' or as 'true French' since, even if they are legally French, everything in their social experience tends to show them that being considered as 'really in their own country' or as 'true French' is reserved for white people (including the descendants of European immigrants).

promising – particularly through the call for 'national preference' in jobs and services, now rebadged the 'national priority' – is not only to maintain but to increase the psychological advantages of status and material conditions associated with whiteness.[73]

The FN/RN has thus managed to make its electoral breakthrough by setting at the heart of the French political arena a divide between 'them and us' based not only on nationality per se (nationals versus foreigners) but also on an ethno-racial criterion (those 'of French stock' or the 'true French' versus those who are 'French only on paper'). The far right has succeeded in constructing a 'people' conceived in nativist terms (that is, one that excludes populations perceived as foreign to the nation), as an alternative to 'the people' that the left and the workers' movement had previously built on the basis of class solidarity (where the principle of exclusion is instead based on the opposition between the exploited and the exploiters, those who rule and those who are ruled over). The previously dominant 'them and us' divide, expressed on a more or less explicit class basis (workers/bosses, people/elites, poor/rich) which had long tended to structure the political field, is far from having disappeared. But it has been pushed into the background by the rise of the far right, and also by two other trends. First is the abandonment over the 1980s and 1990s, by the two dominant left-wing parties, of class-centred reference points, instead turning to wishy-washy rhetoric about 'citizen concerns', and a vague discourse – in fact compatible with the neoliberal logic – opposing the 'included' and the 'excluded'.[74] The other is the radicalisation of the established right and part of the media field in the direction of increasingly virulent xenophobia and Islamophobia.

In addition, national-racial or nativist dividing lines have prevailed all the more easily because capitalist globalisation and the neoliberal policies enacted since the 1980s have generated – and continue to generate – an increase in competition and uncertainty (on the labour market, of course, but also on the local scene or in educational institutions),[75] which itself undermines class solidarity. As the sociologist Benoît Coquard

---

73 See Mathieu Ichou and Ugo Palheta, 'Un salaire de la blanchité? Les revenus salariaux, une dimension sous-estimée des inégalités ethnoraciales en France', *Revue française de sociologie*, 2023, vol. 64, no. 4; Solène Brun and Claire Cosquer, *La domination blanche*, Paris: Textuel, 2024.

74 See Rémi Lefebvre and Frédéric Sawicki, *La société des socialistes. Le PS aujourd'hui*, Bellecombe-en-Bauge: Le Croquant, 2006; Julian Mischi, *Le communisme désarmé. Le PCF et les classes populaires depuis les années 1970*, Marseille: Agone, Contre-feux, 2014.

75 See Chapter 2.

points out,[76] when conditions become more precarious and the future more uncertain, we do not simply see atomisation or individualisation, but a retreat into a restricted affinity group ('true friends', family and so on). After all, the fewer economic and/or educational resources people have, and the more crucial local interpersonal connections become for getting by, the more individualism appears as a luxury. If this focus on friends and family – what Coquard calls 'just we ourselves' – is not generally politicised by individuals and is more a matter of how they go about their daily lives, it can resonate, particularly at election time, with the far-right imaginary. This is because the principle of national priority (or preference) claims that the state must ensure that the individuals deemed as *really from here* are served first – whether in terms of jobs, housing, benefits and so on – and that the state is responsible for ensuring that this is the case. In other words, this means locals or nationals, and more specifically the 'real French': 'our own people' before, and against, 'others'.

However, these dynamics do not account for the FN/RN vote and partisan attachment to the far right within the ruling classes, nor indeed the growing financial and media support that this party receives from big business. The first factor worth mentioning in this ruling-class support is the long-standing but growing porosity between the right and the far right, particularly since the rise of Nicolas Sarkozy in the 2000s. In his bid to 'siphon off' the FN vote, Sarkozy acclimatised a growing proportion of the traditional right-wing clientele – who are particularly drawn from the business wing of the better-off classes (company bosses, professionals, private sector managers) – to far-right 'ideas', rhetoric and affects. The homophobic movement against equal rights ('Manif pour tous') both demonstrated this porosity and undoubtedly increased it among those who identified with these protests. Indeed, this encouraged an enduring complicity between young activists from the conservative right and the far right (who have now become senior members of the RN, Reconquête and LR, or even media personalities).[77] Furthermore, support for the far right – from voting to activist involvement – is often rooted in family traditions that can be reinforced by schooling. From private schools in the west of Paris to certain law faculties or business and management schools, well-born young people have every chance of meeting (socially) similar people who may share the same worldview

---

76   See Benoît Coquard, *Ceux qui restent. Faire sa vie dans les campagnes en déclin*, Paris: La Découverte, 2019.

77   See Nicolas Massol and Marylou Magal, *L'extrême droite, nouvelle génération. Enquête au cœur de la jeunesse identitaire*, Paris: Denoël, 2024.

(at once elitist, conservative or even traditionalist, and sometimes ultranationalist and racist). Added to this is an older mechanism, at work since the 1980s: the FN/RN, an outsider in the political arena but also one of the leading parties, is able to offer quick and easy career advancement, in the form of leadership positions and elected office, to individuals who belong to the administrative or economic elites but are too impatient to take the long route to top positions within the traditional right. As Bruno Mégret said in the 1980s, 'It's better to be number 2 in the FN than number 30 in the RPR.'[78]

To note the cross-class nature of the FN/RN is surely not sufficient grounds to dismiss the myth of the 'party of the working classes' and propose some other, more appropriate characterisation. A party whose leadership is located on the borders of the petty and middle bourgeoisie, but which has a mass electoral base, recruited for the most part from the traditional petty bourgeoisie, from social strata that sociologists have described as 'petit-moyens'[79] and from more economically stable segments of the white working classes (often dual-earner working-class couples who have managed to become homeowners), the FN/RN can only overcome this contradiction by an intensification of nationalist, authoritarian, xenophobic and racist values. This enables it to substitute an imaginary national-racial community for a class community whose material and symbolic foundations have been greatly weakened (organisations, mobilising capacities and so on). Nevertheless, this contradictory social anchoring is sure to create difficulties in terms of developing an economic and social policy orientation, which necessarily requires a selection of priorities more or less favourable to the different classes and class fractions.

The Front National/Rassemblement National's Unidentifiable 'Anti-Capitalism'

It is well known that, in the 1980s, the FN was an extremely virulent supporter of neoliberalism, working to import and popularise in France the precepts advanced by Thatcher in Britain and Reagan in the United States. Far from the anti-Americanism which he championed from the first Gulf War onward, Jean-Marie Le Pen presented himself as the 'French

---

78 See Lebourg and Beauregard, *Dans l'ombre des Le Pen*, pp. 157–8.
79 Voir M. Cartier, I. Coutant, O. Masclet et Y. Siblot, *La France des petits-moyens*, Paris: La Découverte, 2008.

Reagan'. He even pathetically sought to obtain, if not the US president's endorsement, at least a photo with him – which he achieved in 1987 (just as Marine Le Pen sought in January 2017 to secure a handshake with the recently elected Donald Trump, in this case without success). For the first two decades of its existence, the FN was obsessed with 'economic statism'. It alleged an imperceptible convergence between France and 'international communism'; so bold were its claims in this regard that it did not even limit the 'collectivist danger' to the communist movement or even the Union of the Left.[80] Rather, just as the far right sees allies of the 'flood of migrants' everywhere, Jean-Marie Le Pen presented all other political parties and leaders – including Giscard d'Estaing, during his presidency – as agents of a 'Marxist revolution', which was not only a threat for the future but was already at work in the present. Mitterrand's rise to power in 1981, supported by the Communists up until 1984, led to an obvious radicalisation of this discourse, though it might be added that this was not only the work of the FN.[81]

The FN's neoliberal stance was perfectly consistent with the political objective that it set itself at the time: to appear as the only right-wing party of its kind and to peel off a significant proportion of the electorate from the main right-wing parties of the day (the RPR and the UDF), particularly among small employers (shopkeepers, artisans, farmers) and parts of the workforce hostile to the left and the labour movement. This involved constant criticism of the 'welfare state'[82] and the claim to stand for trampled-upon 'freedoms'. This did not mean civil liberties, which were not under threat, but two freedoms that are obvious markers of the right: the freedom of employers (in particular to dismiss their employees without constraints or accountability), and the freedom of parents to send their children to private schools if they so wished. In 1978, the FN adopted a manifesto entitled 'The Right and Economic Democracy', which officially became its economic programme in 1984. Reading it

---

80   Alliance between the Socialist Party, the Mouvement Radical de Gauche and the Communist Party.

81   He stood side-by-side with a more established but already revanchist right, which pretended to fear 'Soviet tanks in rolling down the Champs-Élysées' in order to better justify the pressure exerted by the business community, in the form of massive capital flight, notably to Switzerland, where Jean-Marie Le Pen opened 'an account credited with 2.2 million euros, including 1.7 million in the form of gold ingots and coins'. See 'Jean-Marie Le Pen a eu un compte caché en Suisse', *Le Monde*, 28 April 2015.

82   In 1981, the FN claimed that the 'Welfare State' led to the 'Boss-State' and then to the 'Kapo State'. See François Ruffin, *'Pauvres actionnaires!' Quarante ans de discours économique du Front national passés au crible*, Amiens: Fakir Editions, 2016, p. 29.

shows that the FN clearly preceded the RPR and the Socialist Party in its ardent neoliberalism, and for a long time surpassed them in its virulent calls for ever more privatisations, deregulations, flexibilisation and tax cuts. Similarly, up until the Maastricht Treaty, which it opposed, the FN had nothing to say against the unremitting build-up of the European single market. This was seen as a means of putting an end to social rights and trade union counter-power, and the European Union above all considered a necessary means for confronting the Eastern Bloc, at the time the main enemy of almost all the far-right parties in the West, including the FN.

The FN leadership made its first about-turn in the 1990s. This was a purely opportunistic move, seeing as it sought above all to occupy a political space and electoral niche left vacant by the Socialist Party's turn to neoliberalism (gradually giving this party a more bourgeois activist base)[83] and by the decline of the Communist Party, which was especially pronounced among the working classes.[84] This shift in the FN's economic and social line, towards the critique of economic globalisation and the EU, was heightened from 2011 onwards when Marine Le Pen succeeded her father as FN president, in the wake of the 2007–8 financial crisis. The result was a threefold shift: (1) the FN's programme now placed more emphasis on socio-economic issues than on other fields (immigration, law and order, and so on), even though the far-right party still devoted less focus to them than other parties; (2) the socio-economic measures were gradually (if partially) decoupled from the other ones (halting immigration was no longer presented as the main means of social and economic transformation); and (3) on the economic front, the message shifted from a (brutal) neoliberal orientation to a (soft) policy of limiting some of the effects of neoliberal policies, particularly on pensions.

So, the transformations begun in the 1990s, and amplified by Marine Le Pen in the 2010s, were not only an apparent shift in tone. The FN/RN's socio-economic programme has indeed changed significantly between the 1980s and the present day, to the extent that studies have estimated that '76 percent of the measures proposed by [Le Pen's] Rassemblement Bleu Marine in the June 2012 parliamentary elections were on the left-wing side of the economic axis', compared with just 18 percent in 1986.[85]

---

83   See Lefebvre and Sawicki, *La société des socialistes*.
84   See Mischi, *Le communisme désarmé*. As we said earlier, this in no way means that the traditional Communist Party electorate has gone over to the FN.
85   On this point, see Gilles Ivaldi, 'Du néolibéralisme au social-populisme? La transformation du programme économique du Front national (1986–2012)', in Crépon,

During the 2010s, the FN adopted a series of policy proposals that had traditionally belonged to the left: retirement on a full pension at age sixty, an increase in salaries and lower-income households' pensions, higher taxes on the richest and large companies and so on. It is also worth noting that all this has since been abandoned, in order to appeal to employers and LR's electorate. In June 2024, during the campaign for the parliamentary elections, Jordan Bardella even announced that he would not immediately repeal the pension reform railroaded through by Emmanuel Macron. This was, nonetheless, a policy item that the RN leadership had presented as central for months, even if the party's actual proposal would only have restored the right to retire at sixty for people who started working before the age of twenty and made forty-two years in social-security contributions. Similarly, for a time, the FN/RN criticised privatisation (after having called on the right in the 1980s to go further down this road), and now instead stood for a 'strategic state' and called for re-nationalisation in certain sectors (transport, energy, even banking). Since 2022 the party's manifestos have borne no trace of these calls for re-nationalisations.

Even earlier, during the FN's 'social' period (2012–17), its proposals never went further than repealing particularly unpopular laws (the 2016 Labour Law, or the pension reform). No measures to protect employees against job insecurity or to reduce inequalities have appeared in its manifestos since Marine Le Pen took over: the very words 'precarity' and 'inequalities' are absent from these programmes and from the speeches of its spokespersons. In short, the party postulates that protectionism – but also 'national priority', in other words the deepening of existing legal discrimination in favour of French citizens and against foreigners – will be enough to put an end to unemployment and precarity. This ignores studies showing that the scale of unemployment in France is only very partially explained by offshoring and the pressure of international competition.[86] But it also ignores any measures aimed at loosening the

---

Dézé and Mayer (eds), *Les Faux-semblants du Front national. Sociologie d'un parti politique*, pp. 169–76.

86 Using precise statistical estimates, Michel Husson shows that international trade and free trade are responsible for only a minority (less than 30 percent) of the loss of industrial jobs in France between the 1980s and the 2000s, the bulk of which can be explained by capitalist management of productivity gains. A protectionist policy would, therefore, not be enough to solve the problem of unemployment, or remove the need for an anti-capitalist employment policy or the theoretical and practical construction of a post-capitalist horizon. See Michel Husson, 'Protectionnisme et altermondialisme', *Contretemps*, 25 August 2011, contretemps.eu.

stranglehold of employers and actively controlling shareholders, who are never mentioned in the party's programmes or the speeches of its leading exponents, let alone any questioning of their power over companies. With the RN increasingly and visibly seeking to appeal to big business, Jordan Bardella recently went so far as to say that he understood 'Bernard Arnault's [the richest man in France and boss of LVMH] cry of alarm' (against the taxes and regulations that would burden him), even though France has become a tax haven for the richest in recent years and the taxation of corporate profits has never been so low, particularly for the largest companies, which manage to avoid paying taxes to a large extent.

As far as incomes and the cost of living are concerned, there is no question of raising wages or indexing them to prices, or even freezing the prices of essential goods and rents. The FN/RN's proposals have two main thrusts: to take from immigrants (in particular by abolishing State Medical Aid and certain benefits that may be granted to them, or by excluding them from certain forms of assistance), and to lower social security contributions – the same ones which finance the social protection system (health, pensions, unemployment benefits, family allowances) – to 'give the French their money back' and to allow employers to increase wages. However, there is no guarantee that employers will pass on these tax reductions in the form of wage increases. On the contrary, it is much more likely that, in the absence of any state constraint, they will take the opportunity to increase their profits. This will have the effect of either shifting the financing of social protection onto general taxation (and therefore to the population), or of further undermining social protection – leading, in all likelihood, to privatisation (so eagerly awaited by pension funds and private insurance companies in particular).

This is no coincidence, given that the far-right party remains a fierce defender of 'entrepreneurial freedom' (that false cloak of employers' power); a critic of the very idea of socialisation; and a force radically alien to the idea of breaking with capitalism. They never deign to mention the private ownership of big business, nor the class that holds all the economic power thanks to these property holdings, nor the enormous dividends paid to those with shares in big business (which reached a new record in France in 2024). The RN would have to recognise that the enemy is not some vague form of 'globalism' but has very French names and faces: old bourgeois families and major capitalists, the heads of major corporations, members of the senior civil service, media pseudo-experts and the kind of establishment pundits who never stop being wheeled out on panel shows,[87] all of whom have worked over the last few decades to reshape social relations along neoliberal lines. Yet, despite a few opportunistic calls to order generally made when certain offshoring operations – often the choice of French shareholders – are causing a stir in the press, the RN has no other project than that of a 'good' or 'moralised' capitalism. To use the traditional language of the far right, this means a 'people's capitalism', that of the 'small' against the 'big', in other words that of national, small and medium businesses (SMEs) as against that of multinational trusts. Of course, to make this distinction is to overlook the close interconnections between these two components of French capitalism, and indeed the strong dependence of the smaller businesses on the larger ones. It also glosses over the fact that these are companies subject to the same imperatives of capital accumulation, and that often have even worse working conditions than large companies do.[88]

Above all, a 'people's' or 'moralised' capitalism is a contradiction in terms. As long as there is capitalist ownership and management of the means of production, the economy is necessarily subject to the logic of profit and society dependent on decisions taken by a tiny minority – made up not of 'globalists', but of owners of capital. Oligarchic capitalism is the only type there will ever be. By remaining a prisoner of the structural logic of this mode of production and exchange, we can only swap the political leadership currently in power for a new leadership, which will undoubtedly be even more brutal and authoritarian. So, contrary to myth, there is no anti-capitalist, let alone socialist, horizon in the FN's programme. Its line on the subject remains the same one formulated in the 1990s through the slogan 'social priorities without socialism': in other words, rhetorically bewailing various ills connected to layoffs, household incomes, inflation, the deterioration of working and living

---

87   See Olivier Cyran, Sébastien Fontenelle, Mathias Reymond and Mona Chollet, *Les éditocrates*, Paris: La Découverte, 2009. See also: Serge Halimi, *Les Nouveaux chiens de garde*, Paris: Raisons d'agir, 1997; Henri Maler and Mathias Reymond, *Médias et mobilisations sociales*, Paris: Syllepse, 2007.

88   One variant is to praise (good) industrial capitalism, while radically dissociating it from (bad) financial capitalism – an absurd distinction given how far these two types of capital are now intertwined. The same rhetoric can be found well beyond the FN: in the context of the 2008 financial crisis, all parties were forced to develop a rhetoric critical of the financialisation of economies, even those whom we would least suspect of wanting to confront market finance. We remember Sarkozy's rants against finance, which naturally came with zero consequences. This demonstrates once again that Le Pen's party is, on many points, ideologically indistinguishable from the 'system' it claims to denounce.

conditions and so on, but without any plan to break with the source of this deterioration, namely capitalism. Seeking to find an equilibrium point, the organisation's then number-two leader – Nicolas Bay, who has since moved to Reconquête and then back to Marion Maréchal – took up this slogan almost verbatim when he said, in October 2017: 'Social policy doesn't mean socialism.'[89]

While it is important to remember that Marine Le Pen's 'neither right nor left' line was the same one taken by all fascist parties, it is also crucial to avoid muddying the waters by imagining this involves some sort of 'left-leaning' or 'quasi-socialist' tendency.[90] Even if this was a claim sometimes made by left-wing defectors (by Mussolini, Doriot or others, but not in Germany), fascism was never socialist.[91] Its aim was not human emancipation through the socialisation of the means of production and exchange, but a 'national renaissance' of an essentially moral and spiritual nature. The term 'national anti-capitalism' is itself misleading, because it leads us to take the fascists at their word. As Karl Polanyi wrote, 'it is in the nature of a fascist upheaval not to change anything in the existing economic system [capitalism]. It *is the raison d'être* of fascism to perpetuate the existing economic system.'[92] Going further, Zeev Sternhell has shown that the 'synthesis of the "national" and the "social"', itself 'a code word for this third way between liberalism and Marxism that would lead to fascism',[93] is the product of the fusion between an authoritarian and nationalist radicalisation of the right and a spiritualist revision of Marxism. This stripped Marxism not only of its materialist anti-capitalism (for which a radical transformation of economic structures is a crucial, albeit not sufficient, condition for revolutionising society) but also of its link with the rationalist heritage of the Enlightenment and its revolutionary humanist character.

After Marine Le Pen became the FN leader in 2011, the party stepped up its criticism of 'economic liberalism' and globalisation, regularly asserting its claim to be the party of the ordinary people, the workers, the people and so on, and adopting certain manifesto focuses traditionally associated with the left. The party's evolution in this respect is

---

89 See 'Nicolas Bay: "Le social, ce n'est pas le socialisme"', *La Dépêche*, 9 October 2017.
90 Grégoire Kauffmann, *Le Nouveau FN. Les vieux habits du populisme*, Paris: Seuil, 2016.
91 See in particular: Ishay Landa, *The Apprentice's Sorcerer: Liberal Tradition and Fascism*, London: Brill, 2010.
92 Karl Polanyi, *Essais*, Paris: Seuil, 2002, p. 425.
93 Sternhell, *Ni droite ni gauche*, p. 128.

not simply the combined product of the deepening social crisis and the decline of the Communist Party (insofar as this has indeed opened up an electoral space now up for grabs). It is also a response to the revival of social struggles which began in France in December 1995 and which has somehow reinvigorated the radical left, both politically and intellectually.[94] Marine Le Pen and company, unlike many other far-right leaders in the Western world, were forced to adapt to a national context in which mass, radical social movements became a frequent occurrence. This was particularly noticeable in the mid-2000s, marked by a massive mobilisation of young students and high school pupils (but also of trade unions in solidarity), forcing the government to back down on a neoliberal project to make the labour market more flexible (the CPE mentioned above), and by a dynamic and united left-wing campaign turning a majority of the population against the European Constitutional Treaty in the 2005 referendum on the subject. The FN/RN leadership could not fail to see that neoliberalism was being strongly contested, and Marine Le Pen – less dependent than the old guard on the party's traditional line – was the quickest and most skilful at this attempt to recuperate such talking points. However, the FN/RN has in no way developed an anti-capitalist orientation.[95] This also has some relation to the fact that this has always been and still today remains a party of notables – particularly in its leadership bodies – which has constantly sought to build connections with business circles.[96]

While the FN/RN has a higher vote among the working classes – which implies that a significant proportion of its electorate is made up of blue-collar and white-collar workers, even taking into account differential abstention – this had only limited effects on the social composition of its activist base, of the candidates it put forward in local, regional[97]

---

94 On this period, see in particular: Stathis Kouvélakis, *La France en révolte*, Paris: Textuel, 2007. See also: Razmig Keucheyan, *The Left Hemisphere: Mapping Critical Theory Today*, London: Verso, 2014.

95 This is as true of the FN as it is of the entire European far right, whose economic positions vary according to their country's place in the European division of labour. See on this point Joachim Becker and Rudy Weissenbacher, 'L'hétérodoxie de droite: la politique économique de la droite nationaliste européenne', *Contretemps*, 26 January 2017, contretemps.eu.

96 See Blandine Hennion, *Le Front national, l'argent et l'establishment*, Paris: La Découverte, 1992. For the time being, the FN's efforts to court business leaders have not been very successful, since its influence is currently only really felt among small business owners (even though the far-right candidate was interviewed for the first time by the bosses' federation MEDEF during the 2017 presidential elections, proof that things are changing on that side of things, too).

97 To take just one example, in the 2015 regional elections, the proportion of

and above all national elections, but, above all, on its party machine. The popular vote for the FN is therefore only very partially reflected in its organisation, in particular because its leadership has no systematic desire to encourage the emergence of activist cadres and leaders rooted in the working classes. Among the new RN MPs, there are quite a few white-collar workers (around 15 percent of those elected in 2022), particularly in the security (police) and health and personal services professions, but none hold leadership positions within the organisation or the parliamentary group. It should also be noted – based in particular on the recent thesis by Safia Dahani – that the RN's leadership apparatus is not only hyper-centralised, hierarchical and patrimonial (it is Marine Le Pen who appoints and dismisses the leadership, even more so than her father before her), but also largely disconnected from the party's elected representatives, including at the national level.[98]

Apart from a few figures who have gained a certain working-class legitimacy by highlighting their social background and/or the fact that their parents were communist activists (Steeve Briois, Stéphane Ravier and so on), but who have never themselves been workers (or communists for that matter), the FN/RN has in no way replaced the Communist Party as a workers' party or a party of the working classes, even though a significant proportion of workers vote for it. Whereas the Communist Party deliberately sought to create a political elite rooted in the working classes, relying in particular on its workplace cells, the FN/RN reduces workers and employees to the role of spectators or third-rate actors: electoral clientele, possibly activists assigned to the tasks deemed the most thankless (things like sticking up posters).[99] What is more, while party leaders demagogically mobilised the rhetoric of workers as *victims* of globalisation, they generally remained silent on or violently opposed the struggles waged by workers to safeguard or improve their working and living conditions, and even more so on the prospect of social and

---

blue- or white-collar employees among FN candidates was 29.3 percent, compared with 17.9 percent for the right and 18.8 percent for the left (though the radical left did better with 41.4 percent). See Martial Foucault, 'Élections régionales 2015: portrait de candidats', CEVIPOF, November 2015, no. 15, cevipof.com.

98 See Safia Dahani, 'Une institutionnalisation dans la tradition. Sociologie d'un parti patrimonial, le Front National', PHD Thesis, University of Toulouse, 2022, especially Chapter 3.

99 For a comparison between the Communist Party and the FN in their relationship with the working classes, see Julian Mischi, 'Essor du FN et décomposition de la gauche en milieu populaire', in Mauger and Pelletier (eds), *Les classes populaires et le FN* (abridged English translation: 'France's Far Right Is Gaining Where the Left Has Crumbled', *Jacobin*, 12 February 2024.

political emancipation for the subaltern classes. For the RN, therefore, workers are only of value as a 'class-object',[100] that is, as the object of a discourse formulated from the outside, a purely ideological instrumentalisation, and not as an (even potential) subject of collective, political action in their own interests.

These underpinnings in the traditional middle classes and certain fractions of the ruling classes are confirmed if we look at the party elites. Both before and after the rise of the far-right party, the vast majority of its senior personnel were drawn from the ranks of employers, the professions (particularly lawyers) and private sector managers – far from the image of a 'working class' or 'popular' party. If the far-right party remains aloof from the struggles waged by working-class people and expresses only few demands that respond to their specific interests, this is primarily because its leaders are socially far removed from the working classes. There are not many specific data points on these questions. But the ones available all converge, whether they concern FN/RN candidates or the delegates to its party conventions. As early as 1973, 57 percent of the FN's candidates in parliamentary elections were bosses in industry and commerce, managers or professionals (compared with 10.6 percent for the Communist Party at the same time), and only 2.7 percent were blue-collar workers.[101] Similarly, in the 1980s, the FN leadership included no blue-collar workers and virtually no white-collar ones.[102] Marine Le Pen's rise to the party presidency did not change this. The political bureau of the FN/RN, even when renewed at recent congresses, was almost entirely made up of individuals belonging to the ruling classes. More specifically, it relied heavily on the business wing of the intermediate and ruling classes (small businessmen, estate agents, sales representatives, the professions, private sector managers).

The policy zigzags that came out into the open after the defeat in the 2017 presidential election reflected the tension between the FN/RN leadership's persistent roots in the property-owning classes, at least among the less internationalised fringes of French capitalism (small

---

100   See Pierre Bourdieu, 'Une classe objet', *Actes de la recherche en sciences sociales*, 1977, nos. 17–18.

101   See Lebourg and Beauregard, *Dans l'ombre des Le Pen*, p. 96. See also the figures given by Colette Ysmal: 'Sociologie des élites du FN (1979–1986)', in Nonna Mayer and Pascal Perrineau (eds), *Le Front national à découvert*, Paris: Presses de la FNSP, 1989.

102   See the data on Front leaders compiled by Guy Birenbaum and Bastien François: 'Unité et diversité des dirigeants frontistes', in Mayer and Perrineau (eds), *Le Front national à découvert*, pp. 99–106. See also the data gathered by Alain Bihr for the 1980s–1990s: *Le Spectre de l'extrême droite*, p. 31.

businessmen and the professions), and the opportunistic desire to appeal to the working classes. The latter are socially worlds apart from the party leadership and are seen by its leaders not as a potential political player but as a pure and simple pool of votes. But, if Florian Philippot – who embodied the social-sovereigntist line – was sacked after the 2017 presidential election, and if the leadership decided to abandon certain measures emblematic of the 'social turn' of the 2010s (wage increases, the return of pensions at age sixty, nationalisations, euro exit and so on), this was not just a change in Marine Le Pen's mood. Above all, it was because the FN/RN's new 'social' line made it difficult to appeal to middle and upper-class voters on the right. What is more, this line only partially corresponded to the aspirations of the FN/RN electorate, including even its working-class electorate. In this regard, we should overcome a common misconception – expounded by Pascal Perrineau under the label of 'leftist-Le Pen-ism' and refuted as early as the 1990s.[103] For the blue- and white-collar workers who vote for the FN/RN (and even more so, those of its voters who do not belong to the working classes) are not, in most cases at least, former left-wing voters or even voters who continue to be on the left because they are attached to social measures (in particular the redistribution of wealth). On the contrary, these are the working-class voters who are among the most pro-business, the least in favour of progressive taxation (via income tax or corporation tax) and the least sympathetic to trade unions and strikes.[104] Among these voters, a determined racism (attacking immigrants and minorities) tends to compensate for class fatalism: in other words, scepticism, indifference or even hostility towards collective action as it continues to be promoted by the social and political left.

From a strategic point of view, after 2017, the FN/RN began not a break but a rebalancing operation, inspired by the proposals of Nicolas Bay, who, for a while, became a key figure.[105] On the one hand, it toned

---

103 For two early critiques see Pierre Martin, 'Qui vote pour le Front national français?' in Pascal Delwitt, Jean-Michel De Waele and Andrea Rea (eds), L'extrême droite en France et en Belgique, Brussels: Complexe, 1998; and Nonna Mayer, Ces Français qui votent FN, Paris: Flammarion, 1999. For a recent critique, see Florent Gougou, 'Les ouvriers et le vote Front national. Les logiques d'un réalignement électoral', in Crépon, Dézé and Mayer (eds), Les Faux-semblants du Front national.

104 As Michelat and Simon explain,

when socio-economic attitudes have any influence on the probability of voting extreme right, this vote is, like the right-wing vote (albeit to a lesser degree), more frequent among those, including blue-collar workers, who espouse (neo)liberal options than among those who reject them.

See their 'Appartenances de classe', p. 11. See also Collectif Focale, Votes populaires.

105 His contribution written during summer 2017 can be read in Alexandre

down its social-hued critique of 'globalism', the (vaguely) redistributive agenda adopted in recent years and its praise for the 'strategic state'. It now again highlighted some of the older neoliberal clichés about 'welfare scroungers' or 'fraudsters' (which had been somewhat relegated to the background), and placed greater emphasis on measures that benefit employers and disadvantage employees (cuts in employer contributions and taxation, undermining of trade union rights, making benefits more tightly conditioned in the name of combating 'fraud' and so on). On the other hand, Bay pushed forward a more identitarian critique of 'globalism', focusing on the threat to national identity and security posed by immigrants and minorities – and, of course, their 'woke' sponsors on the left – rather than on the effects of precariousness and impoverishment on the working classes (in particular by abandoning the prospect of euro exit, but also calls for nationalisations). So, on the one hand, this meant a neoliberalism that could present itself as more acceptable in light of the harshness of Macron's regressive reforms (on pensions, for example);[106] and, on the other, an identitarian and xenophobic critique of 'globalism'.

From the interwar period to the present day, it is an essential characteristic of far-right movements that they have no fixed doctrine on economic and social matters, or rather that they are capable of shifting from one doctrine to another, sometimes without transition and always depending on the target audience. The study of these fundamentally 'catch-all' movements cannot therefore rely solely on an analysis of their manifestos, given the strictly instrumental value they attach to any particular proposals made;[107] they are ever-ready to make obviously contradictory promises to different social categories, or to make sudden and radical changes of direction if this will enable them to expand their audience. The FN itself confirms this tendency, since its various programmatic turns have had no other objective than to inflate its electoral scores. Nicolas Bay did not justify his proposed turn on the basis of arguments of principle – for or against Frexit, for example – but by identifying a new electoral clientele that the FN could attract by

---

Sulzer, 'FN: la contre-proposition de Nicolas Bay à celle de Florian Philippot', *L'Express*, 21 July 2017.

106   This reflects the FN's internal contradictions, as confirmed by a survey of FN activists carried out at the moment of its last congress in March 2018, which the newspaper *Les Echos* summed up as follows: 'Reading the responses, you get the impression that the far-right party is going to have to come up with a synthesis between Jean-Pierre Chevènement and Ronald Reagan'. See Guillaume de Calignon, 'Les questions économiques divisent les militants du FN', *Les Échos*, 11 March 2018.

107   See Paxton, *The Anatomy of Fascism*.

moderating its position on this issue. Today, as in the past, fascist, fascistic or neofascist currents have never been encumbered by a doctrine or a programme fixed once and for all time. In their ideology and style, they combine a challenge to the 'system' (which is never specifically characterised, so everyone can project onto this term as they please) with a claim to re-establish order. They combine a subversion of the codes of conventional politics and a desire to be part of immemorial traditions. They combine the vision of a radiant future and the nostalgia for a glorious past. They appeal to both the people and the hatred of popular mobilisation. Making all these elements coexist is the great strength of the far right, allowing it to adapt quickly to changes in its economic, political and ideological environment, but also to the different demands arising from a differentiated society.

However, one constant should be remembered, because it is a crucial one: when fascism came to power – in other words, when it transformed from a movement into a regime – it lost much of its chameleonic character. Even though it claimed to overcome the antagonism between workers and bosses through a form of co-management, as synthesised in a corporatist ideal that was never really put into practice (neither in Italy or Germany, nor in Salazar's Portugal or under the Vichy regime), once in power, it never failed to favour capital over labour by crushing any form of organisation defending workers' interests,[108] and by casting aside any pledge that might alienate business circles.[109] Mussolini's fascism was thus skilfully built on a programme that sounded quite left wing in economic terms, including demands against private property that were immediately forgotten once his party was in power. This was the price of forging an alliance with the big landowners, part of the traditional elite and the Italian bourgeoisie.[110] Similarly, while, in opposition, fascism criticised the big trusts' domination over the economy, praised small-scale production and called for a resurrection of the medieval corporations, the Fascist state pushed for greater concentration of capital, which could only be achieved at the expense of small businesses, and therefore of the petty bourgeoisie. In this way, fascism as regime systematically thwarted all the 'social' proposals of fascism as movement. Above

---

108   With an extremely rich bibliography, see in particular: Timothy Mason, *Nazism, Fascism and the Working Class*, Cambridge: Cambridge University Press, 1995.

109   On the relationship between Nazi political power and the major industrial groups, see in particular: Alfred Sohn-Rethel, *Economy and Class Structure of German Fascism*, London: Free Association Books, 1987.

110   See in particular: Paxton, *The Anatomy of Fascism*.

all, it built a capitalism of unequalled brutality, based on the destruction of civil society by a state Moloch that either abruptly or gradually suppresses all the social and democratic gains of the working classes, annihilating or stifling all popular protest.[111]

This is because, while fascism drapes itself in revolutionary clothes and is eager to mobilise the rhetoric of breaking with the old order, it does not in fact aspire to any kind of social revolution, that is, the abolition of relations of exploitation and oppression. Rather, it strives for spiritual change: a *national regeneration*.[112] However, when the fascists came to power, the 'fascist revolution' was forced to move from spiritualist fantasies to the rather more rugged ground of concrete political decisions, and thus in particular to arbitrate between the major social interests. This necessarily meant making choices in favour of some and against others. Contradictions inevitably arose, or grew sharper, and this, in turn, prompted the fascist government to intensify its repression of opposition, including within its own ranks, as it embarked on a spiral of authoritarian radicalisation. The result: fascism more or less rapidly became the dictatorship of a small clique, which claimed to be the sole embodiment of the national interest. This is also why the plebeian elements of far-right movements – the ones most attached to the anti-bourgeois dimension of the original fascist message (greatly different from the discourse that directly preceded their rise to power) – were ruthlessly and swiftly dismissed once the fascists had gained command of the state, so as not to stand in the way of their alliance with the bourgeoisie. This was the pattern in Mussolini's Italy, in Hitler's Germany and in Salazarist Portugal. The spiritual impulse thus became a state terrorism; and, while the bourgeoisie was deprived of the political personnel whom it had traditionally preferred, its economic power was strengthened. For it had been freed from the counter-power of the workers' movement and the legal constraints that had hitherto prevented it from achieving an untrammelled exploitation.

It is obvious that, if the RN came to power, it, like all the far-right movements before it, would renounce the proposals that troubled big business. This is because there is nothing *anti-capitalist* or *socialist* in

---

111   On this apparent contradiction, see Daniel Guérin's chapters on 'fascist demagogy' and 'the economic politics of fascism', in his classic book: *Fascisme et grand capital*, Paris: Libertalia, 2014 (*Fascism and Big Business*, New York: Pathfinder, 2016 [1939]). See also: Leon Trotsky, *What It Is and How to Fight It*, New York: Pathfinder, 1969.

112   Among many other historians of fascism, Zeev Sternhell notes: 'Such is the nature of the fascist revolution: it is a political, intellectual and moral revolution, but not one reshaping the structures of society or the economy.' See *Ni droite ni gauche*, p. 78.

its political matrix. But it is also because there is no 'third way' between capitalism and socialism, other than a merely imaginary one. Especially in times of deep economic stagnation, if you do not take the path of confronting the dominant class and even breaking with private ownership of companies and the dominance of a market logic, you will necessarily end up submitting to the power of (big) capital. So, the RN in power would, no doubt, opt for a particularly regressive mix of neoliberalism and ultra-authoritarian statism. Using far more violent means than successive governments over the last three decades, it would attack ethnic minorities and workers. It would do this by suppressing their fundamental rights (trade union freedoms, freedom of organisation and assembly, the right to strike and so on), while enlisting the bourgeoisie to its cause with the promise of increased profits.

It is ever less common for political commentators, but even left-wing or trade union activists and organisations, to speak of the FN/RN in terms of fascism or neofascism. This is often said to be a schematic, unduly militant way of looking at the party, which overlooks a whole series of traits characteristic of fascism but absent from Marine Le Pen's party. Yet, in our view, this is indeed the best way of grasping this party's distinctive properties.

Fascism is specifically characterised by the desire – embodied by a leader and supported by an organisation – to strive for the rebirth of a mythologised and essentialised nation. Ridding this nation of all forms of otherness and protest that threaten its imaginary identity and its fantasised unity is meant to put a stop to the decadence currently said to be driven by an indiscriminate mix of capitalist cosmopolitanism and left-wing internationalism, 'stateless' finance and 'uprooted' immigrants, 'globalism from above' and 'globalism from below', to use Marine Le Pen's words.[113] The RN's politics clearly fit into this framework, marked by the desire for a spiritual revolution that would launch a national regeneration. They do not only, or simply, fit into the (quite common) reference to the people, which can be detected in different forms across all political currents. In Marseilles, on 19 April 2017, after calling for a 'national insurrection', Marine Le Pen said:

> We are under threat of a dilution of our national identity. Let's ask ourselves: are we going to be able to live as French people in France for much

---

113 On this point, see Chapter 1.

longer? At a time when entire neighbourhoods are virtually becoming foreign territories? When they are trying to force down our throats rules and ways of life from elsewhere?

Yet, this point has to be qualified in several ways. First of all, even if the FN/RN is based on a political and strategic matrix that has its roots in French fascism and has hardly changed since the party's foundation in 1972, despite successive facelifts, it is hardly just a replica of historical fascism. Its organisation has never managed to develop into a genuine mass movement, capable of being present everywhere, beyond the electoral or media arena. Unlike Indian fascism, for example, whose organisation centres on a massive and many-branched movement (the RSS, the 'National Volunteers Organisation', of which the BJP is the political shopwindow), the FN/RN's influence in civil society remains weak, and is expressed through informal ties rather than through organisations with far-reaching popular roots. Its influence is based on the intensive and skilful use of social networks and the collusion of the mass media, rather than on the mobilisation of activists. Indeed, in most areas, its activists remain few in number, poorly trained and weakly structured – even if Éric Zemmour has tried, for his part, to build a more activist-based organisation, with closer links to far-right extra-parliamentary movements. However, the FN/RN surely is taking root in society and building up its ideological muscle, as can be seen from the strength and spread of its vote and the growing support it enjoys among the ruling classes. At this stage, the FN/RN could be described as an inorganic fascism from above, adapted to an era of capitalism in which the great neoliberal destruction has set back the mass organisations and the collective causes they carried forth. Hence this party is less inclined towards the radiant utopia of tomorrow – a new order and a 'new man' – than haunted by the spectre of a 'clash of civilisations' or a 'racial civil war'. The FN/RN is rather more oriented towards the retrospective exaltation of a mythologised past. Yet it is also true that, in this, it takes advantage of the weakening of the left and its main consequence: the absence of mass investment in a liberatory perspective for transforming society.

To characterise the FN/RN as fascist or neofascist in no way implies that all its activists, let alone its voters, are in favour of installing a far-right dictatorship in the here and now, or that they look to fascism as a model. Nevertheless, we cannot rule out a radicalisation process that could take hold of part of society in exceptional crisis circumstances (as we saw in Greece in the early 2010s with the neo-Nazis of Golden Dawn and, in another form, with Trumpism), or, at the end of a more gradual process of political polarisation, particularly as the ground has been prepared by which xenophobia and racism have been both generalised and made more 'respectable'. Moreover, in the past, it was far from necessary for fascist movements to obtain the support of a majority of the population, let alone for a majority to favour the establishment of a dictatorship, for them to rise to power. In Germany, the maximum support the Nazis could muster before being lifted to power was 37 percent (much more than Mussolini in Italy, who never achieved any great electoral success before King Victor Emmanuel III called on him to form a government). While many of these parties' voters undoubtedly shared a revanchist ultra-nationalism and a more or less visceral antisemitism, their motivations were also varied. For the most part, they were far from any total adherence to the policies pursued by Hitler in the following years, in particular expansionist war aims and – still less – the 'Final Solution'.[114] This evidently was not enough to stop the Nazis from conquering political power and, by allying themselves with large sections of the conservative right (which held most posts in the Nazi-led governments), holding on to power long enough to lead to the disaster of another world war and genocide. We are obviously not at this point yet. But the fact that FN/RN voters have only a very partial knowledge of its programme, or that most of them probably do not want a dictatorship, can hardly be cited as grounds to deny or minimise the danger.

It should be added that the RN has no unchangeable 'nature'. Like any party, it is not set in stone. It could even go through profound changes, depending on both its internal dynamics and its external environment. There are surely grounds to think that, in the years to come, it could evolve into a party of the conservative right. The growing sway of elected representatives over the RN could trigger a kind of notabilisation process, gradually driving its leadership to abandon part of its fundamental project of reshaping society on an ultra-hierarchical, anti-democratic,

---

114   William Sheridan Allen recalls in his book the 'mixed' feelings that NSDAP voters had towards him, perceiving him as a mix of 'decent' people and 'thugs'. See *The Nazi Seizure of Power: The Experience of a Single German Town 1930–1935*, London: Eyre & Spottiswoode, 1966. More generally, see Ian Kershaw, *Popular Opinion and Political Dissent in the Third Reich, Bavaria, 1933–1945*, Oxford: Oxford University Press, 1985. For a critique of the idea that the 'masses' 'wanted fascism', see Nicos Poulantzas, 'À propos de l'impact populaire du fascisme', in Maria-Antonietta Macciocchi (ed.), Éléments pour une analyse du fascisme, vol. 1, Paris: 10/18, 1976 ('On the Popular Impact of Fascism', in James Martin (ed.), *The Poulantzas Reader: Marxism, Law and the State*, London: Verso, 2008, p. 258–70).

racist and reactionary basis. Nevertheless, in recent years, it is more that LR and the Macronist right have aligned themselves with FN/RN, than the other way round. Le Pen's party continues to wage a political battle to achieve power on its own, or by picking off whole chunks of the right (which it did achieve in part by prompting Éric Ciotti's split from LR, and sealing an alliance in which his followers took a subordinate position). If the FN/RN leaders were simply opportunists looking for positions in the institutions, they would long ago have joined the parties of the traditional right or entered coalitions as an auxiliary force, denying or watering down some of their positions in order to gain a seat at the table. However, since its creation in 1972, the FN/RN has, for the most part, maintained its political independence, only exceptionally joining forces with the right (and never in a national-level pact).

Finally, there is the question of violence. Once again, it would be wrong to imagine a clean break between Jean-Marie Le Pen's FN and Marine Le Pen's RN. Right from the party's foundation, the objective of creating an electoral shopwindow for the far right meant that the all-too-visible street battles with the left had to be calmed down, if not rejected on principle. Nonetheless, for a long time, the FN had a militarised security service in the form of the DPS – the 'Protection and Security Department', also known in Jean-Marie Le Pen's day as 'Depends Only on the [Party] President' – which used military techniques and recruited former soldiers, police officers and security guards. In addition to the traditional functions of a stewarding operation (protection of leaders, meetings and public appearances), according to accounts gathered at the end of the 1990s the DPS sometimes carried out offensive actions, mainly directed against anti-FN militants (known as 'punitive missions').[115] In the more recent period, for which less information is available, it would appear that the DPS – hit hard by the Mégret split – was gradually marginalised by Marine Le Pen because of its members' attachment to her father, in favour of the private security firm run by Axel Loustau (former leader of the GUD, an unrepentant neofascist activist and close associate of hers).[116]

---

115   See the hearings held during the parliamentary enquiry into the DPS in 1999: 'Sommaire des comptes rendus d'auditions du 10 fevrier 1999 au 17 fevrier 1999', Assemblée nationale, assemblee-nationale.fr. See also an article on Claude Hermant, a member of the DPS for six years and recently sentenced to seven years' imprisonment for arms trafficking (some of which was allegedly used by Amedy Coulibaly in the Hypercacher massacre): Renaud Dély and Karl Laske, 'Confessions d'un fantôme', Libération, 6 June 2001.

116   See Olivier Faye and Abel Mestre, 'Crise au FN: Marine Le Pen écarte le service d'ordre historique au profit d'un proche', Droite(s) extrême(s) blog, Le Monde.fr, 3 September 2015 . On the links between Marine Le Pen and Axel Loustau, see Marine

But it would seem that it has also stopped carrying out offensive actions such as the punitive expeditions against 'enemies' just mentioned.

For the RN, now is the time for fighting a 'war of position' in Gramsci's sense – an approach not focused on seizing power by insurrectionary means but, rather, gradually gaining hegemony in preparation for its rise to the highest office. Nevertheless, there are links between the institutionally oriented far right and extra-parliamentary currents. In addition to the intellectual influence coming from organisations such as the Institut Iliade (founded by neo-pagan networks stemming from the Nouvelle Droite) and Academia Christiana, a division of labour seems to have been established between the FN/RN, which claims a monopoly on institutional efforts, and extra-parliamentary groupuscules. As the electoral shopwindow and flagship of the fascist fleet, the FN/RN is the ship whose electoral power gives confidence to the small militant vessels that gravitate around it, in complex relationships of competition and cooperation. With these others, it shares a worldview based on 'the Great Replacement' (or being 'drowned' in the planned 'flood of immigrants') and 'race war'. In this way, the FN/RN objectively delegates the use of violence to these groupuscules, particularly when it comes to confronting student protests. To take just a few recent examples: in spring 2018, the FN's main leaders welcomed the Génération identitaire initiative at the Col de l'Echelle mountain pass between Italy and France, aimed at symbolically but also physically opposing migrants' arrival on French soil. During the same period, while fascist militants were regularly attacking students who mobilised as part of a national movement, Louis Aliot appeared on TV calling for the 'blockaders' to be 'kicked out by armed force' and welcoming the government offensive against the ZADistes at Notre-Dame-des-Landes. This shows, once again, that, in the face of social protest, the FN/RN always stands on the side of order, supporting governments that want to use force and maintaining an ultra-authoritarian project that aspires to go further and faster in clamping down on all opposition. We should not forget the FN/RN's massive electoral following within the state's repressive apparatus, especially in the police and particularly the most violent units (notably the so-called anti-crime brigades).[117] As party leaders see things, this makes it superfluous

---

Turchi and Mathias Destal, *'Marine est au courant de tout . . .'. Argent secret, financements et hommes de l'ombre*, Paris: Flammarion, 2017.

117   See Didier Fassin's study: *La Force de l'ordre. Une anthropologie de la police des quartiers*, Paris: Seuil, 2011 (*Enforcing Order: An Ethnography of Urban Policing*, Cambridge: Polity Press, 2013).

to set up militias dedicated to harassing and repressing opponents. Finally, cultural work is also largely carried out by the Bolloré group's media, with their swarms of reactionary columnists and pundits, and by influencers – particularly 'manosphere' figures and Islamophobes – who have massively expanded their reach on YouTube, Instagram or TikTok in particular. These latter play a role both in spreading fascist(-adjacent) ideas and affects and in constantly intimidating the left and liberation movements (digital militias).

The broad public anathema against political violence and the FN/RN's goal of winning high office thus force it to limit as far as possible the prospect of violent acts that are too visibly reminiscent of its roots in the most brutal far-right traditions. It therefore suppresses the rise within its own ranks of groups aspiring to play a role equivalent to that of the SA within the Nazi party (a function that François Duprat assigned to revolutionary-nationalist groups in the 1970s when he was a major figure in the FN).[118] Nonetheless, the RN is preparing people for the intensified use of violence by frequently resorting to the rhetoric of 'civil war'. As Marine Le Pen herself put it:

> For forty years at least, any clear-sighted and objective observer has been able to see the problems mounting. For too many years, from intimidation to intimidation and from anti-French attacks to terrorist acts, the prospect of civil war is no longer just a fantasy.

The FN/RN claims to be the only party capable of *preventing* civil war, while constantly fanning the flames of Islamophobia, Roma-phobia and xenophobia, pointing to the spectre of an Islamist 'fifth column' or the destruction of the French nation. Its leaders have been claiming for

---

118   François Duprat wrote:

> Our revolutionary conception is also very simple: we must be able to combine a combat organisation with an organisation centred on training and command. Without the SA, the NSDAP would never have been able to seize power, but without the Politische Organisation the SA would have been no more successful than Kapp and Luttwitz's Freikorps during the 1920 putsch ... Assuming that the revolutionary-nationalist movement has the forces necessary for a violent and sustained struggle, if these forces are disciplined and organised, it can rally the right-wing masses, who are always looking for a force that can reassure them of their position. [The economic crisis must deepen, the state must weaken, and] a radical solution may then become acceptable to millions of French people ... A Revolution can only be achieved if many peaceful conservatives cease to be tempted by the perpetuation of the reigning order. [If the Revolution is carried out by a *coup de force* made possible by the crisis], only the movement capable of mobilising large numbers of combative and disciplined militants in the streets will be able to achieve a victory and save our civilisation.

Quoted in Lebourg and Beauregard, *François Duprat*, p. 204.

decades that France is 'drowned', 'occupied' and 'colonised' by elements considered 'anti-national' and 'unassimilable'. What kind of policy would such an organisation pursue, if it rose to power? Without even mentioning the effects of encouraging a racist and reactionary intensification among the population itself – in particular among the social-electoral base of the far right – do we seriously think that such a party would simply maintain the status quo? Would it conclude that previous governments have gone far enough already in attacking oppressed groups and liberation movements? This seems implausible. In this respect, it is probably not the FN/RN's fascist past that should worry us, but its fascist future, once it has reached high office.

Conclusion

Fend Off Disaster, Revive Anti-fascism

> On the contrary, it is necessary to direct one's attention violently towards the present as it is, if one wishes to transform it. Pessimism of the intelligence, optimism of the will.
>
> Antonio Gramsci, *Prison Notebooks*[1]

Fending off the possibility of disaster, first and foremost, requires an understanding of the threat actually faced. This danger goes far beyond the multiple attacks on social rights and democracy by neoliberal governments, or even the structural violence of current institutions – from the invisible (because hidden) suffering produced by the labour market, to the brutality associated with the 'legitimate' use of force by the repressive state apparatus. This danger has a name, which political journalists, media experts and most specialists in the contemporary far right have decided to stop saying: *fascism*. The fact that it is so difficult for many intellectuals to frankly acknowledge the fascist threat, when everything suggests that it is bearing down on us ever-more forcefully, is in a sense surprising. But such downplaying of the danger – a minimisation which is particularly striking in the French case – has much to do with the difficulty of confronting head-on neofascist forces and everything that feeds them, whether that means neoliberal policies, hardening authoritarianism or structural racism.

---

[1] Antonio Gramsci, *Selections from the Prison Notebooks*, London: Lawrence & Wishart, 1971, p. 175 fn.

Clearly, the fascism of the present does not look the same as the fascism of the past. But there is no mistaking the reality: in order to triumph, the fascist project of – national, racial or civilisational – regeneration through a purge of society does not need to be carried out by hordes organised into paramilitary militias parading around in brown shirts or marching at a goose-step. This is not to deny that the last fifteen years have, indeed, seen the development of mass violence committed by far-right terrorists and armed groups who routinely attack minorities and/or the left (from India to the United States, via Israel, Turkey, Greece and Brazil), and even political institutions (attacks on the Capitol in Washington, and in Brasilia). In many countries, we have also seen a radicalisation of the mainstream right, visible in France in the case of Éric Zemmour – once a conservative journalist but now converted into a Trumpised neo-Pétainist – but also in the form of Macronism, which, in its desperate search for a stable electorate, has constantly drifted towards the far right, to the point of forming a government which was entirely at its mercy. At the same time, a section of the far right – from Marine Le Pen's RN to the Austrian FPÖ and Giorgia Meloni's Fratelli d'Italia – has worked for (self-)normalisation by appropriating the consensual codes of political communication and abandoning the most visible aspects of their organisations' fascist parentage. In this latter case, appearing respectable first and foremost means making themselves unrecognisable, albeit without giving up on their ethno-nationalist ideological cement.

Moreover, even if we confine ourselves to the two most emblematic cases (Italian and German fascism), to which should be added all the varieties of fascism of the interwar period (from French Doriotism to the Croatian Ustaše, not forgetting the likes of Austrofascism, the Romanian Iron Guard and the Portuguese Blue Shirts), fascism as a phenomenon has always been multiform. It already took many different forms in the interwar period, and its rise followed various different avenues. Nazism, for example, had to wait around ten years before gaining political power, but it imposed its totalitarian dictatorship in a matter of months. Italian fascism, on the other hand, came to power quickly after its first emergence, but took several years to rid itself of all organised opposition. The whole history of fascism shows its distinctive capacity to adapt to different national contexts and its ability to seize opportunities in the most heterogeneous political situations. We find a further illustration of this in June 1940, when the French far right, supported by a large part of the right and some of the left, took advantage of the military defeat to impose the Vichy regime within a matter of weeks. This was a hybrid dictatorship combining reactionary and fundamentally backward-looking aspects with modernising and technocratic tendencies, but also borrowing many of its features from fascism.

The main aim of this book has been to change the way we think about our present historical situation. It is highly unlikely that the years and decades ahead will see a return to the calm exchange of the reins of power between governments, perpetuating the social order by essentially peaceful means and, indeed, with the active consent of the majority. Rather, it must be seen that social and political polarisation is likely to increase, precisely because of the hegemonic instability that is the hallmark of late capitalism. To borrow a famous phrase from Marx and Engels, 'all that is solid melts into air': the social compromises that had allowed capitalism to entrench itself have been broken, or are in the process of being broken up, by the neoliberal offensive; inequalities are growing everywhere and exploding on a global scale; political institutions and forces appear increasingly illegitimate; democratic forms, even simply parliamentary ones, are being hollowed out; states are operating in an increasingly authoritarian fashion, in particular through the growth, militarisation and autonomy of repressive apparatuses; and nationalism is being sharpened by an alliance with racism (in particular Islamophobia). Added to this is the fact that some organisations – in France, the Front National, now the Rassemblement National – have succeeded in cohering the resentment of millions of people around a project that combines intensified nationalism, white revanchism (often allied to masculinism or even traditionalism) and the ultra-authoritarian desire to silence all dissent. This project combines nostalgia for a lost golden age in French society, in which inequalities were unquestioned and the nation glorious, with a racism that demonises immigrants and minorities, and points towards a world freed from the supposed 'tyranny of minorities', the 'flood of migrants' and the 'great replacement'. It necessarily leads to a proposal that does not always dare to speak its name: a policy of racial assertiveness, aimed at maintaining white supremacy, often coupled with the anti-feminist, homophobic and transphobic backlash movement.

Building a common understanding of the danger we face is a first step, but it is not enough. For it is inevitably followed by another question: how can we build an anti-fascism for our time? What lessons can we learn from the battles waged against this plague throughout the twentieth century? How can we be true heirs to twentieth-century anti-fascism without simply reproducing its past forms or, worse still, mimicking its gestures? In the following lines, we shall try to formulate some – doubtless too brief – considerations on anti-fascist strategy. Even this presupposes a few preconditions. First of all, it is important to reject the reduction of anti-fascism to a simple anti-FN/RN rhetoric reserved for the final days of the election campaign, and which lets off the hook the parties whose policies and rhetoric continue to encourage the far right's rise. Secondly, when it comes to anti-fascism, anti-capitalism, feminism or anti-racism, the activist's determination to 'do something' will not alone suffice, and even less so mere moral indignation. Fighting fascism requires assessing the balance of power and studying the terrain of the struggle, dividing the enemy and uniting the forces of opposition, giving them the right direction and seizing the opportunities that present themselves – in short, thinking strategically.[2] Finally, we need to remember the distinction drawn from military thought between strategy, that is, the coordination of various efforts to achieve some long-term objective (in this case, the crushing of neofascism), and tactical choices, that is, one-off operations aimed at achieving partial victories against some particular neofascist force.

Two temptations must first be avoided, as the combination of both will inevitably lead to defeat. The first is an anti-fascism which can be described as bourgeois because it is limited to defending the existing order. It thus aims to build a 'republican front' and claim that any alliance is well and good – including an alliance with the right – to avoid the fascist threat. It is doubtful that we can talk about strategy here, since this orientation generally boils down to pure electoral tactics, without generally being integrated into an overall perspective of anti-fascist struggle. The problem here is not so much a moral one, or indeed a stand of principle against the use of electoral means as such: it may be individually galling, but nonetheless politically judicious, to use the ballot box to temporarily defeat an enemy that we consider more dangerous than the devil we know.[3] However, in this specific case, a consistent anti-fascist movement should be as clear as possible that a call to vote against some fascist candidate is in no way equivalent to an alliance. This implies maintaining complete political independence and

---

2   See Daniel Bensaïd, *Penser agir*, Paris: Lignes, 2008.

3   Leon Trotsky's warning is often quoted, and rightly so:

When one of my enemies sets before me small daily portions of poison and the second, on the other hand, is about to shoot straight at me, then I will first knock the revolver out of the hand of my second enemy, for this gives me an opportunity to get rid of my first enemy. But that does not at all mean that the poison is a 'lesser evil' in comparison with the revolver.

See 'For a Workers' United Front Against Fascism' (December 1931), marxists.org.

developing an uncompromising public critique of those organisations which, claiming to be a remedy for fascism, have enabled its rise through their socially destructive and racist policies. Any political alliance with bourgeois organisations would only fuel the feeling that the far right is the sole anti-systemic force.

One of the main weaknesses of this anti-fascism is its short-sighted electoralism and, at a deeper level, its delusional belief that the dominant political forces and 'republican' institutions – and the state in general – are capable of repelling the fascist threat in the long term. Let us be clear: no 'republican front' will put an end to the fascist dynamic once it has set in motion. This is particularly true when the forces that make up this front keep on borrowing their arguments, their electoral proposals and their policies from the far right, even as they claim to be fighting it. Similarly, no capitalist state, however robust it may appear and however 'democratic' it may present itself as being, can guarantee that a fascist movement will give up on its project once in power just so that it can comply with certain constraints (however minimal) set down by law. The history of fascism demonstrates exactly the opposite. By creating such illusions, the 'republican front' approach weakens anti-fascism to the point of rendering it impotent. It reduces it to a purely *defensive* posture, which should only be used as a last resort. It is too often forgotten that the defeat of the German workers' movement faced with Nazism was primarily the result of such a 'strategy', that is, the one pursued by the German Social Democrats. Yet this same party enjoyed unparalleled political and military power. Fascism developed precisely by presenting itself as an *offensive* solution to the crisis of an economic and political system whose oligarchic foundations it in no way challenged. On the contrary, fascism's aim is to destroy all the elements of popular counter-power which, however embryonic or distorted by class collaboration, generally do exist in capitalist society.[4] To tie your hands in alliances with political forces, which themselves build this system's oppressive force, is to strengthen the illusion that the far right is a real alternative. This is to doom yourself to defeat. To imagine that the constitution will protect

---

4 Trotsky was also clear on this point:

   In the course of many decades, the workers have built up within the bourgeois democracy, by utilizing it, by fighting against it, their own strongholds and bases of proletarian democracy: the trade unions, the political parties, the educational and sport clubs, the cooperatives, etc. . . . Fascism has for its basic and only task the razing to their foundations of all institutions of proletarian democracy.

In 'What Next? Vital Questions for the German Proletariat' (January 1932), marxists.org.

us from fascism if it comes to power is to perpetuate the illusion of a neutral state, and thus to set ourselves up for destruction.

But there is also a second political attitude towards the fascist threat which – although based on opposite premises – itself leads into a dead end by evading the necessary anti-fascist struggle. Present in certain socialist tendencies as well as in parts of the anarchist movement or the autonomist milieu, this temptation can take different forms depending on the political framework to which it is attached. However, it always boils down to opposing and substituting the revolutionary aim for the anti-fascist struggle, as well as for the anti-racist, feminist or environmentalist struggles all cast as so many illusions and diversions. While it is true that only radical social transformation can truly and permanently rid us of the danger of fascism, the problem is how to get there. So, it is important not to contrast immediate aims and the final goal, but, rather, to pose the question of what mediations will lead towards the revolutionary outcome. To say that 'anti-fascism is a red herring'[5] because it postpones the only real alternative to the rise of fascism – the 'revolutionary upsurge'[6] – is hollow verbiage. We know only too well what such maximalism cost the Italian and German communist movements in the past. Why build unity for the anti-fascist struggle, when the 'system' is out of breath and revolution is imminent anyway? Revolutionary optimism, the illusion that 'after the fascists, it'll be our turn', obtuse workerism or the focus on party-building as an end unto itself, all served to justify sectarianism and dodge the immediate tasks.

But, once we have steered clear of the dead ends of opportunism and sectarianism, how can we positively define an anti-fascist strategy for our times? One first imperative is the need to prevent the creation of a far-right organisation with a rooted presence across the country and the ability to violently harass protest movements (trade union, anti-racist, feminist and so on). The FN/RN remains an institutional party with a weak activist base: over the last decade, it has not succeeded in crystallising the growth of its electoral audience in the form of a mass movement. Nevertheless, it is clear that the far right as a whole has real potential for organisational development, given the huge gap between its vast electorate (essentially the FN/RN) and its militant troops (including violent

---

5 This formula is used by Éric Hazan and Kamo in *Premières mesures révolutionnaires*, Paris: La Fabrique, pp. 103–4.
6 'It is the revolutionary upsurge, *the fraternal awakening of all energies*, as Rimbaud puts it, that will send the apprentice fascists back to their nothingness': ibid., p. 104.

groupuscules). Yet it is the fusion between the fascist project and such a movement that would really signal the emergence of a complete fascist movement – not the return of explicit references to historical fascism, which far-right leaders are well aware represent a cumbersome hangover from the past. Zemmour's Reconquête has tried in recent years to build an organisation that has far more of an activist profile than the FN/RN, often acting in concert with violent groupuscules. It seems crucial that we halt construction of such a movement by nipping in the bud all attempts to give it a rooted presence. Wherever such initiatives develop – whether in workplaces, high schools and universities, city centres, suburbs or villages, whether under the banner of the FN/RN, its satellites or small sects – the far right must be denied the right to speak and exposed for what it is: a resurgence, in new conditions and forms, of fascism. This can only be done by building united mobilisations and outmatching the fascists in numbers, preparation and discipline – ideally, stopping them from appearing in public, or, at least, reducing them to a marginal position by discouraging their supporters. This may involve forms of action which, even when they are essentially non-violent, are bound to be presented as 'violent' or 'anti-democratic' by mainstream media. There are sure to be plenty of ideologues who will lecture anti-fascists that such actions are detrimental to the fight against the far right. Yet this is the only way to prevent a fascist movement from building its forces, gaining confidence in its strength and developing beyond the electoral arena.

The question of violence is almost always posed in the wrong way, because it is considered on a moral, depoliticised level. If we remain on this level, we doom ourselves to an easy but above all selective indignation: what about state violence, whether it is used in France (police crimes, the repression of demonstrations and so on) or during military interventions in Africa or the Middle East? Above all, this means forgetting all the moments in history when violence served as an essential means of protection, and even liberation, in the face of oppression. Think of the Paris Commune and its uprising against the French ruling class (which ended with the murder of tens of thousands of insurgents in the middle of Paris). Remember the Resistance's armed struggle against the Nazi occupiers (using what were at the time considered 'terrorist' tactics). Or, indeed, the struggle waged by the Algerian people against French colonialism. So, it is not violence in itself that is the problem, but the political objectives the far right uses it for: crushing minorities, instilling fear in those fighting for social and political liberation, preventing them from organising and protesting, imposing an order based entirely on oppression. While violence clearly cannot be valued for its own sake, it surely cannot be ruled out in the face of an enemy whose project *is* intrinsically violent, which attracts large numbers of violent individuals and whose ideology encourages attacks on minorities and social movements. Any initiative to set up popular, anti-racist and pro-feminist self-defence structures should therefore be encouraged. This also presupposes that trade union and political organisations and collectives should strengthen and combine their capacities in this area.[7]

This is all the truer given that, in the last century, the repressive state apparatus proved time and again that it was no bulwark for public freedoms, democratic rights or the safety of the oppressed. The police and army in particular, but also the judiciary, have generally shown an indulgent neutrality towards the far right, and, in many cases, have collaborated directly with fascist forces when the latter have engaged in systematic attacks against the socialist and communist movements or against minorities. To be convinced of this, we need only read Angelo Tasca's account of the fascist counter-revolution that took place in Italy from autumn 1920 onwards.[8] In particular, he describes how the state's repressive forces systematically disarmed the workers' movement, supplied arms and ammunition to the Fascist squads and rarely arrested their members, even though they were guilty of numerous crimes and appalling violence. Even the perpetrators of murders, which were routinely committed during punitive expeditions in the countryside or towns against trade unionists, labour-movement activists or Socialist elected representatives, almost never had any kind of police trouble (or else they were soon released). As for Nazi activists, they benefited from a staggering leniency on the part of the German justice system, with almost all the murders committed by the assault sections going unpunished (not to mention Hitler himself, spending just thirteen months in jail for the attempted putsch in Munich in 1923).[9] To turn back to our

---

7   See Elsa Dorlin, *Se défendre. Une philosophie de la violence*, Paris: Zones éditions, 2017 (*Self-Defense: A Philosophy of Violence*, London: Verso, 2022). Note also the self-defence organisations built by the French Socialists in the 1930s (partly in reaction to the Communists' own): Matthias Bouchenot, *Tenir la rue. L'autodéfense socialiste 1929–1938*, Paris: Libertalia, 2014. He stresses several points in particular: the organic link between these structures and the elected leadership of these organisations, their centralised command and the self-imposed discipline that had to govern their operation, but also the physical training of the members, collectively taken in charge by the organisation.

8   Angelo Tasca, *The Rise of Italian Fascism*, London: Methuen, 1938.

9   On all this, see Johann Chapoutot, Christian Ingrao and Nicolas Patin, *Le monde nazi*, Paris: Tallandier, 2024.

present situation, we should not forget that the far right already has the – sometimes fervent – support of large sections of the state's repressive forces, with its electoral scores among the police and gendarmes already exceeding all other occupational categories (in 2021, it was estimated that 74 percent of active police officers were preparing to vote for the RN in the coming presidential elections). We can also assume that this far-right support is all the stronger the more we look towards the services responsible for the most brutal tasks of maintaining order – the anti-crime brigades, for example,[10] whose officers know full well that they would have an almost totally free hand if the RN came to power. Their mandate would probably be to carry out 'clean-up' operations against minorities and forces of social protest.

However, we should reject the temptation to reduce anti-fascism to the (necessary) practice of self-defence. This dimension may have been particularly pronounced in certain historical circumstances, for instance the anti-fascist resistance in Parma in 1922,[11] the famous 'battle of Cable Street' in October 1936 against the English fascists led by Mosley or the huge organisations for the defence of the Social Democratic and Communist parties in Weimar Germany. But anti-fascism must be conceived above all as a political struggle which combines different components: self-defence, of course, but also the cultural battle, strikes and street demonstrations, the electoral struggle or even certain forms of 'guerrilla' court actions. Contrary to the simplistic view that sees only its paramilitary units, historical fascism won power through a multi-cornered strategy. We should not exaggerate how coherent it was. But it combined – in different proportions depending on the type of fascism and the national context – intensive use of the electoral arena; tactical alliances with sectors of the ruling classes (big landowners, industrial capitalists) and forces on the conservative right; nationalist propaganda on all fronts through various media (print press and radio); *and* the use of street violence against minorities, the left and the trade union movement.[12] So, it is impossible to defeat fascism through a simple defensive tactic of stopping the far right gaining a street presence. This is particularly apparent in the contemporary French situation: as we emphasised above, the RN is advancing less

---

10   See, for example, Didier Fassin's ethnographic study in which he followed an anti-crime brigade for almost two years: *La Force de l'ordre*, Paris: Seuil, 2011 (*Enforcing Order: An Ethnography of Urban Policing*, Cambridge: Polity Press, 2013).
11   See also: Pino Cacucci, *Oltretorrente*, Paris: Christian Bourgois, 2005.
12   See, for example, William Sheridan Allen's localised analysis, which shows all these elements of fascist strategy at work: *The Nazi Seizure of Power: The Experience of a Single German Town 1930–1935*, London: Eyre & Spottiswoode, 1966.

through grassroots mobilisation and building a strong presence on the ground (except in certain areas, such as the Pas-de-Calais mining basin)[13] than through deft propaganda that exploits the pervasive spread of racism and xenophobia through mainstream media and politics.

The FN/RN is not some groupuscule that can be resisted – or still less crushed – just by stopping it from raising its head in public. We have seen already how far it can grow without having a vast network of locally based activists. Stopping the resilient rise of the FN/RN requires a comprehensive political and cultural battle involving several elements. Firstly, the left needs to break the catastrophist narrative of the inevitable victory of the far right. The far right was soundly defeated in the early parliamentary elections of July 2024, indicating that it did not at that stage have a majority that would allow it to reach high office. But it also suffers from persistent weaknesses (local roots, the training of its personnel, its cadres, its intellectual attraction, capacity to mobilise and so on) and it is not true that it 'naturally' benefits from some supposedly irreversible right-wing drift in French society. We need not only point out how routinely the FN/RN votes against all measures favourable to the working classes (freezing prices and rents, raising wages, creating new taxes on the richest and the profits of big business and so on), but also to refute its xenophobic and racist 'arguments' on immigration, Islam and so on. We need to keep reminding ourselves that the FN/RN does not provide good answers to the political crisis because – contrary to the words of former Socialist premier Laurent Fabius – it is not asking 'the right questions'. To take positions on the far right's chosen terrain in the name of answering the 'real problems' it supposedly raises, or to seek to outmatch its xenophobic or Islamophobic demagogy – as the right and part of the left have been doing since the 1980s – is to doom oneself to strengthening it by feeding the spread of its 'ideas'.[14] FN/RN voters are not simply lost sheep who have misunderstood their interests and are in need of enlightenment. Lastly, it is imperative that we develop and popularise a project for society's future, alternative to both authoritarian neoliberalism and fascist (or fascist-leaning) ethno-nationalism. This must be combined with a credible strategy for defending social and democratic gains, winning political power and bringing about social change.

Just like self-defence, the battle of ideas will remain insufficient if it is not organically connected to the construction of a political alternative

---

13   See Haydee Sabéran, *Bienvenue à Hénin-Beaumont*, Paris: La Découverte, 2014.
14   See Pierre Tevanian and Sylvie Tissot, *Dictionnaire de la lepénisation des esprits*, Paris: L'Esprit frappeur, 2002.

to break with the destructive policies pursued over several decades and, more profoundly, with the present order of things. It will not be enough to break down the so-called arguments and truisms on which the far right bases its discourse (counting on rationalist optimism), or to reverse its de-demonisation with a re-demonisation (as per a certain moralist temptation). Its rise, insofar as it derives from far-reaching socio-economic, political and ideological transformations, must be confronted politically, by building a united front targeting not just the FN/RN but all the policies that encourage its advance. The New Popular Front built in the urgent situation following the dissolution of the National Assembly in June 2024 could offer such a framework. But to develop, such a front would not only have to bring together multiple organisations – from political parties to associations and trade union forces – but also become a priority for them. This would firstly mean the creation of local committees, so as to draw in a popular involvement which extends well beyond the members of these organisations alone. Its aims should be conceived as both defensive and offensive: seeking to stimulate and coordinate resistance against the far right, but, at the same time, popularising the need for a social alternative, involving a political rupture – and, therefore, the conquest of power. In addition to the factors highlighted throughout this book, the FN/RN has also developed as a result of the inability of protest movements to coalesce and to constitute themselves as a credible and radical alternative to authoritarian neoliberalism.

Social resistance to the neoliberal, authoritarian and racist steamroller did not spontaneously give rise to a political alternative. Nonetheless, the intensity of popular struggles in France since winter 1995 has enabled a left that seeks a rupture to grow stronger and break the hegemony of the left that supports neoliberal capitalism, whose outright betrayals under the presidency of François Hollande greatly fuelled the rise of the far right. The strong electoral results for Jean-Luc Mélenchon and La France insoumise in 2017 and 2022, and the formation of the NUPES (New Ecological and Social Popular Union) and the New Popular Front, have prevented the French political field from closing in on the false alternative between Macronism and Le Pen's camp. Nevertheless, the French left faces two kinds of dangerous temptation. On the one hand, is a focus on elections and institutions, which can degenerate into unprincipled electoralism as it gets closer to the coveted seat of power. Elements of its programme that are too much at odds with the neoliberal, securitarian or racist consensus risk being sidelined. But, even if the left holds to its programme, the focus on the electoral-institutional sphere can lead it to underestimate the need for a broad base in society and a significant capacity for popular intervention. As many left-wing experiments in the last century have shown, holding the levers of political office in a capitalist system is not the same thing as dominating the state, let alone having 'power'. In addition to the myriad obstacles that most of the senior civil service would put in the way of an alternative course, there are the more strictly economic weapons that the ruling class can mobilise to bring a government to its knees (media campaigns, investment strikes, capital flight, international pressure and so on). It should also be remembered that the ruling class has never hesitated to use illegal and violent means when its economic power was really under threat.[15] Yet the other dangerous temptation is that of skirting around the electoral question, in the form of outright rejection of elections (elections considered a 'fool's errand') or using them in a narrowly propagandistic sense (elections as a 'forum' for putting forward ideas). In the name of the – quite correct – idea that winning political power through the ballot box is not enough to embark upon a process of social transformation, some end up ditching any prospect of conquering and exercising political power, pre-emptively sparing themselves the enormous difficulties inherent therein. This leads to various means of making up for the strategic vacuum thus created, such as the consoling mythology of the general strike – supposedly opening the way to the construction of a new power, totally external to political institutions and the state[16] – or the comforting call to 'live differently', to build alternatives to capitalism here and now (cooperatives, self-managed spaces and so on), to 're-root' ourselves.[17]

These dilemmas reflect the political and strategic crisis in which the left and social movements have been mired for some decades now.[18] The

---

15 In addition to the example of Chile – where a military coup jointly prepared by the Chilean ruling class and Washington put an end to the reformist-socialist experiment led by Salvador Allende – we can think of Syriza's arrival in power in Greece in January 2015. This is relevant in terms of both the Troika's blackmail and Yanis Varoufakis's statements about the systematic blockages in the ministry he 'led'. See also Ralph Miliband's classic book *The State in Capitalist Society*, London: Merlin, 1969.

16 See Nicos Poulantzas's critique of this illusion that popular power stands wholly external to state power: *State, Power, Socialism*, London: Verso, 2014. See also the criticisms levelled by Henri Weber, then leader of the Revolutionary Communist League (LCR): 'L'État et la transition au socialisme. Interview de Nicos Poulantzas par Henri Weber', *Critique communiste*, 1977, no. 16, contretemps.eu ('The State and the Transition to Socialism', in James Martin (ed.), *The Poulantzas Reader*, London: Verso, 2008, pp. 334–60).

17 See Ugo Palheta, 'Les influences visibles du Comité invisible', *La Revue du Crieur*, June 2016, no. 4.

18 See Bensaïd, *Penser agir*.

absence of a shared utopian horizon and a common strategy has led to the over-valuing of different tactical choices, held up as irreconcilable strategic options.[19] This gives rise to false binaries: strikes versus elections (or, more broadly, the street versus the ballot box), trade unions versus politics, concrete alternatives versus political ones, the local (or national) versus the global, physical confrontation versus peaceful means of struggle and so on. This undeniably throws up obstacles to the antifascist front we mentioned earlier, and, as a result, we lack any collective framework in which to debate the strategic aims of such a front and the tactical means needed to achieve them. There is also the question of the political content of a united front, and therefore its boundaries. Unity is a struggle, both to maintain it against the sectarian temptations present in all organisations and to define the common line. Within the NFP we can see the extent to which a crucial confrontation is taking place between a line of support for neoliberal capitalism (vigorously defended by François Hollande and Raphaël Glucksmann) and a line of anti-liberal, anti-racist and anti-productivist rupture (defended in particular by LFI). All our arguments in this book point in the direction of an anti-fascism that maintains a frontal fight against the far right, while also linking this to three other fundamental political focuses:[20] opposition to neoliberalism; the battle against the authoritarian hardening of the state; and the fight against xenophobia and racism. These axes of intervention are likely to encourage the building of unity on the basis of broadly shared causes, and point to a series of fruitful clarifications. For opposition to neoliberalism is only meaningful if it aims to break with capitalism (of which neoliberalism is only a particular, temporary configuration). Likewise, the fight against the authoritarian hardening of the state only becomes effective insofar as it aims to win real democracy (and not simply a return to the 'normality' of liberal democracy).[21] Finally,

---

19   The 'black bloc' tactic, which emerged in a particular context to respond to specific objectives (in particular, to defend occupied spaces), could thus be made into an absolute, fetishised pseudo-strategy valid in any context. See Salar Mohandesi, 'On the Black Bloc', *Viewpoint Magazine*, 12 February 2012.

20   Further considerations on the political situation in France and other elements for a strategy of social transformation can be found in the afterword, written by Julien Salingue and myself, to Daniel Bensaïd's book: *Stratégie et parti*, Paris: Les Prairies ordinaires, 2016.

21   The conquest of democracy presupposes a politicisation and democratisation of the economy, in at least two senses: power in and over the firm by those who work there and produce all the wealth (in other words, what is generally called self-management), but also the construction of genuine popular sovereignty over the major economic choices, and thus the socialisation of ownership of the means of production,

the fight against xenophobia and racism is only truly effective through the determination to break down their institutional structures (without stopping at an educational mission aimed at deconstructing individual 'prejudices' and 'stereotypes').[22]

These clarifications cannot be imposed a priori as a condition for joint action. It cannot be demanded of whoever wants to fight the far right that they must already be convinced of the need for revolutionary change. This would be a condemnation to marginality. Only mass struggles can break the steel cage of resigned acceptance of the world as it is, and create the conditions for radical politicisation on the scale of millions of people. It is only through such struggles that these millions – on the basis of specific reasons for indignation, sector-based demands or local causes – can imagine going much further in the direction of large-scale social transformation. But such radicalisation does not happen spontaneously through a shared struggle alone, however massive it may be. It can only be achieved if these mass movements take root in the longer term in workplaces, neighbourhoods and educational institutions. It can only happen if they build active solidarity and create new links, if they organise the circulation of tactics for the struggle, intensify people's desire to fight back and, finally, imbibe revolutionary ideas. This presupposes the need for political debate in their ranks, and the intervention of activists, collectives, organisations, media platforms and intellectuals demanding and demonstrating the possibility of a way out of capitalism, the conquest of real democracy and the dismantling of the structures of racism. We must also stress the close link – and thus the imperative alliances – between the anti-fascism that is being rebuilt and the political anti-racism that has developed in France over the last twenty years. Particularly in the form of Islamophobia, racism is central to the political field's shift towards the far right, to the legitimisation of authoritarian hardening and to the rise of the FN/RN – and, indeed, this dimension is too central for it to be relegated to second place. One of the most urgent challenges for social movements in France, and for the anti-fascist movement in particular, is to make the fight against structural racism part of their political agenda. This means not only publicly highlighting the role of the state in perpetuating racism and the role it plays in the capitalist

---

exchange, information and communication. On these questions, see Alexis Cukier, *Le Travail démocratique*, Paris: PUF, 2018. See also Ellen Meiksins Wood, *Democracy Against Capitalism*, Cambridge: Cambridge University Press, 1995.

22   See Ugo Palheta, 'Pour vaincre l'extrême droite, il faut prendre le racisme (et l'antiracisme) au sérieux', *Contretemps*, 15 October 2024, contretemps.eu.

system, but also prioritising struggles that are all too often neglected: against Islamophobia, police crime and systemic discrimination.[23] Only on this condition can the political effort to build a *white bloc* be stopped by the creation of a *subaltern bloc*, uniting the white and non-white popular classes around a project of political rupture and the perspective of an anti-capitalist, democratic and decolonial power.

Such a rupture and such a perspective may seem a long way off, given how much some of us are caught up in the day-to-day material difficulties and uncertainties that come with neoliberalism. Others (though they are sometimes the same people) are already devoting their efforts to defensive battles, to save what can be saved from the social and democratic achievements of the last century. But this future orientation must be at the heart of these struggles: not as a natural outcome that will happen in due course so long as we are patient, and not as an idle utopia disconnected from the present, but as a strategic objective for all protest movements. Clear-sighted recognition of the possibility of fascist disaster, if it coexists with an awareness of our ability to avert it, may serve as an incentive for us and those around us to take political action. If this disaster only has some chance of happening because of our individual indifference, our collective passivity or our strategic errors, then the outcome depends first and foremost on ourselves.

No one can predict the moment when a world turns upside down and goes off the rails, when it is 'midnight in the century' and a new era arrives, made up of experiences and struggles that are only apparently similar to the ones we have known before. It is even doubtful that such a break in time can be observed when it happens, if not several months or years later, and thus inevitably too late.

Moreover, any idea that we can prepare for this is illusory: no training course, no survival manual, will make us politically or ethically equipped to deal with disaster. Reason and the human imagination are often reluctant to envisage the worst of outcomes, instead preferring to follow the well-trodden paths of an unpalatable but familiar present. So, they are powerless to anticipate the new forms of tyranny and the ways in which radical dehumanisation, the absolute denial of human dignity, the in-principle rejection of equality, and contempt for common humanity creep in. They cannot discover in advance everything that insidiously

---

23   On this last point, see Félix Boggio Éwanjé-Épée and Stella Magliani-Belkacem, 'Ce que pourrait être une gauche antiraciste', *Contretemps*, 20 June 2012, contretemps.eu.

lends itself to a policy of apartheid, explosions of purifying violence and mass crimes.

Fascism is the product of the breakdown of a system that knows no rationality other than maximum short-term profit. It is the process in which all the long built-up despair is transformed into the hallucinatory hope of a rebirth, all egoism coagulates into a totalitarian desire for unity and all individual impotence metamorphoses into a fantasy of collective omnipotence. This is done not in order to finally put an end to oppression, but, instead, to rage furiously against everything that seems to threaten this imaginary unity. Willed into being by all those who see their salvation in a regenerated national-racial or civilisational community, the eviction of minorities and the banishment of all dissent, fascism is the illusory act of redemption – and the assurance of catastrophe.

We may be accused of pessimism. That would be a misunderstanding, for this book is entirely based on the hypothesis that the deadly dynamic that has set in motion is, even now, still reversible. While the worst of outcomes is possible, it is never a certainty, provided at least that the enemy ceases to be trivialised, normalised and legitimised; provided, above all, that we get organised and take action.